Cinesonica: sounding film and video

MANCHESTER
1824

Manchester University Press

Cinesonica: sounding film and video

ANDY BIRTWISTLE

Manchester
University Press

Manchester and New York

distributed in the United States exclusively by Palgrave Macmillan

The right of Andy Birtwistle to be identified as the author of this work has been asserted by him in accordance with the Copyright, Designs and Patents Act 1988.

Published by Manchester University Press
Oxford Road, Manchester M13 9NR, UK
and Room 400, 175 Fifth Avenue, New York, NY 10010, USA
www.manchesteruniversitypress.co.uk

Distributed in the United States exclusively by
Palgrave Macmillan, 175 Fifth Avenue, New York,
NY 10010, USA

Distributed in Canada exclusively by
UBC Press, University of British Columbia, 2029 West Mall,
Vancouver, BC, Canada V6T 1Z2

British Library Cataloguing-in-Publication Data
A catalogue record for this book is available from the British Library

Library of Congress Cataloging-in-Publication Data applied for

ISBN 978 0 719 08111 8   hardback

First published 2010

The publisher has no responsibility for the persistence or accuracy of URLs for any external or third-party internet websites referred to in this book, and does not guarantee that any content on such websites is, or will remain, accurate or appropriate.

Typeset in Charter ITC
by Servis Filmsetting Ltd, Stockport, Cheshire
Printed in Great Britain
by the MPG Book Group

for Bi-yu

Contents

List of tables and figures

Tables

Figures

Preface

Like many people who choose to write on the subject of film sound, the initial motivation for my own research was a feeling that the sonic had been somewhat neglected in discussions of film and video – a theoretical and critical inadequacy that concerned me both as a teacher and as a filmmaker. My fascination with film sound arises not only from a love of cinema, but also from the experience of making films, videos and audio works. As a practitioner I gained an awareness of the way in which film and video texts are woven from the visual and sonic materials that constitute them, and experienced the pleasure of recording sound and of making creative choices between different sounds during post-production – responding in different ways to their qualities, placing and shifting them in relation to one another, combining and separating them, suturing or fusing them with images. Although this book does not engage with my own practice, and is not exclusively concerned with issues of film production, this involvement in filmmaking and video production nevertheless reveals itself in my choice of research topic, and informs the work done with the case studies that follow. The experience of making films, and of working with students of media production, can be seen to inform the particular issue that I have chosen to tackle in this book: namely, the ways in which we might critically engage with the materiality of film and video sound. Thus my own critical and theoretical negotiation of video and film attempts to consider what any practitioner is necessarily very close to – the materials that constitute the medium. This concern with the materiality of film and video sound also relates to my own personal history in other ways, especially with regard to the changes in technology that have impacted on low-budget and no-budget filmmaking over the last two or three decades. Having originally trained as a filmmaker, shooting on 16mm and cutting on a Steenbeck flatbed editing table, I emerged from full-time

education in the early 1980s to find myself in a rapidly changing media environment, where film's position in the independent
sector was being challenged by video; a decade later I witnessed
the shift from analogue to digital video. What these changes in
technology foregrounded for me, personally, was the materiality and sonic specificity of each format: the crackle of the optical
film soundtrack, the impacts made by a soundtrack constructed
primarily through editing rather than mixing, the hiss of analogue
video, the crisp resonance of digital sound. The question raised in
my mind by these differences was how we might come to terms
with the various qualities of sound – how we might make sense
of them, and engage with them at a critical and theoretical level.
The problem I faced in relation to the existing body of literature
on film sound was not only that it was heavily biased towards the
visual aspects of narrative cinema, but also that it was dominated
by critical and theoretical models that formulated film as a signifying text. However, my experience of making films and videos,
and of listening to them in cinemas, galleries, lecture halls and at
home, suggested to me there are ways of knowing sound, ways of
registering its materiality, that have little to do with the attribution
of meaning. Sounds and sonic practices are not always most profit-
ably negotiated by way of theoretical interventions founded on a
concern with signification and representation; settling down in a
cinema to enjoy the warm glow of a crackly optical soundtrack, my
first thoughts are rarely, 'what does this sound mean?'

If my particular relationship with film and video can be seen to
have influenced my research interests, so too my own history has
informed the methodology employed and developed in this book,
in terms of its structure, my choice of films, videos and theoretical resources, and the attitude adopted towards the project as a
whole. When I was an undergraduate film student one of my
lecturers told me that the reason he made films was because
he disliked them – which I understood to mean that he disliked
mainstream commercial filmmaking (to which his own praxis was
presumably opposed). While I didn't wholly believe the sincerity
of my lecturer's claim, he was nevertheless expressing a view of
independent film practice that was widely held at that time. The
early 1980s was a highly politicised era, in which an understandable emphasis was placed on oppositional politics. For many like
myself, interested in the social function of independent cinema,
the issue of the relationship between film form and ideology was
of central importance to film practice. Informed in part by the

debates of the 1970s – particularly those associated with structural film – there was a tendency at this time to conceptualise a
radical poetics of film, and thus politicised film practice, in terms
of opposition to dominant, hegemonic cultural forms; thus many
aspects of materialist film practice were often simply inscribed
against naturalistic and narrative modes of representation, understood and valued in terms of their potential to deconstruct or resist
dominant forms of cinema. What I found problematic about this
approach was that one always seemed to end up thinking about
what films *weren't* doing, rather than addressing them in positive terms. At the same time, certain modes of film practice were
privileged over others within the context of a history of radical
poetics – in particular montage, and the so-called 'contrapuntal'
use of sound. Almost thirty years later these established notions of
what might constitute radical film practice remain in circulation,
regularly called upon to theorise both contemporary and historical
work. However, the problem with this way of thinking is that there
are certain modes of film and video practice, and certain aspects of
film and video's materiality, that cannot be understood within this
tradition, and which have consequently been neglected, forgotten,
ignored or dismissed as having no political potential. What therefore emerges from my own background and experience in relation
to the methodological drive of this study is not only a desire to
consider the ways in which sound–image relations are constituted
and understood in terms of materiality, but also a concern with
what exactly might be at stake in the relationship between sound
and image.

Acknowledgements

I am greatly indebted to many people for their help, support and time. The first words of thanks go to Jorella Andrews, Kodwo Eshun, Sarat Maharaj, Irit Rogoff and Rob Stone at Goldsmiths, all of whom have been tremendous sources of inspiration and support. Thanks also to Lisa Blackman and Al Rees for their comments on my research.

I am grateful to a number of people who have generously given their time to be interviewed, have provided me with copies of their work and other research materials, and have patiently responded to my phone calls and emails: thanks to Nick Burton, Tina Keane, Anthea Kennedy, Scott Rankin, John Smith and to Nigel Bewley at the National Sound Archive.

Thanks to John Eacott, Jeremy Strong, Lesley Stevenson, John Drever, Gianluca Sergi and Martin Shingler for giving me the opportunity to road-test some of the ideas presented in this book at conferences, and for the valuable feedback that resulted.

I am grateful to Canterbury Christ Church University for granting me study leave to work on this book. Thanks must also go to my colleagues in the Department of Media, and in particular to David Bradshaw, Ken Fox, Karen Shepherdson, Alex Choat, Eddie MacMillan, Liz Samson and Shane Blackman for their practical help and spiritual support; special thanks to Andrew Utterson for his generosity in sharing knowledge, experience, resources and his interest in all things sonic. Thanks also to Ben Rowley, Alex Gardiner, Mankit Lo, Leon Benning, Alan Meades and to Steve Dwoskin for help with the preparation of photographs for this book.

Throughout the research process a number of people have kindly given their time to deal with my enquiries: thanks to Philip Brophy, Patrick Jordan at *The Commonweal*, Claudia Patsch at Universal Edition and to Peter Cook for help with musical matters.

However, the biggest debts of gratitude are owed to my son Shu-yang for accepting the burden of a father whose attentions have not always been on familial matters, and to my wife Bi-yu, without whose experience, intelligence, love, support, humour and patience none of this would have been possible.

1 Introduction: sound, signification and materiality

This book attempts a coming-to-terms with what I propose are neglected aspects of film and video sound. This neglect, in one sense, manifests itself in the relative lack of critical literature on the sonic. This has been signalled elsewhere, and it is unnecessary for this critical absence to be rehearsed here, since the observation that much remains to be done on sound appears with regular frequency in the steadily growing body of literature on sound in general, and film sound in particular.[1] Rather, the issue addressed in my own study is exactly *how* the sonic dimensions of film and video might be auditioned, addressed, understood and discussed. The key concern of this book is to consider the ways in which we might come to terms with the materiality of film sound, both beyond and in relation to its semiotic or significatory dimensions, and what might be at stake in a critical engagement with this materiality.

Film sound merits study because it is an essential component of cinema. As a number of writers have demonstrated, cinema has *always* been audiovisual: before the general introduction of the recorded soundtrack in the late 1920s, the screening of films was accompanied by various forms of musical orchestration, narration, sound effects and performed dialogue.[2] Given the medium's fundamentally audiovisual nature, logic suggests that sound should make a substantial contribution to the effects and meanings created by cinema. However, the cultural bias towards the image has resulted in the mistaken belief that film is a visual rather than an audiovisual medium. As a consequence of this, sound has often been conceptualised as an add-on or supplement to the cinematic image, and the study of cinema has been, and continues to be, dominated by visual concerns. The challenge taken on by the first wave of modern film sound studies in the late 1970s and early 1980s was to address this cultural bias, and the resultant critical neglect that film sound had suffered. However, the body of literature that has developed since the early 1980s has now established the importance of the study of sound, and it is no longer as necessary as it once was to campaign for sound to be taken seriously. Rather, the task currently facing those working in film sound studies is to consider how thinking on the sonic dimensions of cinema might be developed further, and how areas of critical neglect within the discipline itself might be addressed.

While once there had been a fairly narrow focus on North American and European narrative cinema, the scope of film sound studies has now widened to include film and video emerging from other regional contexts, and an increasing variety of genres and forms. However, although the growing range of films being studied has served to develop understanding of film sound, the way in which the soundtrack has been conceptualised, and therefore the ways which it has been studied, have changed relatively little. Echoing the model of sound proposed by industrial processes of film production, writers tend to analyse the soundtrack according to its commonly accepted constituent elements – music, dialogue and sound effects – sometimes including silence, and quite often focusing exclusively on the role played by music. Unfortunately, in considering these elements of the soundtrack in isolation, the tendency is to neglect their interrelatedness, and more importantly, their changing relationships with one another and with the images on screen. Thus one of the challenges facing contemporary film sound studies is to engage with concepts, and to devise critical approaches, that allow for an increased consideration of the soundtrack as a whole.

Fundamental to the established approach to the soundtrack is the conceptualisation of film as a signifying text. Back in 1992 Rick Altman called for this dominant model of film to be replaced by the notion of cinema as event, thereby extending the range of critical discourse appropriate to the study of film sound (Altman, 1992: 2). While in the intervening period the work of Altman and others has provided alternatives to the formulation of film as text, this model nevertheless continues to serve as the dominant conceptual paradigm in the study of film sound aesthetics. The semiological project has had a profound influence on the landscape, and soundscape, of film studies, and while successive critical moves have distanced the study of film from the interventions made by the first wave of cinesemiology in the 1960s, the conception of film as *signifying* text has retained its influence on film theory and criticism.[3]

Although no longer completely commanding the centre ground of film studies, the complex of signification, meaning and representation that emerged from cinesemiology continues to serve as an important conceptual frame within which film or video are situated critically. Over the last three decades a concern with subjectivity has realigned the film text in relation to issues of reception and spectatorship, but nevertheless, what we term 'the film' seems to remain a clearly demarcated and unchanging entity – it remains a text that signifies. Concern with signification is no longer focused on the internal operations of the filmic text or the precise nature of the cinematic sign, as it was in the heyday of cinesemiology, but rather on the ways in which the signs contained within the film text relate to the various milieus in which they circulate: social, cultural, political, economic, psychological, historical and so forth. Despite the range of perspectives offered by the various strands of post-structural theory, film remains understood primarily as text to be *read*. The longevity of this formulation is, of course, testament to its usefulness.

There has undoubtedly been significant disenchantment with semiology itself as a means by which to engage with the significatory, and the body of post-structural theory can be seen both as a building on and a critique of structuralist modes of enquiry. However, since semiology had a profound impact on the development of the notion of film as text – a model that remains central to the way in which the soundtrack is conceptualised – it is still important to return to Saussure in order to identify what the limitations of a semiological modelling of sound might be.

The semiology of sound and the dematerialisation of the sign

Sound fares badly within Saussurian linguistics, constantly stripped from a project that privileges the seemingly stable, abstract, universal paradigm of language over individual concrete speech acts: *langue* in preference to *parole*. This approach to the study of signification militates against engagement with concrete particularity, the material or the contingent. Thus, although the starting point for the *Course in General Linguistics* is a concern with speech – Saussure states, 'in the lives of individuals and societies, speech is more important than anything else' (Saussure, 1964: 7) – this concern is resolved through the model of language, which itself is identified as a 'well-defined object in the heterogeneous mass of speech facts' and therefore a 'principle of classification' (Saussure,

1964: 9). Saussurian linguistics consequently excludes the material and the contingent in favour of abstract paradigms, which as conceptual entities are necessarily divorced and absent from concrete phenomena, events and objects. Encountered within the conceptual frame of semiology, each individual act of signification is simply rendered a manifestation of an abstract paradigm.

A further distanciation from the sonic takes place when Saussure nominates writing as the means by which language can be successfully navigated: 'we generally learn about language only through writing' (Saussure, 1964: 23). In a telling use of imagery that figures chaos in terms of the oceanic, Saussure comments, 'Whoever consciously deprives himself of the perceptible image of the written word runs the risk of perceiving only a shapeless and unmanageable mass. Taking away the written form is like depriving a beginning swimmer of his life belt' (Saussure, 1964: 32). However, my primary concern with the Saussurian model of signification is not the fate of the sonic within a project that was obviously never concerned with it; rather, this brief return to Saussure serves to highlight a conceptual dynamic that hinders critical engagement with the concrete particularity of events, phenomena and objects situated within significatory networks, and circumscribes the discourse in which the materiality of sonic phenomena might be addressed. The conceptual mode proposed by Saussurian linguistics represses consideration of the material dimensions of the signifier beyond its ability to sustain difference, and thus to create or support meaning through negative differentiation. This is famously expressed in Saussure's formulation, 'in language there are only differences *without positive terms*' (Saussure, 1964: 120). What this focus on difference means in terms of materiality is figured powerfully in an illustration given by Saussure in support of the synchronic study of language. In part, the *Course in General Linguistics* is motivated by Saussure's objections to the diachronic study of language, which had dominated modern linguistics until this point. For Saussure, the study of language is served not by engaging with its evolution, but by removing it from a temporal frame: his interest is in the synchronic, the static, the science of language-states (*états de langue*). Accordingly he comments on language, 'It is a system based on the mental opposition of auditory impressions, just as tapestry is a work of art produced by the visual oppositions of threads of different colours; the most important thing in analysis is the role of the oppositions, not the process through which the colours were obtained' (Saussure, 1964: 33).

What this illustration demonstrates, beyond an obvious prob-lematic dispensation with the temporal, is semiology's inherent tendency to dematerialise the sign. Here there is no way to deal with the materiality of the signifier other than in terms of its ability to support and manifest difference; there is no discourse offered within which colour can be considered, other than its ability *not to be* other colours, and thus to differentiate itself in *negative* terms from others.

This dispensation with materiality takes its place within a broader conception of signification that renders both elements of the sign (signifier and signified) as psychological entities; the signifier is deemed by Saussure to be a 'sound-image' (the *mental* imprint of a sound), while the signified is a concept (Saussure, 1964: 66). Thus Saussure comments, 'Everything in language is basically psychological, including its material and mechanical manifestations, such as sound changes' (Saussure, 1964: 6). The clear inference here is that matter does not matter: the materiality of objects and events barely figures in a system founded primarily upon the notion of the arbitrary sign.[4] Saussure makes this posi-tion clear when he states, 'language is a form and not a substance' (Saussure, 1964: 122). This dematerialisation of the sign must also be seen in relation to semiology's privileging of the signified as the primary term of signification. While not dispensable, the signifier simply takes its place in the sign as that which supports the creation of meaning; the pay-off of signification is the concept that results, the sign's terminal point.

One of the key problems of approaching film and video sound through the concept of signification is that it rather too neatly coincides with the way in which we casually formulate sounds in terms of the objects or events perceived as their source, describing sonic phenomena as the sound *of* something or other. The problem posed by this formulation is that it limits, to issues of representa-tion, the ways in which we might come to terms with these sounds, while simultaneously ascribing to them a secondary status, situat-ing them at the level of attribute, characteristic or effect. Thus an object represented on screen, perceived to be a sound's source, seems to 'explain' the sound we hear, and if that source is absent from the screen, then sound seems to be explained by the fact that it signifies that source in its (visually unrepresented) absence.[5]

One of the concerns that emerges from this return to Saussure, and one of the key issues that dominates this book, is the question of how we might begin to come to terms with the materiality of film sound. Running alongside the significatory is a parallel universe of materiality, with ways of knowing sound, and ways of registering sonic presences that have little or nothing to do with the attribution of meaning, and which cannot be understood through those reading techniques founded upon semiological models. How, then, can these sounds be mapped and negotiated beyond, and as well as in relation, to their significatory dimensions?

Affect and materiality

The work of a number of contemporary theorists suggests ways in which a non-significatory registration of sonic phenomena might be considered critically. Studies undertaken by Vivian Sobchack, Laura U. Marks and Brian Massumi have been formulated in ways that seek to engage with the sensory, both in relation to the significatory and as distinct from it. Vivian Sobchack's work on film has drawn on phenomenology to explore the relationships between bodily experience and contemporary moving-image culture, and considers film in terms of the ways in which it represents and re-articulates our experiences of embodiment and vision (Sobchack, 1992, 2004). Laura U. Marks's research on what she has termed 'haptic visuality' has considered how film signifies through its materiality, in ways that suggest the tactility of vision. In this way, argues Marks, film is able to evoke the sense of touch, smell and bodily presence (Marks, 1998, 2000). Negotiating intercultural cinema through the context of embodiment and the senses, Marks's *The Skin of the Film* explores what can be represented by this form of transsensoriality, proposing that filmmakers working between cultures can engage the sensory to convey cultural experience and memory. And in Brian Massumi's *Parables for the Virtual* (2002), movement, affect and sensation provide the key terms of reference for an examination of bodily and cultural processes that operate through multiple registers of sensation.

The increased interest in perception, embodiment and the senses has been seen by some as part of a broader 'affective turn' in literary and cultural studies. While the nature, magnitude and value of this 'turn' are hotly debated, the growing body of critical literature which explores notions of affect undoubtedly marks a departure from the text-based models of analysis that emerged from the 'linguistic turn' of the 1960s. What this brings to the study of film is an opportunity to examine, within a cultural framework, the spectator's non-cognitive responses to the medium. Since the late

1990s, the interest in affect has been marked within film studies by the sheer number of books that have re-articulated or drawn upon the work of Gilles Deleuze and Felix Guattari, e.g., Ronald Bogue's *Deleuze on Cinema* (2003), Barbara M. Kennedy's *Deleuze and Cinema: The Aesthetics of Sensation* (2002), D. N. Rodowick's *Gilles Deleuze's Time Machine* (1997), Gregory Flaxman's *The Brain is the Screen: Deleuze and the Philosophy of Cinema* (2000), Patricia Pisters's *Micropolitics of Media Culture: Reading the Rhizomes of Deleuze and Guattari* (2001) and *The Matrix of Visual Culture: Working with Deleuze in Film Theory* (2003), Anna Powell's *Deleuze and Horror Film* (2005), Elena Del Rio's *Deleuze and the Cinemas of Performance: Powers of Affection* (2008) and Ian Buchanan and Patricia MacCormack's *Deleuze and the Schizoanalysis of Cinema* (2008). This growing body of literature stands in addition to a host of other studies that situate Deleuze and Guattari's ideas within the context of philosophy or cultural studies. Deleuzian theory seems to provide a radical alternative to structuralist thinking, and to that strain of post-structural theory which is inevitably bound to structuralism in its very attempt to divorce itself from it. The work of Deleuze, in particular, offers a means by which it is possible to engage critically with affect, sensation, desire and embodiment. These, and other related concepts, provide theoretical resources with which it is possible to register, and engage with, the experience and circulation of the moving image beyond the terms proposed by the model of the signifying text.

Despite being a difficult term to define precisely, the notion of affect provides a useful concept with which to explore the ways that viewers and listeners respond and relate to film outside of the cognitive processes by which meaning is created. In psychology the term is used to refer to the emotional tone expressed by a subject, or to the subject's externally displayed mood. However, in its more general usage, 'affect' is loosely understood to be synonymous with emotion or excitement. A useful introduction to the way in which this notion of affect relates to spectatorial engagement with the cinematic text is provided by Noël Carroll, who, writing on the relationship between film, emotion and genre, characterises the 'affective life' as 'the life of feeling' (Carroll, 2006: 217). Carroll suggests that affect comprises a range of phenomena – including automatic reactions (e.g., the startle response) and phobic and sexual responses – in addition to those responses we might more readily identify as emotion (fear, anger, sorrow, etc.) (Carroll, 2006: 217–218). Within the framework he provides for analysing the relationship between film and emotion, Carroll employs the notion of affect to describe and identify a particular set of spectatorial responses to the cinematic event, and to acknowledge the place of emotion and feelings within the cinematic experience. Formulated in this way, affect may be distinguished from wholly cognitive responses to cinema; that is, the notion of affect describes responses to audiovisual stimuli that cannot be accounted for in terms of knowledge or meaning. Critical interest in affect can therefore be seen as a break with the focus on signification that came to dominate the study of film in the wake of the 'linguistic turn' of the 1960s.

I have suggested above that our encounters with the materiality of film include ways of knowing sound and ways of registering sonic presences that have little or nothing to do with the attribution of meaning. The concept of affect therefore presents one set of possibilities for registering and mapping our encounter with film's materiality, suggesting a range of possible connections that may be made between film and the audiospectator, beyond those proposed by significative models of cinema. Many theoretical attempts to negotiate affect, and to distinguish it from cognitive responses to stimuli, formulate the term in ways that give primacy to sensation. Thus, Anne Rutherford's article *Cinema and Embodied Affect*, which considers the implications of an aesthetics of embodiment for film theory, figures affect in terms of 'sensible resonances of experience', and 'a dilation of the senses, a nervous excitation . . . an opening of the pores, a quickening of the pulse' (Rutherford, 2003). Gay Hawkins, theorising cinematic affect in relation to her own response to the film *American Beauty*, situates it in terms of phenomena 'registered somatically, beneath and before consciousness' (Hawkins, 2002). Similarly, in the book *Deleuze and Cinema: The Aesthetics of Sensation*, which explores cinema as a primarily non-cognitive experience, Barbara M. Kennedy draws upon the work of the seventeenth-century Dutch philosopher Baruch Spinoza to propose that, 'affect has an irreducible bodily and autonomic nature. . . . Autonomic here is defined as purely a physical response to something: sensual responses, for example, the skin getting warmer, or the heart beating faster' (Kennedy, 2002: 101). What these various commentaries propose is affect as a sensory and bodily response to the audiovisual stimulus of the cinematic event. Responses of this type cannot be figured in cognitive terms, and thus, at first sight, appear disconnected from those frames of reference proposed by established approaches to cinema founded on significatory paradigms – for example, narrative, identification and representation.

Although 'affective' theorisations of cinema have become more widespread in recent years, the affective dimensions of film were not only recognised, but also theorised, by Soviet filmmakers in the 1920s. In *The Sound Film: A Statement from the USSR*,[6] Eisenstein, Pudovkin and Alexandrov wrote of the power of editing, 'It is known that the basic (and only) means that has brought the cinema to such a powerfully affective strength is MONTAGE' (Eisenstein, 1977b: 257), thereby celebrating the affective impact made on the spectator by film editing. Running through Eisenstein's writing on cinema is a concern with the affective potential of film, the means by which this might be realised and the purposes for which this potential should be employed. To take just one example, of the five types of editing identified by Eisenstein in the 1929 article *Methods of Montage*, only intellectual montage is wholly situated and discussed in relation to the cognitive aspects of cinematic experience, whereas his formulations of metric, rhythmic, tonal and overtonal montage can all be seen to be draw significantly on an appreciation of the affective dimensions of film. Outlining the parameters of metric montage, Eisenstein considers the question of whether or not a perceptible metric beat would be required for this type of editing to have its desired effect on the spectator: 'I do not mean to imply that the beat should be recognizable as part of the perceived impression. On the contrary. Though unrecognized, it is nevertheless indispensable for the "organization" of the sensual impression. Its clarity can bring into unison the "pulsing" of the film and the "pulsing" of the audience' (Eisenstein, 1977b: 73). Here, Eisenstein expresses the idea that the regular 'pulsing' generated by a film edited in this way will be registered as affect by the spectator, and, in common with the contemporary writers referred to above, formulates this phenomenon in sensory terms. Furthermore, he distinguishes the affective power of metric montage from the representational dimensions of film when he adds, 'the content within the frame of the piece is subordinated to the absolute length of the piece [of film]' (Eisenstein, 1977b: 73).

However, while it might be relatively uncontentious to recognise affect as that which Eisenstein formulates as the 'sensual impression' made by the film text on the spectator, understanding the precise nature of this encounter is somewhat more problematic, not least because, as both Massumi (2002) and Kennedy (2002) have pointed out, there is no cultural vocabulary specific to affect.

Drawing on the work of Spinoza, Massumi suggests that affect can be figured as an impingement on the body – a registering of sensory stimuli by and through the body (Massumi, 2002: 31). However, he argues that affect should be understood as *intensity*, relating to the body's passage from one state to another. This proposition distinguishes affect from both the 'content' and effect of that which impinges upon the body, locating it in a 'space' between perception and action; thus affect precedes subjective and cognitive responses to stimuli.[7] Massumi proposes that the validity of conceptualising affect as intensity rather than emotion is demonstrated by the fact that the feelings of sadness generated by a film can, paradoxically, be pleasurable for the spectator. In this way he suggests that it is the *intensity* of emotional response that is registered by spectator as affect, rather than the character of the emotion itself.

Like Massumi, Kennedy draws on Deleuzian notions of affect, which shift the concept from purely psychic formations, in which it is conceptualised primarily in relation to emotion, to '"material" configurations of energy and matter' (Kennedy, 2002: 81). In its Deleuzian formulation, affect is figured in relation to a body reconceptualised in terms of flows, intensities and assemblages. Importantly, it is the Deleuzian disengagement from wholly psychic formulations of affect that allows the term to be articulated by Kennedy in relation to film's materiality. Adopting a similar position to Massumi, Kennedy distinguishes affect from emotion, and in so doing removes it from the field of subjectivity: she comments, 'affect operates beyond subjectivity within the materiality of the film itself, through an immanence of movement, duration, force and intensity, not through a semiotic regime of signification and representation, but in sensation' (Kennedy, 2002: 101). What Kennedy recognises in her own negotiation of affect is the part played by film's materiality in the encounter between film and spectator – an encounter that cannot be figured simply in terms of significatory processes. The strength of Kennedy's approach, and its relevance to my own study, is that it takes into account not only the sensory aspects of affect, but also the way in which the material configurations of film produce affective responses. In this way, it becomes possible to discuss film's affective potential, or its affective dimensions, in relation to its materiality. Accordingly, Kennedy sketches one aspect of affect in what she describes as film's 'processuality':

> the ways in which colours vibrate, clash, coincide, resonate; the
> dimensions of their tones; the blurring of their boundaries; the

linearity across and within the frames; the rhythms and movements felt across the screens; the role of sound within this experience. Not in any psychic or libidinal way as we saw in psychoanalysis, for example, but through the materiality of the film, its compositional elements, connecting with other bodies, corporeal, material, molecular. (Kennedy, 2002: 104)

This understanding of affect reinstates the material play of film into a concept that might otherwise run the risk of divorcing sensation from stimulus. The essential interconnectedness of material stimulus and affective response is certainly recognised by Deleuze and Guattari; hence their pithy observation, 'it is difficult to say where in fact the material ends and sensation begins' (Deleuze and Guattari, 1994: 166). For these writers, affect cannot be distinguished or disentangled from the material events and assemblages that produce sensory response: 'Harmonies are affects. Consonance and dissonance, harmonies of tone or colour, are affects of music or painting' (Deleuze and Guattari, 1994: 164). Taking this lead from Deleuze and Guattari, Kennedy's study of cinema as a non-cognitive experience conceptualises film as a body (denaturalised, conceived as a series of flows and particles) in assemblage with other bodies (the spectator). What we term affect is generated in, through and by this meeting or assemblage. And whereas Massumi figures affect in terms of impingement, Kennedy models the non-cognitive interaction between film and our body as absorption: 'When our bodies absorb the movements of the screenic images, instead of reflecting them, our activity can be described as effort, or . . . as "affect"' (Kennedy, 2002: 169).

Within the context of this book, my own use of the term signals those sensory responses to sonic materiality that cannot be explored through the significatory paradigms that have come to dominate the study of film. However, informed primarily by the notions of affect developed by Deleuze, Guattari and Kennedy outlined above, I also employ the term to engage with those aspects of film sound's materiality that are fundamentally connected to the affect they generate, thereby shifting attention from spectatorial experience to the film itself. Since the primary focus of this book rests on the materiality of film and video sound, the notion of affect is employed in ways that enable a critical engagement with that materiality; as such, affect takes its place alongside the temporal, historical and morphological formulations that I also employ to map and negotiate the material dimensions of film sound.

The potential problem of concentrating exclusively on the notion of affect, as a way of dealing with that which cannot be understood in terms of signification, is that it inevitably places focus on the subject through the concern with embodiment, perception and the senses. While all of these factors must occupy an important place in a critical engagement with the non-significatory, non-linguistic and non-cognitive aspects of cinema, the benefit of what I have so far termed 'materiality' is that it maintains a focus on the text. Having come to film studies through training as a filmmaker, and as someone who continues to produce video and audio work, and who works with students of media production on a daily basis, I am very much aware of the way in which the film or video text is crafted – the way in which the interaction and weaving of its material dimensions creates the sensory stimulus negotiated by the audiospectator. Formulating the film and video text as the meeting point of practices, materials and processes, rather than a source of meanings to be decoded by a 'reader', my own study locates affect as just one of a number of factors to be considered in a critical negotiation of film and video sound.

What is evident from the body of literature produced over the last decade is that the increased interest in affect has not impacted significantly on the study of sound. If indeed there has been an 'affective turn' within cultural studies, then it is certainly not a 'done deal', and in the move to take up the ideas of Deleuze and Guattari there remain substantial critical absences. Much remains to be done even in the task of thinking through Deleuzian concepts in relation to the sonic, and beyond passing references to sound, the work undertaken thus far in film studies has been concerned primarily with the moving image.[8] The critical move made in this book, however, is not simply a switching of sides – a debunking or reversal of established critical positions. What follows is not a wholesale dismissal of the significatory in favour of the material. Rather, my own study is informed by the belief that a critical engagement with film and video sound must be aware of, although not always directly concerned with, both signification and materiality, and importantly, the relationship between these two elements within the film or video text. As Stan Brakhage has suggested, the representational dimensions of film are never entirely lost, no matter how much we might attempt to displace or reconfigure the medium's representational qualities. Although Brakhage made a number of films with recorded soundtracks, his commitment to producing so-called 'silent' work is well known.[9] When asked by Suranjan Ganguly what he had learned from his encounters with the composers Edgard Varèse and John Cage, and from listening to their music, Brakhage commented:

> Primarily what I got from them was the inspiration to make silent film. I was especially attracted to the instrumental aspects of their recorded live-sound (for example, the hiss of tires on a wet street) and the fact that the sound could refer to the source of the recording (a passing car). This is a corollary of film because when you turn on the camera you automatically pick up reference. Even if you shoot totally out of focus, there is a certain quality of say a car's movement which even if reduced to a blob of hexagonal lens-reflecting light is usually recognizable as that of an automobile. (Ganguly, 2002: 154)

For Brakhage, film's capacity to signify through reference to an object-source must be challenged constantly in order to create a 'direct' encounter with vision. This particular approach to the image was determined, in part, by Brakhage's response to the referentiality of recorded sound:

> Take the jackhammer with its electronic echoes in [Varèse's] *Poème Electronique* or the waterdrop sounds that resound within the interpolations in *Deserts*, and consider how these references to the source of the sound are embodied within what is finally a pure sound aesthetic. That has taught me to resist the referent, to take on referential photography and contain it so that the references would not destroy the aesthetic of the film as a film experience. (Ganguly, 2002: 154)

What can be taken from Brakhage's comments is the idea that the significatory can never be neatly excised from cinema, leaving a material balance to be neatly weighed and measured. While the concerns of this book are very definitely focused on the materiality of film and video sound, it is understood that this cannot always be considered in isolation from a medium's representational dimensions. That is to say, the critical engagement with materiality proposed by this book seeks to address phenomena that may or may not support the creation of meaning, but are not in themselves purely significatory.

The materiality of sound

The question of what constitutes film's materiality is far from straightforward and, like the notion of affect, needs some form of clarification within the context of my own approach to the study of film and video sound. The conceptualisation of film as a signifying text, and the resultant focus placed on meaning, neglect two important facts: firstly, that film is a material assemblage, and secondly, that the cinematic event possesses concrete temporal and spatial dimensions. Issues relating to film's materiality have perhaps been most clearly articulated in relation to avant-garde filmmaking practices, particularly those taking their cue from modernism in proposing film practice as a self-reflexive investigation of the medium's own properties. In broad terms, what can be seen as a modernist concern with specificity reveals itself in the pursuit of 'film as film'; that is, film practice that attempts to draw primarily upon the medium's essential characteristics, reducing or eradicating non-cinematic elements, and thus differentiating film from other art forms.[10] The issue of materiality was central to the formulation of structural film practice in 1960s and 1970s, occupying a dominant place in its theorisation.[11] Thus Birgit Hein's characterisation of structural film proposes, 'These works are basically exploring the whole reproduction-process that underpins the medium, including the film material, and the optical, chemical and perceptual processes' (Hein, 1979: 93). Within the context of avant-garde film theory and practice, an important formulation of film's materiality has centred on a recognition of, and engagement with, the qualities of its physical substrate: that is, the strip of film itself, and its unique photochemical properties. For Regina Cornwell, film's material dimension is essentially conceived in terms of light acting on film emulsion in time (Cornwell, 1972: 111). According to this model, film's materiality reveals itself primarily in visual properties such as grain and colour, and in the phenomena of movement and flicker – all of which situate materiality exclusively in relation to film's photochemical support and its passage through the projector.

However, the temporal dimensions of film's materiality alluded to by Cornwell are not limited to film's ability to reproduce or generate movement. The physical aspects of film's material substrate form not only the basis of the film image, but also the medium's structure in time. Accordingly, Malcolm Le Grice proposes that some forms of structural film practice 'establish experience of duration as a "concrete" dimension of cinema, and as the dominant dimension of cinematic experience' (Le Grice, 1977: 118–120). Similarly, for Peter Gidal, duration is understood to be a 'material piece of time', and thus the 'basic unit' of film (Gidal, 1975: 191). We might therefore take Gidal's pithy statement, 'Material must not mean just that which you can touch, some object' (Gidal, 1989: 46), to suggest that an understanding of film's materiality need not necessarily be limited to consideration of the medium's physical substrate. Understood as an event taking place in time, film's concrete temporal dimension renders process and structure part of its material. Within structural film practice, duration is not seen as a neutral and transparent 'container' for time-based images, but becomes foreground as one of film's fundamental properties, one of its material dimensions. And in the same way that film occupies time, so it also occupies space; as Michael Snow points out, 'It is precise that "events *take place*"' (Hartog, 1978: 36). Consequently, the concrete spatial aspects of film exhibition might also be understood to constitute one aspect of the medium's materiality, mapped in part by the physical cone of light emerging from the projector, the screen itself, and the relationship between the two-dimensional screen and the three-dimensional beam of light that is directed at it.

The limitation of the formulations of materiality sketched briefly above, at least in relation to my own study, is obviously their visual bias. To tackle this problem, two key questions need to be addressed: firstly, in what ways might film's sonic element be considered 'material', and secondly, how might this materiality be situated within an audiovisual context? The issue of whether sound *itself* can be considered material, rather than the object it seems to refer to, is addressed by Pierre Schaeffer's notion of 'reduced' listening (Schaeffer, 2004). According to Michel Chion, if *causal* listening involves listening to sounds in order to identify their source, and if *semantic* listening involves listening in order interpret a message transmitted in a code or language, then *reduced* listening (also known as acousmatic listening) focuses on the *traits* of the sound itself, independent of the cause or the meaning of a sound (Chion, 1994: 29). Listening in this way produces a new domain of sound, referred to by Schaeffer as *objets sonore*, or sonic/sonorous objects. Taking Schaeffer's lead, if sound can be listened to and conceptualised as a concrete sonic event, dissociated from its representational functions, then its materiality can be registered in terms of complexity, amplitude, tonal qualities, timbre, duration, development over time and so on. While my own study does not draw directly on Schaeffer's work in this area, the value of the concept of the *objet sonore* is that it addresses the fact that, irrespective of whether or not a sound signifies, it has a material existence in space and time independent of its source. Thus, if we understand sounds to be material events or phenomena, then the notion of sonic materiality refers to the specific qualities, states, forms and structures of those sounds. The qualities of timbre, duration and development over time, which might serve to adumbrate the Schafferian *objet sonore*, provide clear parallels with those aspects of the image that were seen to manifest film's materiality within structural film practice: for example, movement, grain and duration. It is important to remember, however, that the multiple dimensions of sound's materiality are fundamentally interrelated. The quality of reverberation that contributes to the temporal profile of a sound is also inextricably linked with the physical space in which a sound event *takes place*; similarly, the timbral qualities of electronic sound, which serve to identify and constitute its concrete particularity, cannot be divorced from the material technology that produces them. It should also be noted, when thinking through the materiality of film sound, that the soundtrack, as a material assemblage of sounds structured in time, tends to present a multiplicity of sonic phenomena to the listener, rather than discrete, neatly differentiated individual sounds. The experience of listening to the soundtrack reveals its material state to be characterised by flux and flow – a materiality marked by fluid, multiple and shifting sound-to-sound relationships, engendered not only by the recording itself, but also through editing and mixing.

The range of factors to be considered when addressing the complexity and particularity of the material dimensions of cinema are suggested by Rick Altman in a commentary on film exhibition:

> As a material product, cinema quickly reveals the location and nature of its sound track(s), the technology used to produce them, the apparatus necessary for reproduction, and the physical relationship between loudspeakers, spectators, and their physical surroundings. Such an approach encourages us to move past the imaginary space of the screen to the spaces and sounds with which cinema must compete – the kids in the front rows, the air conditioner hum, the lobby cash register, the competing sound track in the adjacent multiplex theatre, passing traffic, and a hundred other sounds that are not part of the text as such, but constitute an important part of cinema's social materiality. (Altman, 1992: 6)

Here Altman maps the material dimensions of cinema not only in relation to its soundtracks, but also in relation to technology, and to the spatial aspects of film exhibition. Importantly, this opens up a much broader range of sounds to critical consideration than those sanctioned by what Altman characterises as 'text-oriented' approaches to cinema. Analysis of film's sonic materiality need not therefore be limited to the multiplicity of sounds recorded *on* the soundtrack, but might also include those sounds produced *by* the soundtrack (such as the crackle of the optical soundtrack), and the technology of film exhibition, heard within the context of particular physical space. While what Altman identifies as the sound of cinema's social materiality does not occupy a significant place in my own study, his suggestions that we open our ears to a range of sounds beyond those sanctioned by the established notion of the soundtrack, and that we consider the role played by film technology in terms of materiality, nevertheless inform my own formulation and negotiation of the material dimensions of film sound.

Audiovisuality

The ways in which film's sonic elements might be considered 'material' having been outlined, the issue remains of how this materiality might be situated within an audiovisual context. If the materiality of sound can in part be mapped in terms of duration, development, rhythm, contrast and so on – as concrete manifestations of what might be more broadly termed 'structure' – then it follows that relationships between sound and image might also be considered as constituents of materiality. That is, if we understand structure to be the concrete particularity of the distribution of events within a temporal frame (rather than an inferred or imposed abstract paradigm), and accept that structure maps an important part of film's materiality (as has been proposed by some writers on structural film), then it is not only the 'horizontal' relationships between sound and sound, and between image and image, that constitute film's materiality, but also the 'vertical' relationships between sound and image. Furthermore, if the concept of materiality relates to the qualities, states, forms and structures of the concrete sounds and images that constitute film, then it should also embrace sound–image relationships.

Central to the formulation of materiality offered by this study is the idea that the material events of film are marked by a relationship between sound and image. Thus I propose that a critical engagement with sound's material dimensions needs to address film and video's *audiovisuality*. I have borrowed Philip Brophy's elegant neologism 'cinesonic' to signal the fact that the sounds with which I am concerned are not isolated sonic phenomena, but are heard within the context of films and videos.[12] This observation appears so self-evident that it hardly seems worth mentioning, but however straightforward this statement may seem – or perhaps because of its very simplicity – the idea it conveys has had relatively little impact on the study of film. Yet for film theory and criticism the consequences of this observation are profound indeed. Michel Chion has almost single-handedly placed this idea on the critical agenda, explaining in his seminal work *Audio-vision* that 'films, television, and other audiovisual media do not just address the eye. They place their spectators – their audio-spectators – in a specific perceptual mode of reception, which . . . I shall call audio-vision' (Chion, 1994: xxv). In his book Chion states that his objective is to 'demonstrate the reality of audiovisual combination – that one perception influences the other and transforms it. We never see the same thing when we also hear; we don't hear the same thing when we see as well' (Chion, 1994: xxvi). My own work builds on Chion's central premise in proposing that any critical engagement with film's materiality must be informed by the idea that what we term 'the film' is marked by a *relationship* between sound and image. Thus what follows is an exploration of that materiality which is best described as film's *audiovisuality*; *Cinesonica: Sounding Film and Video* sets out to sound this audiovisuality by examining the sonic within the context of its relationship with the image.

The notion of audiovisuality may be provisionally considered in relation to three key aspects of the cinesonic text, each having an important bearing on the way in which this book formulates the sonic dimensions of film and video. The first observation to be made regarding this provisional notion of audiovisuality is that the relationship between sound and image is always present in film and video, since sound can never be wholly absent from the cinema or video event. As stated above, a number of studies have shown that film has never been truly silent, since before the introduction of the recorded soundtrack, exhibitors employed various forms of sonic accompaniment to create an audiovisual experience for their audiences. But as Altman suggests, in addition to this performed or recorded soundtrack, sound is also produced *by* an audience, the technology of exhibition and the physical environment in which a film is screened. So, despite the fact that a filmmaker like Stan Brakhage might make the conscious choice not to record a soundtrack for a film, screenings of his work can never be a purely visual experience. The benefit of thinking through the sonic dimensions of film and video in this way is that, in challenging the dominant notion of the self-contained soundtrack, a broader range of sound–image relationships is brought to bear on the study of the cinesonic. What is interesting about these extra-textual sounds is that while they contribute to the cinematic experience, they are often situated below the level of consciousness; as Brian Massumi points out, 'The vast majority of the world's sensations are certainly nonconscious' (Massumi, 2002: 16). If the range of sounds appropriate to the study of film is extended in this way, then we are required to turn our attention to sounds that we normally neglect, ignore and listen through – like the hiss of oxides on magnetic tape, or the optical crackle that marks older film prints.

The second observation to be made with regard to a provisional notion of audiovisuality relates to the idea that film and video are transsensorial media forms. The common conception of film as a binary construct composed of sound and image precludes engagement with the transsensory or intersensory experience of cinema. A number of filmmakers, yet surprisingly few theorists, have concerned themselves with the ways in which the senses of sight and sound combine, mix and sometimes blur in cinematic experience. The work of film theorist Laura U. Marks is a notable exception to this, and recent interest in the sensory has begun to challenge the distinctions previously made between the senses, in relation to our apprehension of various phenomena.

The issue of film and video's transsensoriality brings us to the third observation relating to a provisional notion of audiovisuality. In turning attention to the ways in which sounds and images merge and coalesce, this book does not suggest that no useful distinction can be made between the sonic and the visual, but rather that there are forms of combination and blending that create significant moments of transsensory experience, just as there are strategies of differentiation and dissociation that demand consideration of the sonic and the visual as distinct phenomena. The issue here is not that one type of relationship determines audiovisuality, but rather that film and video are host to multiple, shifting sound–image relations. Accordingly, any consideration of audiovisuality must necessarily respond to the fluid nature of the film text, and to the fact that the relationship between sound and image is never of a single, stable and continuous type, but is instead marked by constant flow and flux. In time-based media like film and video, the changes that take place *within* both sound and image necessarily create a constantly changing relationship *between* these two elements. Furthermore, at any given moment film's audiovisuality may be marked by more than one type of

relationship; it is therefore possible that simultaneous, overlapping, multiple audiovisual modalities might comfortably occupy
any given audiovisual moment. At the same time that we engage
intellectually with the signficatory dimensions of film and video,
the medium's materiality also registers and operates at the level
of affect. Any critical appreciation of cinesonic will therefore need
to embrace the ways in which the visual and the sonic interact,
combine and separate to create the film or video text. What this
demands is an engagement with the contingent rather than the
universal, an engagement with flux, flow and change rather than
the frozen, the static, the immutable.

Sounding audiovisuality

With the above notion of film's materiality in place, I attempt to
sound audiovisuality through its temporal, historical, morphological and affective dimensions. Thus the formulations of materiality
drawn from the work of Altman, Schaeffer and from structural
film theory serve mainly to define the territory of sonic materiality
that my own study seeks to map in other ways. This break with the
established discourse on materiality re-raises the issue of why it is
important to engage in a critical sounding of film and video's audiovisuality at all. My own study does not offer itself simply as an
attempt to account more *accurately* for those elements of film and
video that cannot be netted by Saussurian notions of signification
– a pointless activity in any case, since Saussure never intended his
posthumously published work to be applied to an analysis of the
cinesonic. But it is to Saussure that I once again return to address
the issue of what might be at stake in a sounding of the cinesonic.

Located at the heart of Saussurian linguistics is the figure of
negative differentiation: 'in language there are only differences'
(Saussure, 1964: 120). Central to this approach to language is the
distinction made between what is knowable and what is unknowable, which then maps onto modal distinctions between notions of
essence founded upon differentiation, individuation and abstraction, and phenomena which are noisy, chaotic, unruly, unmasterable and ultimately unknowable. The tension between these
conceptual and ontological modalities reveals itself in the way in
which Saussure removes the troubling presence of sound from the
study of linguistics, the subsequent eschewal of speech in favour
of language, and the modelling of language through writing. The
unmanageability of the sonic dimension of language is clearly a

troubling presence in the *Course in General Linguistics*, and a key factor informing Saussure's preference for writing: 'apart from their graphic symbols, sounds are only vague notions' (Saussure, 1964: 33). But what is it that necessitates the clear removal of sound from the Saussurian project, when it might just as well have been considered a significant constituent of speech? In a discussion of the object of linguistics, Saussure constructs speech (*parole*) as unruly, unmasterable, 'many-sided and heterogeneous' (Saussure, 1964: 9), not simply uncontainable within his own approach to the study of language, but unknowable within *any* scientific project. From Saussure's standpoint, speech lacks unity, 'straddling several areas simultaneously – physical, physiological and psychological – it belongs both to the individual and to society; we cannot put it into any category of human facts' (Saussure, 1964: 9). Within the context of a project based on classification and differentiation, speech becomes a noisy, tumultuous swirling mass that can only be tamed by language (*langue*): 'As soon as we give language first place among the facts of speech, we introduce a natural order into a mass that lends itself to no other classification' (Saussure, 1964: 9). What is particularly telling here is Saussure's use of the word 'mass': speech is figured as the undifferentiated, the confusing and, most worrying of all, the unmasterable. With its sonic base, speech is too fluid, too undifferentiated, too much in flux to be dealt with in the same way as the static, immutable model of writing. Saussure's project not only favours this unchangeability, but also imposes stasis on the phenomena under study by denying their multiplicity, flux and fluidity.

As noted above, the Saussurian model of language is founded upon the inscription of difference. However, the influence of this conceptual model extends beyond Saussure's formulation of the mechanics of signification to suffuse and inform the semiological project as a whole; what cannot be *differentiated* is rejected as an unmanageable, unknowable mass. Returning once again to Saussure's simile of the swimmer without a lifebelt, the threat posed by the oceanic becomes clear: 'Whoever consciously deprives himself of the perceptible image of the written word runs the risk of perceiving only a shapeless and unmanageable mass. Taking away the written form is like depriving a beginning swimmer of his life belt' (Saussure, 1964: 32). The epistemological model of semiology proposes ways of knowing that are wholly reliant upon forms of division and individuation. As such, Saussurian linguistics is simply one, albeit highly influential, manifestation of what

Deleuze and Guattari have termed 'arborescent' thought. Taking
the root system of plants as a way to map and describe 'the most
classical and well reflected, oldest, and weariest kind of thought'
(Deleuze and Guattari, 1988: 5), the authors propose that arborescent thought is founded upon forms of bifurcation, separation and
individuation – just as a root system divides underground: 'Binary
logic is the spiritual reality of the root-tree' (Deleuze and Guattari,
1988: 5). What this arboreal modelling addresses are the deeply
structural problems of structural thinking, of structuralist theory
and of that strand of post-structural theory which, in its opposition
to structuralism, can never be divorced from it. For Deleuze and
Guattari, challenging this model of thought is of central importance to any radical philosophical project: 'We're tired of trees. We
should stop believing in trees, roots, and radicles. They've made
us suffer too much. All of arborescent culture is founded on them,
from biology to linguistics' (Deleuze and Guattari, 1988: 15). And
if one considers how arboreal modes of thought underpin divisive
social, sexual and political constructions of otherness, then it is
clear that a great deal is at stake in any attempt to address their
influence on the ways in which we understand the world.

The question this raises for my own study is how binary formulations and the inscription of difference might impact upon the ways
in which we conceptualise and negotiate relationships between
sound and image; for example, what does this inscription of difference mean in terms of cinesonic formulations such as montage
and so-called 'contrapuntal' uses of sound, or in relation to oppositional and deconstructive filmmaking practices? One of the problems associated with forms of negative differentiation is the focus
they place on a constitutive other – an issue that is particularly
relevant to the theorisation of oppositional and deconstructive
filmmaking practices founded on a resistance to dominant modes
of representation and expression. Negative differentiation's need
for a constitutive other places a problematic reliance on a secondary term – a reliance on that which the phenomenon under
consideration is *not*. The problem with this constitutive outside is
that it has the effect of deflecting attention away from the thing
under consideration, rendering it at best subordinate to this other
term. This displacement is echoed by the sound–source formulation, wherein our attention is constantly diverted from the material sound being auditioned to the real or imagined object or event
it is understood to represent. The challenge these issues raise for
a critical engagement with the cinesonic is to find ways in which

we might constitute and negotiate the object of study in positive terms, avoiding the constant displacement of materiality that occurs in significatory systems. Similarly, if binary epistemological and ontological modalities are reliant upon differentiation, mutual exclusivity and opposition, how then might we engage with the forms of fusion, entanglement, combination and blurring that the notion of audiovisuality might justifiably include?

In addressing what is at stake in a critical exploration of the cinesonic, my own study of film and video sound attempts to address the political dimensions of audiovisual practice, and in particular ideas surrounding the notion of a radical audiovisual poetics. The fact that some forms of audiovisuality may be unknowable within particular epistemological regimes gives them radical potential; that is, they may offer alternatives to hegemonic models of audiovisuality – like that proposed by classical cinema – in ways that contest those models at a fundamental level. In some senses my concern with radical poetics represents a return to the issues of film form that were central to what D. N. Rodowick has termed 'Political Modernism' (Rodowick, 1994). In the 1970s the theoretical interventions made in film studies by semiology, psychoanalysis and Marxism came to have a direct bearing on the way in which film practice was understood as political. One of the important consequences of this particular theorisation of film practice was that issues of 'form' were considered in political terms: 'Ideology was no longer simply considered as the message or content of films; equally important was asking how the spectator was addressed through strategies of filmic signification' (Rodowick, 1994: xii–xiii). By revisiting the issue of the relationship between film form and politics, questions of audiovisuality open out onto what is at stake politically in sound–image relationships, what might constitute a radical poetics of audiovisuality, and how this relates to what has traditionally been understood as political within the context of audiovisual poetics, particularly in relation to modalities of modernism.

Organisation and scope

The way in which this study is organised relates very closely to issues of methodology: my study of cinesonica works through a number of trajectories, each of which can be seen as an attempt to sample and sound the audiovisuality of film and video. The book makes no claim to offer a linear history or totalising 'theory' of the cinesonic, but rather seeks to make a number of interventions into what remains an under-theorised area of the study of film and video. In doing so, the book aims to make creative and productive connections between particular historical moments, film and video production practices, technologies, theoretical and conceptual frameworks, and individual film and video texts. The trajectories that constitute the book draw upon films and videos as primary sources in their own right, on various bodies of critical and theoretical work, and sometimes on the words of the filmmakers themselves. Since the concern of my study is the cinesonic, rather than issues of film genre, the book purposefully engages with a wide range of film and video sources. The majority of the work undertaken on film sound to date has tended to focus on the narrative feature film, and while my own study also considers classical Hollywood cinema, significant reference is also made to avant-garde film and video, animated cartoons and scratch video. Although each chapter makes use of resources drawn from the field of film studies, critical and theoretical work from other disciplines is also brought to the discussion of my chosen topics. Each of these is introduced within the context of the chapter hosting it, but a brief outline might usefully indicate the key theoretical resources upon which the book as a whole draws.[13] Mention has already been made of the work of Deleuze and Guattari, and this study engages specifically with concepts developed in *A Thousand Plateaus* (1988) and in Deleuze's *Cinema 2: The Time-Image* (1989). My own approach to these texts has been to *use* the ideas developed in them, rather than to make Deleuzian philosophy the focus of my study. In drawing upon a limited number of Deleuzian concepts, such as the refrain, territoriality, the line of flight and the fold, my aim has been to explore the ways in which these ideas might deepen an understanding of the cinesonic, rather than an understanding of Deleuzian philosophy. A number of these concepts and terms are already well established in the field of cultural studies, and therefore, in order to maintain focus on the cinesonic, I have tried to minimise the amount of space given over to descriptive accounts of these ideas, and to situating them within their original contexts. Readers who wish to explore these ideas further are directed to the excellent studies listed elsewhere in this chapter, and to Deleuze and Guattari's original texts. Works on music, and the writings of composers, figure in several chapters, and in addition I have drawn upon Jacques Attali's seminal work of cultural historiography, *Noise* (1985), Curtis Roads's work in microsound, in his book of the same name (2001), and Siegmund Levarie and Ernst Levy's *Musical Morphology* (1983).

Each of the trajectories featured in the remaining five chapters of this book stands alone in some ways, but at the same time each forms a part of a larger arc. They appear in a particular order, and are constructed in a certain way, to create a sense of movement over the book as a whole, balancing the act of sampling with the articulation of my chosen samples. At the same time, connectivity is created by issues and figures that echo across the chapters. Ideas relating to noise, montage, negative differentiation, and decon-struction[14] take the form of a refrain, each return of which aims to add both depth and breadth to the study. The nodal points in this study, entitled 'refrain', appear at the end of chapters, so that each subsequent chapter can build on what has gone before.

The notion of the refrain – in the sense of a return – describes the critical stance I have attempted to adopt throughout this study. Whenever we approach a film, video or critical text, we tend to inherit well-rehearsed readings of that text; my critical response to this has simply been to ask the question, 'what if?' Much of what follows can be seen as a form of revisionism, which returns to sets of ideas and particular readings in order to release a potentiality that is locked into a resource, but which has remained neglected because of the way that resource has been used or read; and it is by this kind of critical return that I aim to make an interven-tion into the study of film and video sound. A brief illustration of this approach is given by the way in which I have used Siegmund Levarie and Ernst Levy's work on musical morphology. The notion of musical morphology is not one that in any way dominates the critical landscape of musicology – indeed, Levarie and Levy's work is firmly located in traditions of structuralist thought in ways that might seem unhelpful in the context of my own study. However, their passionately written, highly personal text not only serves as a snapshot of a certain mode of thinking that this book attempts to break with, but in its central figure of morphology provides a critical resource that can be *revisited* to engage productively in a sounding of the materiality of sound–image relationships. Although, in asserting that music can be understood in terms of the stability of certain musical forms, Levarie and Levy's study adopts a structuralist approach to sonic phenomena, the notion of morphology can also be applied to an encounter with the shift, flux and change of sound. Thus the critical approach proposed by this book is not one of debunking or demolishing, but of revisiting and rethinking – approaching both audiovisual texts and critical works as material that is there to be constantly mined and re-mined.

Notes

1 While filmmakers, critics and theorists have been writing on the subject of film sound since the late 1920s, it was perhaps the journal *Yale French Studies* that first considered the place of the soundtrack within the discipline of film studies, in its 1980 *Cinema/Sound* special issue. Elisabeth Weis and John Belton's *Film Sound: Theory and Practice* (1985) did much to consolidate and develop the first wave of film sound studies, bringing together important existing articles on sound and commissioning new pieces; it remains a key text for anyone approaching this topic for the first time. A special issue on the soundtrack published by the journal *Screen* in 1984, and Rick Altman's edited collection *Sound Theory Sound Practice* (1992), both offer stimulating articles on various aspects of film sound. More recently, Jay Beck and Tony Grajeda's edited collection *Lowering the Boom: Critical Studies in Film Sound* (2008) has brought an interdisciplinary approach to the theory and history of film sound in a book that considers various elements of the soundtrack in a range of different film forms and genres. As many writers have noted, the literature on film music is substantial, and is dominated by a focus on narrative fiction film; key works in this area of scholarship include Theodor Adorno and Hanns Eisler's *Composing for the Films* (1994), Claudia Gorbman's *Unheard Melodies: Narrative Film Music* (1987) and Kathryn Kalinak's *Settling the Score: Music and the Hollywood Film* (1992). A small number of studies have focused exclusively on the place of the voice in cinema, most notably Kaja Silverman's *The Acoustic Mirror: The Female Voice in Psychoanalysis and Cinema* (1988), Michel Chion's *The Voice in Cinema* (1999), and Sarah Kozloff's books *Invisible Storytellers: Voice-over Narration in American Fiction Film* (1988) and *Overhearing Film Dialogue* (2000). In relation to film sound technology, there are many studies dealing with the transition from 'silent' to sound film (albeit mainly in relation to American cinema), including Donald Crafton's *The Talkies: American Cinema's Transition to Sound, 1926–1931* (1999) and James Lastra's *Sound Technology and the American Cinema: Perception, Representation, Modernity* (2000). Gianluca Sergi's *The Dolby Era: Film Sound in Contemporary Hollywood* (2004) provides valuable insight into developments in film sound since the 1970s. Michel Chion's seminal text *Audio-Vision: Sound on Screen* (1994) remains the most important work to date on sound–image relations in film and television, exploring the way in which the soundtrack affects perception of the image; these ideas have been developed and expanded in Chion's *Film, A Sound Art* (2009). For a lively and

stimulating alternative to established discourse on film sound, readers are directed to Philip Brophy's *100 Modern Soundtracks* (2004), which offers short critical essays on the use of sound in post-classical cinema.

2 See King (1984), Abel and Altman (2001) and Altman (2004).

3 Throughout this book critical attention is focused on the theoretical lineage of semiology rather than semiotics. C. S. Peirce's work certainly provides an alternative to Saussure's modelling of the sign in his tripartite formulation of the indexical, symbolic and iconic, and an alternative model of signification that proposes a process of infinite semiosis rather than formulating the signified (or rather the *interpretant*) as the terminal point of significatory processes. However, the fundamental division between the material signifier and what it might signify – which is a central concern of this book – remains common to the work of both Saussure and Peirce, even though their formulations of the processes and the elements of signification differ; thus Peirce writes, 'A sign is an object which stands for another to some mind' (Peirce, 1991: 141), while Saussure proposes, 'The linguistic sign unites, not a thing and a name, but a concept and a sound image' (Saussure, 1964: 66). Similarly, while Peirce proposes a division between sign and interpretant, Saussure proposes one between signifier and signified. In relation to the central concerns of this book, the specificity of Peircean Semiotics does not fundamentally challenge the issues raised by my analysis of Saussurian linguistics, but rather illustrates them in different terms. To avoid any confusion that might arise with regard to these two traditions, I have chosen to use the adjectives 'significatory' and 'significative' throughout this book, in preference to the more familiar 'semiotic'.

4 Saussure acknowledges that language is only one particular semiological system, and that there are others which embrace signs that are not arbitrary, but motivated in some way, e.g., bowing. However, his *preference* for arbitrary signs is clearly expressed: 'Signs that are wholly arbitrary realise better than the others the ideal of the semiological process; that is why language, the most complex and universal of all systems of expression, is also the most characteristic; in this sense linguistics can become the master-pattern for all branches of semiology although language is only one particular semiological system' (Saussure, 1964: 68).

5 This latter type of sound is commonly described as off-screen sound, a term that signals the dominance of retinal regimes over the ways in which cinema is described and understood, since what this means, in fact, is that a sound's perceived *source* is off-screen.

6 This article first appeared in English translation in *Close Up*, October 1928, Vol. 3, No. 4, pp. 10–13. However, reference is made throughout this book to the translation by Jay Leyda, published in Eisenstein's *Film Form* (1977b).

7 This is not to suggest, however, that there is no relationship between the affective and the cognitive. While affect can be usefully distinguished from cognitive responses to stimuli, the two exist in relationship to one another. As Paul Gormley states, 'Thinking about the differences between affect and knowledge/meaning in purely binaristic and totalising terms is impossible' (Gormley, 2005: 33). Massumi suggests that the relationship between meaning and affect is one of 'resonation or interference, amplification or dampening' (Massumi, 2002: 25). Similarly, Eisenstein does not propose that meaning and affect are in any way mutually exclusive, but rather that film's affective and representational potential may exist and operate simultaneously; for example, a representational image may also register with the spectator at an affective level, as a result of the way in which it has been edited. Nevertheless, distinguishing the cognitive from the affective is a useful strategy when, as in my own study, the aim is to explore areas beyond the significatory.

8 A notable exception to this is a study by Laleen Jayamanne (2001), which considers Spike Lee's use of music in *Do the Right Thing* (1989) in terms of Deleuzian notions of territoriality.

9 See Brakhage's essay *The Silent Sound Sense* (1960).

10 A view of modernism proposed, for example, by Clement Greenberg in his famous essay *Modernist Painting*: 'It quickly emerged that the unique and proper area of competence of each art coincided with all that was unique in the nature of its medium' (Greenberg, 2002: 775).

11 See, for example, Regina Cornwell's *Some Formalist Tendencies in the Current American Avant-garde Film* (1972), Peter Gidal's *Theory and Definition of Structural/Materialist Film* (1975) and *Materialist Film* (1989), Sharits's *Words per Page* (1972) and Peter Wollen's articles *The Two Avant-Gardes* (1975) and *Ontology and Materialism in Film* (1976).

12 Brophy coined the term for the *Cinesonic International Conference on Film Scores and Sound Design*, held annually in Melbourne since 1998.

13 Although not referenced extensively in my own study, there is a growing body of literature relating to the emerging field of sound studies, concerned in particular with auditory culture and sonic arts. This body of work presents an interdisciplinary approach to the study of sound within a cultural context, drawing upon musicology, architecture, electro-acoustic composition, urban studies, communication and media studies, phenomenology, social sciences, psychology and other disciplines to engage with subjects such as the role of sound in historical and social thought, contemporary and historical soundscapes, music, voices, technologies and auditory experience and sensation. Bull and Back (2003), Erlmann (2004) and Augoyard and Torgue (2005) draw on a range of disciplines to offer a variety of perspectives on the study of auditory culture, while the work of Kittler

(1999), Lastra (2000), Day (2000), Taylor (2001), Thompson (2002), Weiss (2002) and Sterne (2003) situates specific sound technologies within histories of auditory culture. Recent critical commentaries on sonic art, which seek to locate art works and sonic practices in relation to broader contexts of auditory culture, include LaBelle and Roden (1999), LaBelle and Migone (2001), Weiss (2001) and Toop (1999, 2004).

14 It is understood that the term 'deconstruction' has a very precise meaning in the field if literary studies, associated with Derridean theories of reading. While not entirely divorced from this notion and history of deconstruction, the term is used in this book in a more general sense to signal those artistic and critical practices that, in the wake of structuralism, sought to deconstruct particular (often hegemonic) cultural practices and objects. My own use of the word seeks to embrace a plurality of deconstructive practices, including the strategies associated with so-called 'counter cinema' and 'Brechtian' techniques, both of which sought to uncover and reveal the illusionistic nature of particular representational forms. Of particular relevance to this study are those deconstructive practices and theories that seek to disentangle the sonic from the visual within the audiovisual constructions of cinema.

2 Sound Source Object

Listening ears

Scattered along the British coastline are the crumbling remains of a sound technology that never really was. Between the First and Second World Wars a series of experimental concrete sound mirrors was constructed to serve as an early warning system against airborne attack from mainland Europe. Sound was gathered at the focal point of these acoustic reflectors by means of trumpet-shaped sound collectors, connected to the listener's ears by a stethoscope arrangement of rubber tubes – a system to be replaced in later experiments by microphones, amplifiers and headsets. The personnel posted at these listening stations would monitor for the sound of enemy aircraft heading towards Britain over the English Channel, providing a sonic forewarning of imminent aerial attack that would allow the relevant authorities to take appropriate defensive action. At the heart of this technology, a forerunner of radar, lay a notion about the relationship between sound and its source that ultimately turned out to be the technology's failure. The value of these 'listening ears', as they are sometimes referred to locally, was founded upon the belief that one sound could be separated from a host of others, and could be attributed to a particular source: in this case, approaching enemy aircraft.

These now crumbling concrete structures represent a manifestation of the common conception of sound as an attribute of a source. What motivated interest in these particular sounds was the fact that they signified the approach of enemy aircraft, but the failure of this project points to modalities of sound that challenge significatory formulations of sonic phenomena. Somehow, the sound of an aeroplane was to identify the presence of an unseen enemy in vast, fluid, undifferentiated expanses of sea and sky. However, the problem with the acoustic mirrors is obvious to anyone visiting them today. For those constructions with an elevated or exposed coastal position, the swirling white noise of wind, rain and waves masks and envelops all other sounds until it is too late – until the enemy is upon you. The oceanic sound of wind and waves, and the flux of meteorological systems, mix, conceal and homogenise all sonic phenomena within their grasp. And for those acoustic mirrors located some distance back from the coastline, it was the environmental noise created by the development of road transport and the expansion of coastal communities between the wars that interfered with air defence listening.[1]

If the foundation of this technology rested on the notion that sound is attributable to a source, then its failure reveals two ways of conceptualising and approaching sound that seem opposed and mutually exclusive. The first constructs sound in terms of isolation, individuation, differentiation and an associated cognitive foregrounding. As the mode attributing sound to a source, it is the conception underlying the most common linguistic formulation by which we describe sonic phenomena as 'the sound of' something or other. In contrast, the other conceptual mode proposes sound as undifferentiated, fluid, protean, dispersed and oceanic: a conception of sound that is primarily associated with sonic phenomena relegated to the background of conscious perception, or alternatively, disruptively foregrounded as noise. But even if somehow it had been possible, under optimum conditions, to differentiate these sounds, their detection gave no information about the height, speed and direction of approaching aircraft. The crude sound–source model adopted by this technology was not able to describe or map the spatial and temporal dimensions of the unwinding sonic event, and was thus of limited value to those trying to prepare defence against an enemy attack. Put another way, the significatory model upon which the acoustic reflectors were founded was unable to engage with the material dimensions of the sonic event; unable to engage with the flux, flow and movement of sound in space and time.

The relationship between sound and source manifested by these concrete structures relates directly to the signifier/signified model proposed by Saussurian linguistics. If sound is considered to be an attribute of an object-source, when divorced from that object, sound becomes conceptualised as a signifier of that source in its (visual) absence: barking signifies dog, while rumbling possibly suggests the approach of enemy aircraft. Sound therefore enters into networks of representational thought, serving as a proxy for something that is absent from its own concrete manifestation, and divorced from its own materiality. Transposed to the cinematic, this sound–source formulation has a powerful influence on the way in which we think through sound–image relations. In some respects the screen, through its representational visual imagery, seems to offer itself as a collection and succession of object-sources, to which sounds are appended. But in cinema, sounds are appended not to objects, but to images. This introduces into the sound–object formulation a further significatory dimension, to which is added the fact that the sounds we hear at the cinema, designed to accompany the images, are usually recorded; the dog listening attentively to his master's voice is not listening to his master's voice at all, but rather to its recorded analogue.

Sounding the untranslatable

The cinesonic is not entirely served by an essentially linguistic model of film as signifying text. When film is conceptualised as such, along the lines proposed by the dominant linguistic models of signification, we engage in an act of translation, attempting to transpose the material audiovisuality of cinema into the immaterial paradigms of language. But what of those elements of the audiovisual experience that resist this act of translation, and which cannot be neatly processed by attaching the label 'signifier'? There are a host of cinesonic elements and practices and relationships that do not necessarily *make sense*, but which can nevertheless *be sensed;* that is, there are aspects of the cinesonic that do not function primarily through signification, or whose contribution to cinematic experience is not wholly exhausted by the concept of signification. The material dimensions of the cinesonic are sensed and experienced beyond their ability to support the significatory processes that often seem to dominate our understanding of cinema, since this materiality resides not only in the film text itself, but also in the temporal and spatial complexity of the audiovisual event, and our own perceptual relationship with it.

These neglected dimensions of audiovisuality might be usefully formulated with Sarat Maharaj's notion of the untranslatable as the 'left-over' of translation (Hall and Maharaj, 2001: 45). Maharaj describes that which cannot be processed or contained within any particular epistemological system in the following terms: 'When one language, one experience, one visual or retinal regime gets translated into another, it has to be re-jigged to fit into the system of thinking of the other and something is "left out". This remainder – at least this is what logically appears when you analyse translation – inhabits the space of the untranslatable' (Hall and Maharaj, 2001: 45). Applied to the case of a cinema conceptualised as signifying text, the 'left-over' that remains unaccounted for by the logic of the sign could be, for example, the material aspects of the signifier, or the non-significatory temporal and affective dimensions of the cinesonic event. As a time-based medium, film occupies duration, but if we choose to think of film only as a signifying text, translating its audio-visuality into chunks of meaning, the experience of duration is 'left out' or 'left over'. To engage critically with the cinesonic, it becomes necessary therefore to think beyond the significatory formulations of what a sound means or represents. However, in a representational art form like cinema, the significatory cannot be neatly excised, leaving the material balance of non-signification to be neatly weighed and measured, since the meaningful and the meaningless exist in close relation to one another (and not simply in terms of mutual definition). So, for example, when we listen to an actor speaking in an 'old' film, in addition to the semantic meaning of the dialogue relayed to us by the technology of cinema, the technology itself is made present in a quality of sound that might signify era of production, mode of production and so on. At the same time, this quality of sound – the warm, oceanic, enveloping rumble of optical crackle that marks older film prints – is also registered by the audiospectator as affect. The problem with a purely significative modelling of the film text is that it has no way of dealing with either the materiality of this sound, or its powerful affective dimensions, both of which are left out and left over by the process of translating it according to linguistic paradigms of signification.

As Saussure's preference for language over speech indicates, in order to ensure the success of the semiological project, the material balance of translation needs to be contained, repressed or excluded. But since all signification begins with a material manifestation, this is not easily done. In the Saussurian model of linguistic signification, the materiality of a signifier simply exists to manifest difference, and after doing so 'evaporates' in deference to the signified, which being a conceptual entity has no material dimension. However, the materiality of the signifier does not evap-orate, and its troubling presence cannot be completely repressed or excluded. This material 'other' of the significative is sometimes sounded as noise in relation to the semantic, as Maharaj suggests in his discussion of the 'left-over' of translation: 'The remainder which cannot be put into words might be something you can visualise or something that can be suggested through sonic stuff, through '"sounding of that difference"' as a kind of turbulence, as a cloud of disturbance around clear-cut linguistic meaning' (Hall and Maharaj, 2001: 46). The 'untranslatable' aspects of materiality might thus be inscribed within and against significatory modes as a destabilising form of turbulence.

This particular relationship between materiality and meaning is demonstrated by the films and videos of John Smith, Scott Rankin, Anthea Kennedy and Nick Burton, whose work, in a variety of ways, presents a direct critical engagement with proc-esses of signification, albeit by means of their destabilisation. A consideration of the approaches to film and video practice adopted by these filmmakers is particularly relevant to a sound-ing of cinesonic materiality, since, in the process of destabilising signification, materiality begins to reveal itself. What their work shows is that not only can the materiality of sound disrupt sig-nification, but also this disruption may manifest the material. In Smith, Kennedy and Burton's films, this critical engagement with signification is largely undertaken through the deconstruction and denaturalisation of filmic modes of representation, while in Rankin's work the focus is on personal, cognitive and linguistic relationships, and the ways in which these relationships influence our thought processes and perception of the world. In the work of these film and video makers, cinesonic materiality is sounded where signification breaks down or is tested, where it proves resistant and difficult, or where it is revealed not to be that simple relationship of equivalence proposed by the signifier/signified binarism. The case studies that follow consider the points at which destabilisation occurs in the field of the cinesonic – moments in which the disturbance and breakdown of signification begins to sound the space of untranslatable materiality, marking what is 'left over' and neglected in studies of film sound dominated by the concept of the signifying text. Equally importantly, this work also serves as a means by which to log the disjuncture between film practice and its theorisation. By engaging critically with the limitations of theoretical modes that draw predominantly on significatory models of meaning, the films themselves become models through which it might be possible to figure some of the neglected spaces of cinesonic materiality. In this sense, what follows is a search for productive failures, in terms both of significatory film practice, and of the potentially creative disjunctures between film practice and its theorisation. As the surrealist poets Paul Eluard and Benjamin Péret once observed, 'Cherries fall where texts fail' (Eluard and Péret, 1995: 129).

Maharaj's notion of the untranslatable clearly signals the limitations of significatory models when he writes, 'Beyond the *sense* of word and image are sounds which cannot be entirely drawn into the net of signification and cannot entirely be decoded and deciphered as meaning this, that or the other. These larger sonic pools – the penumbra of the untranslatable . . . for which we have to venture beyond language . . .' (Hall and Maharaj, 2001: 39–40). This 'penumbra of the untranslatable' is clearly a potentially huge field, largely unmapped in terms of critical enquiry. How, then, should we begin to traverse its terrain?

The sound–source formulation, by which we attribute sounds to perceived or actual objects, provides a productive departure point from which to begin a sounding of this 'penumbra'. As stated above, this common cinesonic model occupies a privileged position in terms of the way sound–image relationships in film have been conceptualised, representing what Maharaj refers to as 'the net of signification'. As such, the sound–source formulation serves as a primary example of the significative modelling of sonic phenomena; but as Walter Murch has observed, sounds are not 'completely explained' by the objects that seem to create them (Chion, 1994: xvi). And indeed, what some film sound practices demonstrate, particularly those taking their cue from developments in modernism, is that the very act of conceptualising sounds as signifiers, and of attempting to resolve their identity into a simple significatory function, produces a turbulent excess that demands to be heard.

John Smith: signification and self-reflexivity

The work of John Smith explores both the significatory potential of sound, and its material flux and fluidity. Smith has been
producing films since the early 1970s, and although he is usually
categorised as an avant-garde or experimental filmmaker, his use
of low-key drama, humour and an interest in storytelling mark
a point of contact with some aspects of mainstream film and television. However, while engaging with narrative, Smith's work is
clearly influenced by the concerns of structural film, which was a
dominating presence in British independent film culture when the
filmmaker was a student at the Royal College of Art in the early
1970s.[2] Thus his early films have been described by A. L. Rees as
part of that movement's 'second-wave' (Rees, 1999: 117).

For Peter Gidal, one of the key theorists and practitioners of
structural filmmaking, and also Smith's tutor at the Royal College
of Art, structural film was conceived in terms of the tension
between film's representational dimensions and its materiality:
'The dialectic of the film is established in that space of tension
between materialist flatness, grain, light, movement, and the
supposed reality that is represented' (Gidal, 1978: 1). For Gidal,
this approach to film practice necessitated a rejection of illusionism in favour of a concern with the material dimensions of the
cinematic event. What resulted was a pursuit of 'film as film',
demanding an active viewer situated in opposition to the passive
consumer of mainstream cinema. In this respect, structural film,
as formulated and practised by Gidal, was a political project,
designed to resist the psychological manipulation of the viewer
that was considered central to the operation of classical cinema.
This praxis is firmly located within the context of what Rodowick
has termed the 'political modernism' of the 1970s, in which the
relationship between film and ideology became a central concern
for avant-garde film practice (Rodowick, 1994). Thus, structural
film was to engage directly with what Gidal proposed were the
oppressive dimensions of representation: 'Representation matters,
it is realism of another kind. A materialist experimental film practice engages on that level with the illusions of representation and
the illusory (and real!) constructs of viewing film, or anything,
as if it were natural' (Gidal, 1989: 7). The issue of representation became a key arena in which the significatory and primarily visual dimensions of film were discussed in political terms.
Representation was thus situated as the site of political struggle,

in which the material dimensions of cinema were positioned in an oppositional relationship to 'illusionistic' and 'naturalistic' forms of signification: 'Without a theory and practice of radically material-ist experimental film, cinema would endlessly be the '"natural"' reproduction of capitalist and patriarchal forms' (Gidal, 1989: xiii). While for Gidal and others this entailed a radical negation of normative modes of film construction, a wholesale rejection of narrative and an oppositional stance to illusionism, Smith's own praxis adopted a different attitude to the ideas underpinning structural film practice:

> I guess it wasn't that I was resistant to it, it was that it wasn't all there was for me. I have always been fascinated in or attracted to illusion-ism in cinema: being drawn into a surrogate, substitute experience. But also what really makes that work for me is being able to pull out of it, so that the films are a kind of interplay . . . between looking at the stuff as material and moving in and being immersed in it. It's that kind of edge that I'm interested in, between immersion and dis-tance.[3] (Smith, 2002)

The role played by sound in film, and its relationship with the image, are key concerns of Smith's praxis. His films engage with the way in which sound creates or accepts meaning, working to loosen the bond between sound as a material signifier, and that which it might signify. A technique commonly used by Smith is to offer up an image or a sound that seems to have a single identifi-able source or a particular meaning. He will then work to decon-struct the relationship between signifier and signified, throwing it into question and objectifying its terms. *Om* (1986) presents us with the image of a young Buddhist monk sitting alone in a dark space. Shaven-headed, and dressed in saffron robes, he looks directly at the camera as incense smoke rises in the foreground of the shot. He takes a deep breath, and then begins to chant the single sound-word-tone 'om' (Figure 2.1).

As the duration of the unbroken chant extends further and further, we begin to sense that the sound we hear cannot possibly have been produced naturally by the monk. The sound runs for an impossible length of time; the monk should be exhausted, and thus what we hear can only be the result of film technique. He contin-ues to look into the camera, the resonant humming tone broken only once by the insertion of a comic 'tiddly pom' into his chant. Suddenly the torso of a barber armed with electric clippers enters the frame. The young monk's head is shaved clean, and now the

humming sound of the chant is also 'taken' by the electric clippers
(Figure 2.2). But there is yet another level of indeterminacy at
work here: this hum could be either the objective sound from our
point of audition, or the subjective sound of the clippers as heard
by the monk. Finally the head is shaved clean, a click signals that
the clippers have been switched off, and the sound of the chant/
hum cuts out, leaving only the ambient sound of the room. The
barber takes off what at first seemed to be the young monk's robes,
but is now revealed to be a barber's cape, beneath which we see
the braces and polo shirt of a British skinhead (Figure 2.3). The
young man looks at himself in the camera/mirror, leans towards
the source of the rising smoke, previously assumed to be a burning
stick of incense, and lifts a cigarette to his mouth to take a final
drag before stubbing it out.

In this way Smith reveals the ambiguity of sound and image,
foregrounding the ability of each to both create *and* accept
meaning. The tone we hear at first is unquestionably that generated by the chanting monk, but this interpretation of the sound
is subsequently undermined by a number of factors. Firstly, the
duration of the chant suggests that the sustained tone is a product
of film technique, not a reliable document of a profilmic event.
Secondly, the introduction of the electric clippers 'takes' the sound
previously assumed to have been made by the monk, but in such a
way that what we hear could be either an objective or a subjective
auditioning of the perceived source. Central to what is at work here
is the possibility of a cinesonic polysemia, figured in terms of slippage, extension and movement. What is significant about Smith's
films is that these multiple meanings are not always packaged out
separately, as in a pun, but rather coexist as a series of possibilities
coalescing around the material signifier. In this instance what we
are presented with are not simply two or three separate 'meanings'
for the tone we hear, given one after the other, but rather an accretion of meanings that resists definitive resolution. The indeterminate nature of the relationship between the sounds and what they
may signify seems to be resolved towards the end of the film, when
the clippers are switched off and the humming tone ceases. Yet,
this is an impossibility if we recall how the sound was originally
created, initiated it seemed by the chanting monk. Part of the film's
joke rests on the impossibility of wholly attributing the sound we
hear to any single source, and in this way Smith loosens the grip
of the source on sound, problematising the relationship between
signifier and signified. Here is a puzzle that we can never solve; all

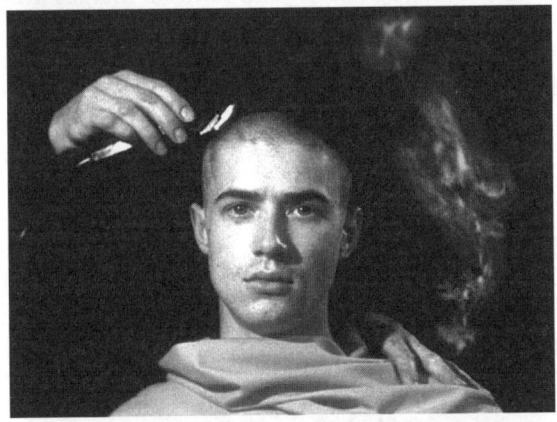

2.1–2.3 *Om*

we can do is shuttle between one possible meaning and another. This establishes an oscillation between the material sound and a number of points demarcated on a horizon of possible meanings, thereby revealing a quality of undecidability in sonic phenomena. But of course this is an undecidability situated within a contained locus of specified meanings, concordant with a conceptual position that suggests a signifier *can* imbue, or be imbued, with meaning; there is no opening of the floodgates here to what is unknowable within the semiological project.

Movement and meaning

In Smith's film *The Black Tower* (1985–87) we are challenged to make connections between sounds and images that initially appear to resist meaning. The narrative of *The Black Tower* centres on an unseen protagonist who is haunted by a tower he believes is following him around London. Much of the film features a black screen, to which Smith cuts when the troubled protagonist describes his sightings of the tower on journeys around the area in which he lives: visits to Hackney Marshes, Brixton Prison, and a trip out of town to the country. The amount of black screen in the film brought complaints from viewers when Channel 4 first showed the film in Britain in 1988. The station's call log for the evening of transmission records the following comments:

> 'Why the hell isn't this a radio production? I'm in the media, and I've come home after a 15 hour day expecting to see something decent, not this unmitigated rubbish.'
> 'What is this? Is there something wrong with the programme? When advised, demanded to know why no warning was given out.'
> 'What's going on, I can't understand this at all.'
> 'I've watched this upside down and sideways, but I can't make head or tail of it. Doesn't make sense.'[4]

These viewers' comments articulate a response to the turbulence generated by something that cannot be understood in significative terms. What motivates most of these callers to contact the TV station is the fact that they are confronted with something that, to quote one of the callers, 'doesn't make sense'; that is, something that doesn't resolve itself in the act of signification. The absence of images is figured by another of the callers as some form of transmission failure. This is, of course, what makes TV companies anxious about silence and blank screens, worried that a channel-hopping audience will assume the station is 'down' and turn to another. That which does not signify can thus present a very real disturbance to what seems to occupy the most privileged position in film – namely, the creation and transmission of meaning. In extreme cases, like Smith's extended use of the black screen, this failure to signify equates with the unthinkable of television and film: their demise, cessation, negation.

In voice-over, the protagonist tells his story and we trace his progress from unease to breakdown and eventual death. The voice-over narration in traditional documentary forms, sometimes referred to as 'the voice of god', directs our reading of a polysemic image by anchoring meaning. Smith acknowledges and foregrounds this power of resolution when dealing with images or sounds that seem to lack meaning, such as the black screen. The black screen has a special status in film, rather like that of silence on the soundtrack, marking either a temporary suspension of the film or its cessation. The fade to black between scenes presents a 'bracketed' moment, a pause that takes us out of what seems to properly constitute 'the film' and into a void which, despite being part of the material experience of film, seems at the same time not to belong to it; this form of participation without belonging is evidenced by the fact that we are barely aware of black screens during their 'extra-textual' appearances. However, what Smith does in *The Black Tower* is to use sound to move us to a position where we become consciously aware of the black screen's material presence. At the same time, through the use of sound, Smith is able to make the same black screen take on specific meanings, rather than simply serving as 'empty' space between the shots that make up the film. After initially spotting the tower near his home, the protagonist describes his surprise at seeing it again inside the walls of Brixton Prison, and at several points on his journey home. The sequence ends:

> NARRATOR: I decided to take another look at the tower from my house when I got back, but by the time I got there it was dark.
>   (Cut to black)
>   There was no moon and I couldn't see it over the rooftops. That night I dreamt that I was imprisoned in the tower. My body was paralysed and only my eyes could move. At first I thought that I was in complete darkness, but after a while I noticed a greyish speck which remained in the same place when I moved my eyes. I realised that I was facing a flat black wall. I got the feeling that the room was in fact brightly lit, but I couldn't be sure.

At first the black screen seems to mean nothing: it does not hold our attention or engage our thoughts at a narrative level. But in response to the suggestions of the voice-over, this same black screen comes to represent night, and then the black wall of the protagonist's dream. So persuasive is this voice-over that we may search the screen for the grey mark described by the narrator. There is a humorous, reflexive element to this device, which situates Smith's practice within the traditions of structural film, and reminds us of Peter Gidal's comment, '"Empty screen" is no less significatory than "carefree happy smile"' (Gidal, 1975: 189). Listening to the film's soundtrack played over loudspeakers, the audiospectator finds themselves gazing at a visually inert TV monitor or cinema screen, and is thereby confronted with the material conditions of film or TV exhibition. In the absence of an image, our attention may be directed to the screen itself, the means by which images would normally appear on it, and also perhaps to the fact that film's sounds and images are recorded and reproduced independently of one another. Within the context of structural film practice, the 'empty' screen can therefore be constructed as an anti-illusionist device, working to heighten awareness of the material conditions of film exhibition, and creating a self-reflexive foregrounding of the audience's perceptual response to the event *taking place* within the physical space of the cinema. In Smith's work, which prompts the viewer to invest the screen with meaning, the oscillation set up between meaning and materiality has the effect of making the viewer self-aware, conscious of the perceptual and cognitive contribution they make to cinematic experience. Thus, the viewer becomes a witness to their own desire to invest the untranslatable and the material with significance, and to the ease with which this process takes place.

Smith also employs a tactic of delayed resolution to articulate the relationship between sound and source, signifier and signified. Following the sequence described above, we are presented with a brisk series of monochrome screens, each accompanied by a different sound (Table 2.1).

No explanation is given for the match between sound and image, and there seems to be no obvious connection between the two; what sutures them together is simply their synchronous cutting. What is notable, in terms of the difference between the ways in which we perceive sound and images in this sequence, is that we are quite easily able to accept these monochrome screens as visual abstractions; we are not necessarily concerned with the

Table 2.1   First monochrome sequence from *The Black Tower* (John Smith, 1985–87)

Shot number	Image	Sound
1	black screen/monochrome	hissing
2	dark red monochrome	buzzing
3	black monochrome	footsteps
4	bright red monochrome	birds, hum of distant traffic
5	black monochrome	crackling
6	yellow monochrome	watery sounds
7	light brown monochrome	hiss and bubbling
8	blue monochrome	watery movement

'source' of the images, and would not feel the need to identify what they represent. Imagery of this kind will be familiar to many from work by other avant-garde filmmakers, most notably the 'flicker' films of Paul Sharits and Tony Conrad. In contrast, however, the worldly nature of the sounds triggers a desire to fix them in terms of a source, and thus determine what they signify. We recognise the sounds as potentially representational, even though we struggle not only to *identify* them (which means to identify their source) but also to conceptualise them without the help of an image to reign in their polysemic play. In this first monochrome sequence the relationship between sound as signifier and its meaning is loosened, if not lost altogether; and when sound is severed of its source, the listener is forced to engage with its materiality. Since the sounds themselves are unidentifiable, suggestive only in a vague way, we are compelled to listen closely to each sound, observing its morphological development over time, searching for features that might resolve its ambiguity and anchor its meaning. The reaction generated by these sounds, in combination with the abstract monochrome screens, sets up a desire to connect sound and image in an attempt to resolve their identity with respect to one another. But there is little support here for the audiospectator, since there is no sense of predictability or patterning in the relationships between sound and image. The viewer is invited to make links between the soundtrack and the monochromes, almost forced by the editing to do so, but the screen offers only the blueness of blue, the redness of red and the grain of the film stock. Although colours often have strong cultural associations, in their refusal to support these associations the sounds strip away the possibility of connecting sound and image in this way. In short,

Table 2.2   Second monochrome sequence from *The Black Tower* (John
Smith, 1985–87)

Shot number	Image	Voice-over
1	black monochrome/ screen	The Teasmade woke me up at eight-thirty . . .
2	dark red monochrome	and I jumped out of bed and rushed across the room to switch it off.
3	black monochrome	It had rained again during the night but I drew open the curtains to discover that the morning sky was bright and clear.
4	bright red monochrome	Shivering, I quickly put on my clothes . . .
5	black monochrome	and lit the fire.
6	yellow monochrome	In the kitchen, I poured myself some fruit juice . . .
7	light brown monochrome	and made porridge. While waiting for it to cook I . . .
8	blue monochrome	did the washing up from the night before.

audiospectators are left to fend for themselves, and in the absence
of any meaningful context for what they see and hear, are simply
confronted with the blank materiality of both sound and image.

However, Smith does not allow this to go on for too long, since
the montage is fairly rapid and is followed by a second sequence,
in which the visuals of the first are repeated, but are accompanied
by voice-over (Table 2.2).

Words are now matched to the colours, but still no resolution is
offered in terms of the meaning of the visual track. We may make
some connections, the cut from black to red signifying daybreak
for example, but these do not carry the weight of final resolution.

The third variation of the sequence finally resolves image and
sound in relation to one other, as the sounds heard in the first
sequence are attributed to a source previously represented only
by visual abstraction. Thus the dark red monochrome, which was
accompanied by the sound of birds and the distant hum of traffic
in the first sequence, and by the line 'I jumped out of bed' in the
second, is revealed to have been a close-up shot of a red blanket,
which is thrown off by the protagonist as he is shown getting out
of bed in the third sequence. In this final sequence each of the
monochromes is shown to have been a close-up detail of some

part of the protagonist's home: one of the black monochromes is identified as a detail of the dark interior of the bedroom, revealed as such when a Teasmade is seen switching on, illuminating its surroundings; another of the black monochromes is shown to have been a curtain, which is then pulled back to reveal a window looking out onto a tree; the bright red monochrome is shown to have been a close-up shot of a shirt, covering other garments lying on the floor; the last of the black monochromes is revealed to have been a shot of an unlit fire, which begins to glimmer as flames take hold; the yellow monochrome is shown to have been the side of a ceramic mug, revealed as such when a hand enters the frame to pick it up; the pale yellow monochrome is shown to have been a close-up of porridge cooking; while the blue monochrome is revealed as a shot of a kitchen worktop when a cup dripping with soap suds is placed on it, in the third and final sequence. In each case we are able to retrospectively relate sound to image: the buzzing sound is the Teammate's alarm, the crackling sound a fire burning in the hearth, the watery sounds are dishes being washed, the hissing and bubbling sounds are porridge being cooked, and so on. Thus, in contrast to the polysemy of *Om*, the dominant structuring device of this sequence is the *deferral* of significatory resolution.

Two other techniques used by Smith represent variations on this problematisation and objectification of the relationship between signifier and signified, sound and source. Smith often uses sound to shift the audience from one perceptual viewpoint to another. In another sequence in *The Black Tower*, the protagonist, feeling under pressure from the continual appearance of the tower, decides to leave London for a while. Smith cuts to a shot of a house and lamp-post surrounded by trees and bushes, accompanied by an atmos track of bird-song, suggestive of a peaceful semi-rural location (Figure 2.4). A short time later we return to this shot, this time located within a dream sequence. On this occasion the shot is held for a few seconds, but Smith then jump-cuts to another shot that matches the first exactly, except for the presence of a large tower block in the centre of the frame (Figure 2.5).

At first the tower block shot is inserted as flash frames into shots of the semi-rural scene, which hence remains the dominant image. However, as the sequence progresses, so the balance between the 'tower block' and 'rural' versions of the shot changes, so that the 'tower block' version becomes dominant, with the 'rural' scene inscribed momentarily into this new 'reality'. This creates

2.4–2.6 *The Black Tower*

a noticeable shift in our reading of the image, the edits becoming highly visible markers of the means by which this has been achieved. We then hear the noise of an explosion and see the tower block crumbling into a heap of rubble in the centre of the frame, sending up a growing cloud of dust (Figure 2.6). Smith created this sequence by filming the demolition of a block of flats at Hackney Wick, returning some time later to shoot exactly the same scene from the same spot, minus the now demolished tower block. As the tower block collapses we hear a rumble and crackle as a growing cloud of dust fills the image. The voice-over comments, 'I was woken by the smell of burning and opened my eyes to see the rising smoke. I stamped out the flaming edge of the newspaper'. Since the protagonist has apparently fallen asleep reading a newspaper, the rumble/crackle we hear is now understood to be that of the burning newspaper 'leaking' into the dream of the collapsing tower block. Rather than an accretion of meanings, what we witness here is a simple transition from one meaning to another as Smith foregrounds sound's representational latitude, and its polysemic capacity to support a range of interpretations.

Theorising Smith's use of sound

Smith's work with sound in *Om* and *The Black Tower* centres on polysemy, shifts in meaning, the attribution of meaning and the deferral of meaning, in which 'meaning' is, on the whole, equivalent to the perceived or represented source of a sound. In this way Smith's work engages directly in a destabilisation of the model of sound–image relations that informs much of classical film practice. By exploring the relationship between sound and image, and the way in which they come together to create meaning, the films demonstrate what Phillip Drummond has referred to as modernism's 'explosion of the semiotic' (Drummond, 1979: 12); Smith's films examine the nature of cinematic signification, confronting the processes and apparatus of sign production, resulting in a subtle undoing of cinema itself. It is this notion of deconstruction that has served as the dominant critical framework for many of those writing about Smith's films. Critics have tended to emphasise the way in which his work reveals the constructed nature of film, and how this anti-illusionist stance situates his own work in opposition to a classical, mainstream film practice, which by contrast remains illusionistic and essentially manipulative. Thus Rees writes, 'as a joint product of the aesthetics and the techniques which they embody, the films assert a personal vision which is never finalised or fixed, and open a narrative space in which the viewer can question the construction of the film as a manipulated spectacle' (Rees, 2002: 16). Similarly, Rees situates the spectatorial self-awareness that results from the techniques used by Smith in relation to dominant forms of cinema:

> In John Smith's films, the spectator is a producer as well as a consumer of meaning, bound in to the process but simultaneously distanced from the 'naturalness' of the film dream. This feature alone marks off John Smith's films from the lure of cinema (to which his richly visual images nonetheless allude) and locates him firmly as an artist-filmmaker, who turns the codes of the film medium into a continual questioning of film truth. (Rees, 2002: 30)

Elsewhere, Nicky Hamlyn pairs self-reflexivity with deconstruction in his analysis of the way in which Smith deploys strategies of cinematography to construct narrative in *The Black Tower*:

> As the narrator slips into a paranoid state, the viewer comes increasingly to realise that the film's meanings have been constructed through carefully selected framing. The utter simplicity and transparency of this strategy forces the viewer to confront his own gullibility, but equally to take pleasure in noticing the details which give the game away, and to understand how easy it is for him/her to be deceived. (Hamlyn, 2003: 87)

Like other critics, Hamlyn also situates Smith's own particular type of film practice in relation to the model of mainstream cinema. In a commentary on how Smith's cinematography differs from that of other filmmakers concerned with revealing and foregrounding film's materiality, Hamlyn writes:

> Where many filmmakers have striven to foreground the medium by, for example, scratching the emulsion, or filming the act of filming, Smith has always insisted on technically immaculate, seemingly straightforward images. But these images are so created precisely in order to challenge mainstream cinema and TV on their own ground. The high quality pictures are put in the service of thoroughly subversive structures, which question their own veracity as much as they challenge the mainstream. (Hamlyn, 2003: 57)

This critical perspective is very much in harmony with Smith's own conceptualisation of his work. In interview, Smith has commented, 'I'm interested in work that invites us to question what we are told. It's to do with engagement rather than consumption' (Elwes,

2001: 13). And on the issue of the relationship between materiality and representation, Smith states, 'I wanted to play with the
edge between immersion in a psychological narrative and seeing
the film for what it is – a material construction, an assemblage of
assorted parts' (Elwes, 2001: 15).

The critical location of Smith's work would seem to position the
figure of film sound's materiality primarily in relation to the processes of signification and the creation of meaning. While Smith's
cinesonic strategies aim to reveal the material construction of film,
that materiality is always aligned with a concern with meaning. That
is, although the material dimensions of the cinesonic prove to be a
destabilising source of turbulence in relation to the significatory,
materiality itself never sets the agenda; rather, materiality serves
to adumbrate processes of signification. Though the attribution and
creation of meaning might be disrupted or delayed in Smith's work,
meaning is never entirely displaced. Auditioned from this perspective, the materiality of Smith's soundtracks is ultimately absorbed
and resolved in processes of signification. Rees (2002), Elwes
(2001) and Mazière (1983) all make the point that one thing that
distinguishes Smith's films (and defines them in contradistinction to
mainstream classical cinema) is the 'space' they offer the spectator
to do their own work; but ultimately the work that is done by the
spectator is to invest Smith's sounds and images with meaning.

In its primary concern with meaning, it is clear that an important
element of the deconstructive tradition that has informed Smith's
work is founded on structuralist modes of enquiry which emerged
from the 'linguistic turn' of the 1960s. The attraction of structuralism, which not only informed Gidal's take on structural film but
also dominated British film theory in the 1970s, relates perhaps
to the way in which it provides theoretical support for a mode of
modernist art practice concerned with uncovering and undoing.
Thus, the founding ideas of structuralism become politicised in
lending support to a Brechtian tradition of unmasking, revealing
and deconstructing hegemonic cultural objects. This set of ideas
continues to inform Smith's work, offered by him as a rationale for
its political value. What is evident from Smith's analysis of his own
praxis is that it emerges from a particular moment in the history
of British independent film culture, when the ideas of structuralist
theory informed a radical poetics of film practice:

> The notion of making the process clear in the work is kind of politi-
> cal in relation to Brecht and use of alienation and these sorts of

things. When I look back on it I also think it's kind of quite religious
in a way. You were sort of taught these things, these notions at film
school by the people that I came into contact with as a student, and
I kind of took these things onboard totally. And I sort of completely
believe in them – I have to make work which actually refers to
its process in some way. I see that as a political dimension of the
work.[5]

The relationship between theory and practice mapped by
Smith's films thus creates a distinct context in which the material
dimensions of the cinesonic experience can be discussed. What we
observe in the work, the theoretical resources it draws upon and its
subsequent theorisation by critics is the centrality of deconstruction. Clearly there is a self-reflexive dimension to Smith's approach
to deconstruction, in the sense that his films work to reveal their
own artifice – however, this form of deconstruction is primarily
motivated and informed by a concern with the illusionistic, manip-
ulatory powers and truth claims of dominant cinema. Thus Smith's
own praxis is constantly haunted by the figure of a cinema that
works to conceal its construction: that is, an absent, mainstream,
classical cinema. As a political project, his praxis assumes an
oppositional stance in relation to the hegemonic cultural objects
and institutions of this dominant form of cinema. Importantly,
the politically informed deconstruction undertaken in this work is
mapped very closely to film's semiological dimensions, particularly
in relation to the strategies by which Smith examines sound–image
relations founded on the sound–source model. Consequently,
although the figure of materiality never seems far from the concerns of this type of deconstructive film practice, its articulation
by the discourses surrounding it orients this materiality almost
exclusively in relation to regimes of signification. In other words,
materiality only matters in so far as it reveals processes of signification, thereby supporting modernism's 'explosion of the semiotic'.

Beyond deconstruction

When considered *outside* of the deconstructive traditions in which
the films have been predominantly situated – which serve to locate
the filmmaker in relation to the debates of structural film, and
in an oppositional relationship to mainstream cinema – Smith's
work points to ways of figuring the materiality of the cinesonic,
other than in support of or in opposition to processes of signification. Thus the *play* between sound and image in Smith's work

demonstrates something that might seem remarkably uncontentious, yet is profound in its implications: namely, that what
constitutes a crucial dimension of sound film's materiality is the
relationship between sound and image. Smith's deconstruction of
sound–image relations allows the audiospectator to do their own
work, albeit within carefully controlled parameters. As Mazière
observes:

> This is not to be interpreted as a free for all, that the subject con-
> structs the film in isolation according to his wishes, desires, etc. . . .
> but that working with a specific set of units, variables, motifs, images
> and words one can produce films which engage the viewer in an
> active, critical and pleasurable activity. It is in the construction of the
> films that a reading space is left, by denying a hegemonous structure,
> an orientated multiplicity is produced. (Mazière, 1983: 44)

While oriented towards a critical engagement with signification, the films compel the audiospectator to recognise that what
we term 'the film' is constituted by a relationship between sound
and image, rather than the simple addition of these two elements. In giving the audiospectator the opportunity to do their
own work, Smith's deconstruction of the sound–source cinesonic
model foregrounds the *dynamic* nature of significatory processes,
thereby adumbrating the flow and flux of sound–image relations.
The polysemic nature of Smith's audiovisuality, its latitude and
play, eliminate the possibility of a one-to-one equivalence of signifier and signified, which might otherwise suggest that pre-given
meaning is located exclusively within a particular material image
or sound. Of course, there are moments in a film when the image is
dominant, and where sound occupies a secondary, accompanying
position; similarly there may be moments when sound takes the
lead in the creation of meaning. However, since there is always
a sonic dimension to the cinematic experience – whether this is
a recorded soundtrack, musical accompaniment, or the sound of
the projector – this relationship between sound and image always
exists, and crucially, is in a constant state of flux. As one might
expect, the shifts in meaning that are observed in Smith's work
map precisely to the flux of its audiovisuality. In actively witnessing the shifts in meaning that take place within Smith's films, and
in identifying the role played in this process by sound and image,
the audiospectator is confronted with the flux of audiovisuality,
and hence with a key element of film's materiality. What this play
in the relationship between sound and image also makes clear

is that meaning is an effect like any other; it is the product of a coming together of sound and image, and simply needs to take its place alongside other effects, rather than dominating critical consideration of the film event to the exclusion of all else.

Smith's films make the audiospectator consciously aware of the ways in which the visual and the sonic interact, combine and separate. Rather than grounding acts of signification in notions of 'universal' abstract meaning, Smith's work foregrounds the transitory and contingent nature of the production of meaning, thus offering a 'deconstructive' audiovisuality that signals the flow of sound–image relations, rather than the static individuation of constituent terms. It is this sense of *movement* that Smith's work foregrounds, even if this has so far been understood by critics only in terms of the latitude of meaning. Smith's work therefore demonstrates that the *audiovisuality* of film is comprised of something other than the sum of its constituent parts, differing from, yet constituted by, both sound and image.

The theory and practice of deconstruction have served an important political role in challenging hegemonic cultural objects and practices, as well as in formulating alternative cultural projects. However, one of the shortcomings of deconstruction, both as a filmmaking practice and as a conceptual frame in which to situate that practice, is that in reducing cinema to what it takes to be its constituent elements, it effectively severs sound from image. As the majority of writing on film has prioritised the visual, it is understandable that in an attempt to rehabilitate film sound, deconstructive film criticism and practice have long been at pains to disentangle the sonic from the visual within the audiovisual constructions of cinema. Paradoxically, in staking a claim for sound, the risk being run is that the *relationship* between sound and image is lost. While the visual bias of the critical landscape demands that we focus attention on the traits and dimensions of the sonic as a strategic measure, sound needs to be reinstituted within the context of the cinesonic – that is, in terms of its deployment in relation to the image. What is needed is an approach to sound that is not bounded by the dynamics of individuation, differentiation and specificity, but embraces forms of blurring, combination, contamination, fusion, synthesis and the coming together of the senses. The drawback of figuring film as a binary structure composed of sound and image, or image and sound, is that it precludes engagement with the transsensory nature of cinema. Therefore, in trying to come to terms with the place and role of sound in cinema, deconstruction needs always to be balanced by a creative act of construction. In this way, by logging the lack of fit between theory and practice, between the film event and its dominant conceptualisation, we are forced to search for alternative critical perspectives that may help to sound materiality in other than deconstructive terms.

Anthea Kennedy and Nick Burton: the materiality of direct sound

The disjuncture between certain dominant forms of critical practice and the cinesonic experience of the films they attempt to deal with is usefully illustrated by a consideration of the work of two of Smith's contemporaries. The films of Anthea Kennedy and Nick Burton, fellow students with Smith at the Royal College of Art in the 1970s, and sometime collaborators, also deconstruct the orthodox codes and conventions of film practice, perhaps most notably in relation to the cinesonic in their film *Birdman* (1975). However, the way in which the type of film practice represented by Kennedy and Burton's work has been largely conceptualised does not do justice to what we hear on the soundtrack of their films, and how this relates to the experience of watching their work.

Drawing loosely on the life of the exiled German opera singer and wildlife sound recordist Ludwig Koch, *Birdman* features Koch's son, Val Kennedy, playing the role of his father. The soundtrack is made up of three distinct elements: extracts from Koch's autobiography, read as voice-over by Kennedy; recordings of bird-song made by Koch; and the dense location sound that forms the dominant sonic texture of the film. The recording of this last element of the soundtrack is informed by a 'direct' sound aesthetic. This approach to sound production, more familiar as the sound of news and documentary, involves the transcription of all location sound, resulting in extremely dense recordings that are rich in sonic detail. The film's soundtrack, dominated as it is by noisy location sound recordings, stands in contrast to the well-modulated, well-behaved classical soundtrack, and the dominant sonic key of *Birdman* is one of unruly uncontainability, disturbance and interruption; indeed, Burton describes the soundtrack as 'fairly rough and ready'.[6] Interruption is created, in part, through strategies of editing; for example, in the final scene of the film we hear fragments of a voice-over that seems to make no sense in relation to what is happening on screen, or even to what has been heard previously, and the film ends cutting midway through a voiced-over sentence. This fragmentation is explained by Burton in terms of the disruption of narrative engagement:

> the film is highly structured, and rather one-dimensional in the sense that it was very fixed on the form. And although we were interested in the narrative, the narrative had to be attacked somewhat. An abrupt ending is, of course, a very useful way of non-closure, which was an essential part of the system that we were using . . . the narrative was there as an attraction, as something going on that you might be keen to get more involved with, [but] you were never really allowed inside the pleasure of the narrative world.[7]

In one scene Koch's assistant Pidsley is shown crouching over sound recording apparatus in a suburban garden. As he puts on a pair of headphones, we hear bird-song on the soundtrack – sound taken in fact from Koch's original recordings. Sound and image relations work here to suggest that we now share Pidsley's point of audition. However, the filmmakers question the status of what we see and hear in the film, in relation to the sound–source dynamic, when the technician then removes his headset and the recording of bird-song continues to dominate the soundtrack. Like Smith's semantic manipulations of sound, this play with sound perspective refers the listener to the fact that there are cinematic codes at work structuring sound–image relationships in ways that determine how the audience interpret what they see and hear. As with other scenes in *Birdman*, this particular device works to draw attention to the way in which the cinematic code of sound perspective structures film's audiovisuality to create meaning. In this instance, a destabilisation of the normative modes of sound–image relations serves to denaturalise and demystify the audiovisual dimension of cinematic representation. Furthermore, there is no sense of careful crafting here, of modulating the recording of bird-song to allow room for the location sound that runs beneath. Rather, this feels like a crude mechanical layering, producing a cacophony that forces a confrontation with the concrete particularity of the soundtrack, preventing any unconscious acceptance of the sound as naturalistic representation.

Other techniques are used by the filmmakers to challenge the illusionistic nature of the well-behaved naturalistic soundtrack, in which smooth transitions and the careful balance between constituent elements would normally produce an erasure of its material existence. In a scene in which Koch encounters the Queen of the Belgians painting in a clearing in the woods, the Queen's reply to Koch's greeting is dubbed, in contrast to the direct location sound we have heard until this point. No attempt here is made to bed this post-synched sound into the sonic atmosphere of the rest of the scene; in contrast to the noisy location recordings of Koch's dialogue, we are now confronted with the relatively clean, dead sound of a studio recording in which the background sounds of birds and the movement of actors are entirely absent. This inscription of difference announces the material heterogeneity of the soundtrack, an approach that Burton conceptualises in terms of deconstruction: 'when we dub, it's absolutely obvious . . . everything is clear, everything is what it is . . . that's what it's like watching that film; it's like a car with the body shell off, and you're seeing all the components'.[8] Kennedy also considers this deployment of sound in relation to the project to reveal the constructed nature of the film text, but situates this in terms of a strategy designed to prevent any potential manipulation of the audience: 'If it sounded dubbed, that wouldn't have bothered me. I would have thought it was a good thing that the process had been revealed. I think I preferred that to feeling that I had somehow cheated and therefore had cheated the audience'.[9]

A striking example of this form of deconstruction features another exploration of the sound–source dynamic, in which sound is irreconcilably split from the image that signifies its source. Kennedy and Burton's *The Reichstag Fire Part I* (1976) includes a single six-minute shot that begins with a stationary motorcyclist revving his engine in preparation for departure (Figure 2.7). The close-miked sound of the engine dominates the soundtrack, and in terms of sound perspective is in keeping with the shot distance at this point. The filmmakers obtained this recording by placing sound recording equipment in the panniers of the motorcycle. The camera then tracks with the motorcyclist as he drives through suburban streets and joins a busy motorway (Figure 2.8). However, although the motorcycle falls back from the tracking camera (Figures 2.9 and 2.10), and then overtakes it, leaving the frame entirely (Figures 2.11 and 2.12), the sound recording remains constant: there is no accompanying variation in volume to signal a change in sound perspective, as the sound of the engine continues to dominate the shot, even when the motorcycle – its perceived object-source – is entirely absent. Here we witness a radical separation of the elements that constitute the film text, situating the directors' praxis within a Brechtian tradition that seeks to

2.7–2.12 *The Reichstag Fire Part I*

reveal cultural objects as constructions. In separating sound from image, Burton and Kennedy signal what Altman has referred to as 'sound film's fundamental lie': that is, the fact that the naturalistic relationship between sound and image proposed by classical cinema's use of audiovisual synchronisation is an illusion, and that while sound may appear to be produced by the image, it is in fact independent of it (Altman, 1980: 6).

This approach of allowing naturalistic modes of filmic construction to rupture and collapse informs other aspects of the films' soundtracks. In both *Birdman* and *The Reichstag Fire Part I*, shot in or around the filmmakers' West London home, the continuous sound of traffic permeates many scenes. In addition, every movement of performers and props within profilmic space is captured in crisp sonic detail. The actors' entrances and exits, and their movements around the predominantly domestic interiors, are rendered with a sonic concreteness that foregrounds performance and objectifies the spaces in which these performances take place, thus undermining any attempt to construct a convincing fictive world. Kennedy comments on this aspect of the soundtrack in terms of the decision made by the filmmakers to adopt a direct sound aesthetic: 'I liked to hear the acoustic of the room where the filming was taking place and this is something I miss in post-synched films today. It produced an immediacy and an awareness in the spectator of the filming taking place. You could almost hear the film crew breathing which produced a tension, a frisson'.[10] Direct sound recording is usually associated with documentary, news and certain realist practices. Despite the fact that a sound recordist is almost always listening for particular sounds in a location, negotiating their way through the total soundscape of a space by the use of a directional microphone, the direct soundtrack does not necessarily conform to the sonic hierarchy of classical cinema. In the latter, dialogue is accorded first place above sound effects and music, and is thus provided with a protected sonic space. In the classical film, sound is always marshalled so as not to interfere with dialogue, which as one of the central supports of narrative has a higher status than other elements of the soundtrack. In contrast, background sounds, ambient sounds and sounds without an obvious visual source located within the frame all find a place in direct sound recording. Consequently there is a place here for the idiosyncratic, the unexpected and the unintelligible. These attributes are taken to indicate a lack of mediation, a certain passivity that seems to guarantee the indexicality and objectivity of the recording. Thus,

Kennedy comments of her own work, 'Direct sound seemed like a pure and honest thing to be doing'.[11] The direct sound approach appears at some level to involve a minimum of human agency, unquestioningly transcribing everything that takes place in front of the microphone. For this reason, Michel Chion has commented, 'Many people consider location sound not only the sole morally acceptable solution in filmmaking but also the one that simplifies everything, since it eliminates the problem of having to make choices' (Chion, 1994: 104–5). What Chion suggests is that one of the appeals of this approach for filmmakers is that it is, in some ways, less constructed, less mediated than other modes of sound production. In this respect, the moral dimensions of this practice are roughly concordant with a Cagean approach to sonic construction;[12] that is, direct sound seems not to require us to impose our will on the sonic event or its record, but allows sounds to speak for themselves. These 'undoctored', continuous recordings appear to stand as an unblinking witness to the profilmic event, the inclusion of the aleatory and accidental suggesting that these sound events are autonomous, and not staged for the camera or sound recorder. The corollary of this is that the direct sound recording, unlike well-modulated classical sound, appears not to set out to manipulate the listener. All these factors figure in the value that is attributed to direct sound when heard within the context of news and documentary production, and these are essentially the features that support the notion that news and documentary might somehow attempt to be objective and unbiased.

However, this position on direct sound would obviously be unsustainable in a film practice – like that of proposed by Kennedy, Burton and Smith – in which the moral and political responsibility of the filmmaker is to reveal an artwork's constructedness. Thus, the adoption of a direct sound aesthetic in *Birdman* and *The Reichstag Fire* needs to be situated within another critical context. What is important about the use of direct sound within reflexive film practice is that it produces a proliferation of detail that is confusing, 'irrelevant' and perhaps unintelligible. While this in itself can stand as a mark of fidelity and immediacy, it can also bring the soundtrack to a point of excess. In rendering the manifold elements of image and action in startling sonic clarity, direct sound presents a form of realist documentation that challenges naturalist approaches to sound. Like the exhaustion of realism undertaken by James Joyce in *Ulysses*, direct sound can push realist tropes to the point of saturation and perhaps overload, thereby collapsing the representational into the material. What we observe through this conceptualisation of direct sound is a cinesonic practice that inscribes materiality within and against the significative as a destabilising form of turbulence. Since the microphone, unlike the ear, is relatively unselective, the resultant density of direct sound seems to self-reflexively foreground the materiality of the sound recording. Altman (1985) has contrasted direct sound with those classical soundtracks that work to mask their own construction – soundtracks grounded in a technical and aesthetic tradition of denial and concealment. Thus he ascribes to direct sound an inherently oppositional stance to the naturalistic forms of sound found in studio-produced classical narrative films. Altman's critical stance certainly accords with the dominant conceptual frame in which deconstructive work has been situated, perhaps most notably by the critical writing associated with structural film, attributing as it does oppositional and demystificatory potential to materiality.

When situated alongside other aspects of film style, this auditioning of *Birdman*'s direct soundtrack seems appropriate, since the film's approach to *mise-en-scène* and performance also serve to deconstruct naturalist registers. The film is shot in domestic interiors, in a suburban back garden and in a park, and although Koch arrived in the UK in 1936, no attempt is made to dress sets or locations in a historically accurate fashion. Rather, the fabric of contemporary life, which includes the audible sound of West London traffic, is visible and audible everywhere, from the dress of performers to the presence of contemporary motor vehicles. Other elements of the soundtrack also work to deconstruct naturalistic modes of representation. For example, Val Kennedy's voice-over presents itself as being *read* (which indeed it is) rather than *performed*. At the opening of the scene in which Koch meets the Queen of the Belgians, holding a sheet of paper Kennedy reads extracts from his father's autobiography with exactly the same style of delivery that is heard in the voice-overs, thereby erasing the normative distinctions made between voice-over and dialogue, while simultaneously highlighting the constructed nature of performance. There is a sense in which this sound of reading is self-reflexive and self-objectifying, not only because it makes no pretence to naturalism, but also because the flatness of delivery tends towards a materialising monotony – a tendency that is brought out further by the filmmakers' use of extended duration in passages of voice-over.

Destabilising naturalistic cinesonic codes

When auditioned within the contexts of the film, its historical and cultural milieu, and the rationalisation offered by the filmmakers, *Birdman*'s soundtrack is rather neatly contained by the notion of deconstruction. This is also the case if one considers the film's cinesonic strategies in relation to the issues and debates that have been employed by critics to situate Kennedy and Burton's work on other films (Ellis, 1981, 1992; Cowie, 1981; Christie, 1981). Like Smith's work, the films of Kennedy and Burton represent an undoing of cinema. If we ask ourselves of which cinema this is an undoing, then the answer is a cinema in which cinesonic codes and devices are repressed – a cinema that presents itself, in terms of construction, as transparent. This cinema is, of course, classical Hollywood cinema. For these three filmmakers the use of deconstruction has, at least in part, a counter-cultural, oppositional motivation; it forms part of a broader project to destabilise and challenge dominant, hegemonic models of cinema. For Burton, the adoption of 'formalist' techniques had a clear ideological motivation:

> It was political. When I start talking about it now it seems rather naïve, I guess. Perhaps it was. It was to do with . . . that sense of not wanting that kind of illusion and manipulation of a spectacle. At that time we were at war with the society of the spectacle, and classical Hollywood cinema seemed to epitomise that. That was the appeal. But I have to say there was another kind of appeal . . . it's a cinematic appeal, you know, what you can do with film. There is a great appeal of classical Hollywood language. But there is also a way of exploring those things, the relationship between sound and image, and just pushing them a bit, seeing what will happen if you disturb that harmony.[13]

There is an apparent sense in which counter-cultural cinematic practices of this period were engaged in a denaturalisation of the filmic sign, with the aim of revealing the ideological underpinning of sign systems and signifying practices. As Smith explains, the motivation behind this was – and in his case continues to be – an attempt to destabilise and denaturalise illusionistic film practices:

> These words are probably coming straight out of the 1970s at the RCA, but it's what I've always said and what I think I believe – it's to do with actually being able to engage with the work rather than simply consume it. That you are manipulated, but you're aware that you're being manipulated, and you know how you're being manipulated and the films set out as part of their project to actually tell you

that. So in a dry way the theory behind that is that it enables you to engage, it enables you to question. The work makes everything suspect however 'authentic' it is in terms of documentary material or whatever – it makes you ask questions about it, I hope. So much of the work is on one level documentary, but hopefully you're looking at it in a way that you don't necessarily trust it – certainly that you're aware that you're being presented with subjective material anyway, there's no kind of attempt at objectivity – it's the opposite.[14]

This desire to destabilise naturalistic film practices clearly signals the importance of the concept of deconstruction to these particular filmmakers. However, this positioning of film practice reveals one of the fundamental problems of deconstruction, especially where, as in the case of Smith, Kennedy and Burton's work, it has an oppositional motivation. Deconstructive and oppositional formulations of film theory and practice share the problem of being in some way binary constructs, the primary term of which is absent. This is particularly apparent in the writing on structural film from the late 1970s. For example, although Gidal states that structural film is conceived in terms of a *dialectic*, explored in a space between material and representation, its critical formulation demonstrates a tendency towards antithesis: 'Such film mitigates against dominant (narrative) cinema [. . .] An avant-garde film defined by its development towards increased materialism and materialist function does not *represent*, or *document*, anything [. . .] Structural/Materialist film attempts to be non-illusionist' (Gidal, 1975: 189). These negative formulations are found elsewhere, common in theorisations of independent film practice in this period. Thus Phillip Drummond opens his introduction to the catalogue of the Hayward Gallery's 1979 exhibition 'Film as Film' by stating that, 'Our definition of avant-garde film will clearly hinge upon the qualities we associate with the broader context of "mainstream" or what we might call "dominant" cinema. In this case the avant-garde will then be typified by its "opposition" to norms and values within its "opposite"' (1979: 9). Similarly, Peter Wollen employs the term 'counter-cinema' in his account of Godard's 1970 film *Vent d'est* to describe a film practice that is wholly defined in terms of its opposition to an absent, other cinema – once again, that of the Hollywood mainstream.[15]

Rather like the problem posed by the sound–source formulation, the danger with this mode of conceptualising film practice is that, in a centrifugal fashion, attention is turned away from the object or event itself, to something that is external to it.

Rather than engaging with the concrete particularity of the film text, this critical strategy becomes reliant upon abstracted, absent hegemonic models. What we encounter in deconstructive and oppositional formulations of film practice is thus a problematic dependence on a secondary term, a constitutive other. For example, when John Ellis offers a critical commentary on Kennedy and Burton's 1980 feature *At the Fountainhead (of German Strength)* – a film that continues to develop its directors' interest in German history – he continually refers to the ways in which the film departs from, challenges and deconstructs televisual modes of narrating history. Discussing the film, Ellis writes, 'It both acknowledges television's dominant treatments of this history, and rebuffs them. It uses all the major television strategies . . . but refuses their distinctive discursive closures, and places them in a particular emotional register that is alien to them' (Ellis, 1981: 48). However, what he does not work to establish is the precise nature of the 'particular emotional register' created by the film, which is somehow opposed to a problematic televisual counterpart. Paradoxically, his understanding of Kennedy and Burton's practice is fundamentally oriented by what it is *not*: 'Any cinema calling itself "independent" has to encounter this televisual mode of narrating and organising general political history' (Ellis, 1981: 48). Even when dealing with concrete practice in positive terms, the orientation towards antithesis remains. Situating *At the Fountainhead* within the context of British Independent cinema, Ellis writes:

> Rather than the regime of narrative progression, which tends to unify all the effects contained within the film into a final harmony, some independent films deliberately work in a different way. They promote an attitude of reading the image as a space containing different and conflicting meanings; and the soundtrack as composed of sounds which do not necessarily cohere into an aural 'point of view.' (Ellis, 1992: 259)

This is not to suggest that such theorisations are somehow lazy or irrelevant; on the contrary, these oppositional notions have a crucial radical function within a particular set of historical and cultural conditions, and may continue to have relevance (although the fact that this conceptualisation of film practice grew out a specific period in the history of independent film is mentioned by both Smith and Burton). The value of these formulations is in revealing, examining and challenging existing hegemonic models and structures. In this respect, this type of politicised oppositional film practice, and its supporting theoretical resources, form part of a broader social, political and cultural project that follows through the radical logic proposed by the events of May 1968. Certainly this conceptual frame makes sense of Smith, Kennedy and Burton's work, since the filmmakers were overtly engaged in the deconstruction of a film text understood as a signifying system, and as such, a socially informed construction. However, to allow this one set of ideas to circumscribe all critical consideration of their work is to limit the study of film to issues of authorship, or worse, to consign everything but the contemporary to discussions of film history.

The practice of situating films and filmmaking in relation to an absent 'other' continues to exert a dominant influence on critical thinking. At the time of writing, the website for the British Artists' Film and Video Study Collection featured a research paper by Orlene Denice McMahon entitled *An Analysis of the Soundtrack in the Work of Malcolm Le Grice*. In the absence of critical literature on the sonic dimensions of avant-garde film, this is indeed a welcome contribution to scholarship in this area. The fact that it is featured on this particular website accords the article and the ideas it contains a certain status. However, while it contains many interesting observations on Le Grice's work, MacMahon's article simply reiterates what have become normative critical notions in this field. Thus the paper begins, 'The fact that this type of film-making remains the "most marginal and least understood" [Edward S. Small] means that we must resort to Hollywood and its commercial films as a critical yardstick for analysing avantgarde film. The role of music and soundtrack in avant-garde films is significantly in contrast with the place of music in Hollywood films' (McMahon, 2009). While this kind of theorisation has a role to play in making sense of films like *Birdman*, and in situating them historically, the challenge it lays down is to think of ways in which it might be possible to map and explore the materiality of the film's soundtrack in *positive* terms. The disadvantage of only considering Kennedy and Burton's work through debates that relate to its original historical context is that the film is robbed of any contemporary relevance. Although now rarely screened, Kennedy and Burton's films of the late 1970s still represent an important engagement with the materiality of the cinesonic; it was simply that there was no critical discourse at that time to enable an engagement with audiovisuality outside the confines

of a politically motivated deconstruction informed by structuralism. While these well-worn critical perspectives may or may not
continue to have relevance today, questions relating to the material dimensions of film's audiovisuality, and what is at stake in
it, remain largely unaddressed. However, by returning to these
films it becomes possible to release a potentiality that can make a
positive contribution to a contemporary critical engagement with
notions of materiality.

What immediately strikes the audiospectator listening to
Birdman is the bristling density of its soundtrack: a sonic friction
that constantly engages and envelops the listener. But how do we
engage with the 'rough and readiness' of a soundtrack in ways
other than referring to the well-behaved, well-modulated and
largely 'inaudible' soundtrack of mainstream cinema? One way
might be to consider the affective dimensions of the direct soundtrack, and how these relate to its unexplored significative dimensions. One specific example of this approach revolves around what
we might term the 'sound of technology'. Burton comments:

> We always used Sennheiser 816s, the big rifle mic. What it was, of
> course, was classic news film stuff. And of course it gave you that
> [news] look with the [Arriflex] BL. We shot on BLs and Sennheiser
> 816s. It was just convenient in those days, I guess, that those of us
> that were working that way – and there was a group of us working in
> the same way – wanted that sound. But actually that was what was
> around, too. I think that whole generation were brought up on BLs
> and 816s, which gave you that sound. That's what it was for: it was
> for picking up news. And of course it suited us absolutely with this
> philosophy of direct sound and overtly recording what was there.
> They're very powerful microphones, as well – they're not actually the
> most ideal for more naturalistic sound.[16]

What Burton refers to as 'that sound' defines a certain sector of
low-budget independent cinema, and a certain moment in its
history, reminding the listener of other films made in this period,
other films produced within this particular cultural milieu. This
distinctive quality of sound is produced by a number of factors:
the type of microphone used, whether sound is recorded on location or in a studio, and importantly, how all these are in turn
filtered and rendered by the film's optical soundtrack. This sound
of technology, whether consciously registered by the listener or
not, has a powerful affective dimension, overlaying the film with a
feeling of 'pastness'. In this respect, this neglected dimension of the
cinesonic event has its own significative potential. But is it simply

by convention that the murky, scratchy sound of the optical sound-track refers us to the past? To turn to issues of perception and cognition, a sound like that of optical crackle inhabits a borderline between conscious and unconscious awareness, between significa-tion and a sensory engagement with the material. This sound has a warm, enveloping, oceanic quality that would seem to relate to the affective dimensions of the cinesonic. Furthermore, like the busy ambience of direct sound, this sound of technology has an inescapability that also figures at an affective level. Yet none of these aspects of the soundtrack are addressed by the dominant conceptual modes applied to the analysis of film. Similarly, while deconstruction provides a number of ways in which we might make sense of *Birdman*'s audible sound editing, as a conceptual mode it has no way of engaging with the visceral, affective shocks produced by the film's sonic construction.

What we witness in the films of Smith, Kennedy and Burton are filmmaking practices that seek to address the codes and conven-tions of cinema itself, and which work to destabilise signification within the field of the cinesonic. In Smith's films turbulence is sounded around the sound–source formulation that structures film's representational function, while in the work of Kennedy and Burton this destabilisation focuses on a range of naturalistic cine-matic practices. In contrast, the work of the American videomaker Scott Rankin is less overtly involved in an examination of film language, and more concerned with the issue of language itself. A number of Rankin's videotapes take as their subject matter per-sonal, cognitive and linguistic relationships, and how these influ-ence the ways in which we think and view the world. Investigating the problematic dimensions of the creation of meaning, his tapes demonstrate what is at stake in the model of difference that struc-tures language. Rankin's work provides an alternative sounding of the untranslatable of signification, and another way of mapping the cinesonic event. Through contrast, tension and disconnection, Rankin sets in motion the relationships between sound and image, the linguistic and non-linguistic, and the representational and the material.

Scott Rankin: materiality and language

Rankin's video work employs a range of sonic and visual strategies that construct a tension between the representational function of the sign and its material dimensions. In *This and That (Part*

2.13 *This and That (Part Two)*

Two) (1990) Rankin presents the simple image of a tree, behind which lies the ocean under a clear summer sky. Superimposed over the various elements of the image are the Welsh words *cwmwl*, *terfyngych*, *dwr* and *gwydden* (Figure 2.13). These words are also spoken in Welsh as voice-over. The vocal sounds we hear are presented as signifiers, and we can do the mental work of stitching together sound, word and referent even though we may not personally know the actual meaning of these Welsh words; for non-Welsh speakers, these sounds lack the power to signify by convention. Rankin made the decision to use Welsh in this sequence because he felt that, since the language has relatively few speakers, it would probably not be understood by the majority of his audience:

> I tried many languages . . . I wanted the viewer to not understand the language yet understand the emotional layer and grain of the voice, its tonality, rhythm and emotion . . . Latin, Cantonese, and Sanskrit were considered for their relative unfamiliarity . . . but each had connotations that I did not want. Welsh had a sound that was

to me English-like . . . (although Welsh is not related to English). It seemed the most familiar yet opaque to what I expected would be my audience's language range.[17]

In this way Rankin forces confrontation with signs that seem at first not to signify, in that they fail to deliver the semantic substance promised by the words. However, what Rankin demonstrates is that the materiality of the voice has significative and affective dimensions that exist independently of speech's semantic content: 'On that tape it teases you into reading the images, as if it were a story he's telling us. And then he goes "gwandar", and then you're like, *what*?! Then he gets angry. So it's all mixed to do just that; it's to have the emotional value and rhythm of voice. Stuff like a dog understands'.[18] Oozing out from around the edges of the conceptual designation 'sign' are the sounds we usually describe in terms of 'language' (in the sense of 'tongue'), 'accent' and 'voice' – an excess produced by casting sounds as 'signifiers'. This excess can also be understood as the audible materiality of sound. In this way the opacity of Welsh to the non-Welsh speaker forces a confrontation with the untranslatable material balance of signification.

In another sequence from the same tape Rankin presents an extreme close-up of a mouth enunciating the vowel sounds of Welsh (Figure 2.14). These are not entirely familiar to an audiospectator, like myself, whose mother tongue is English. In what becomes a key trope of *This and That*, phonic difference begins to conjure national difference. On screen, superimposed over the mouth as it produces the sounds, we see the letters identifying these vowels graphically: a e i o u y w. Here, language appears to be reduced to its fundamental building blocks: the phonemes from which speech is constructed. This particular set of vowel sounds is drawn from a language of which I am not a speaker, thereby connoting otherness. An opacity results from the fact that these sounds do not allow me immediate and unconditional access to the language system from which they are drawn, and within which they might *make sense*. However, these are *sounds*, not verbs, nouns or adjectives, and as such I recognise their familiarity since they may form part of my own spoken language. Yet despite their recognisability, the linguistic frame in which these sounds are cast (a e i o u – the set of vowels) means they do not bed into the phonic conventions of spoken English. That is, they do not precisely conform to the absent, abstract model of vowel sounds in which I attempt to situate them as an English-speaking listener. At the same time, the

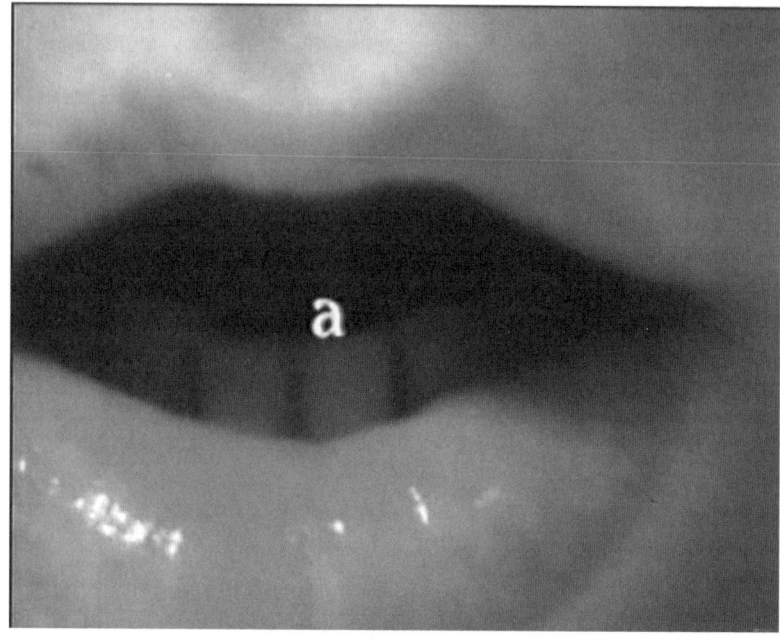

2.14 *This and That (Part Two)*

letters superimposed over the image of the mouth producing these sounds locate them as properly contained by that set of phonic conventions they also seem to resist. Consequently an unresolvable tension is set up between the materiality of these sounds and their place within a linguistic structure. Here it is the untranslatability of one language into another (one 'tongue' into another, but also the moves between writing and speech, the visual and the sonic) that sounds itself as turbulence.

These mismatches resonate with another set of divisions and disjunctures created by the juxtaposition of the written letters and the vowels sounds. The former stand as graphic signifiers, not of the sounds we hear, but of the sound's 'name' – or more accurately, for me, the equivalent vowel sound's name in English. This name, of course, has its own sound, closely related to that of the vowel, but not identical. Thus the elements to be considered here are the graphic symbol (a), its sounded name (pronounced eI), and the speech sound it signifies (pronounced æ in English). However contrary to the expectations of an English speaker, Rankin presents the written letter 'a' with the extended Welsh vowel sound (pronounced a:). Here, the relationship between sound and image points up the fracture that lies at the very heart of language, the opposition that structures the signifier/signified binarism. In his simultaneous uncoupling and recoupling of sound to naming and 'meaning', Rankin skilfully hints at the destabilising nature of difference. While language must be shared, what I hear in this slight variation of the first vowel sound – in its elongation – is the national difference that can be inscribed into even the most simple material sound. This difference is created by a template of language that is imprinted upon a sound simply because of the order in which that sound is presented in relation to others. Designating this particular vocal sound part of the group of vowels 'a e i o u' inflects the material with a sense of difference that constructs otherness; in *almost* conforming to this absent linguistic pattern, these sounds inevitably mark their departure from it.

In a discussion of the performative aspects of language, Deleuze and Guattari propose the concept of *incorporeal transformations*. The term refers to that change which takes place when, for example, a judge's sentence transforms the accused into a convict (Deleuze and Guattari, 1988: 80). What Rankin's vowel sequence reveals is that the linguistic frame into which sounds are placed performs a complex act of instantaneous incorporeal transformation. In running these most elemental of vocal sounds through a linguistic structure, Rankin's tape highlights the fracture between signifier and signified that underpins and structures language, setting in motion the internal instability of the sign. In sounding this turbulence, Rankin signals what is at stake in the significative translation of the material: namely, the creation of otherness and difference.

The sequence continues with the remainder of the alphabet spoken as voice-over. However, unlike the vowel sequence, now an image rather than a written letter accompanies each sound (Table 2.3). In the relationship proposed between sound and image, the sequence works to adumbrate facets of audiovisual materiality that cannot be accounted for by significatory systems founded on the notion of the arbitrary sign. The image of the cow signals a form of representation that corresponds with, and returns us to, the visual nature of the tape we are watching. This particular image is an ideogram, part of an Egyptian hieroglyph, but like the carving, the video image we are watching is also a representation. Both are motivated signs that stand in contrast to the arbitrary nature of the speech sounds accompanying them.

Table 2.3   Opening of alphabet sequence from *This and That (Part Two)*
(Scott Rankin, 1990)

Place in alphabet	Pronunciation	Image
A	aː	

2.15

| B | bʌ | |

2.16

| C | ɛk | |

2.17

Unlike Saussure's formulation of the sign, founded on the paradigm of language, the work of Charles Sanders Peirce allows some engagement with the material dimensions of signification in his tripartite classification of indexical, symbolic and iconic signs (Peirce, 1991). While the symbolic can be considered arbitrary in the Saussurian sense, Peirce's formulations of both the iconic and the indexical challenge the notion of arbitrariness as the founding principle of the sign. Video's images and sounds have both an iconic and an indexical aspect, and thus contrast with the arbitrary nature of vocal speech sounds. This difference between modes of signification situates Rankin's alphabet sequence right on the Saussure-Peirce/semiology-semiotics fault line.

Rankin destabilises processes of signification by bringing these two modalities together, confronting the arbitrary with the motivated sign. Emerging from this tension, what begins to reveal itself in the alphabet sequence is an audiovisual resistance to the incorporeal transformations imposed by linguistic structures. By selecting what appear to be random images to accompany the speech sounds of an alphabet, Rankin severs the naturalistic link between sound and image that characterises the vowel sequence, in which we see a mouth creating the sounds we hear. His editing imposes a linguistic order on these images, since they are marshalled to 'correspond' to an alphabet structure. But at the same time, these images refuse this structure. There seems to be no relationship between sound and image other than a temporal correspondence created by the editing; the sequence of images simply doesn't form an alphabet. The images refuse to be translated, demonstrating a corporeality that is resistant to processes of incorporeal transformation. In addition, a further degree of instability is introduced by the lack of correspondence between Rankin's use of the Welsh alphabet and the absent structure of the English alphabet, against which the former is situated for me, personally, as a listener. Through contrast, tension and disconnection, Rankin sets the relationships between sound and image, between the linguistic and non-linguistic, and between the representational and the material in motion.

The moving images included in the sequence propose a defiantly non-linguistic relationship with the soundtrack. The elongated sound 'ɛŋ' is accompanied by a camera track past a museum display cabinet containing stuffed rabbits. The sound 'ɛl' shows a glass being placed on a table, which then falls off to the sound of the next letter, 'ɛs'. To the sound 'ɒ' a wave crashes, 'pi' milk poured into a glass (Figure 2.18), 'u:' ripples on a pond.

2.18 *This and That (Part Two)*

This audiovisual parallelism creates a bond between sound and image that is arbitrary in a linguistic sense, but is motivated in terms of morphology – that is, in the ways in which sound and image develop over time. This is something more than an arbitrary suturing of sound and image through editing, something more than what Chion terms *synchresis* – the 'spontaneous and irresistible weld produced between a particular auditory phenomenon and visual phenomenon when they occur at the same time' (Chion, 1994: 63). Here the correspondence of the morphological profiles of sound and image creates a brief transsensory effect. This fusion of sound and image is part of a poetics of editing that entirely escapes significative modes of analysis; structuralism, as a mode of theoretical capture, has no way of engaging with becoming, no way of dealing with flux and flow. Indeed, Saussure effectively sidelined temporal considerations of linguistic phenomena by simply proposing the value of the synchronic study of language above the diachronic. One consequence of this is that the audiovisuality of film and video, constituted as it is by the flux and flow of sound–image relationships, is unknowable within significatory regimes. In this respect the audiovisuality of Rankin's alphabet sequence demonstrates what Sarat Maharaj has termed the 'elusive liquidity' of the untranslatable. Maharaj's positive formulation of the untranslatable provides an alternative to those notions of materiality that as simply position it in relation to significatory processes as oppositional and turbulent (Hall and Maharaj, 2001: 46). Rankin's simple inclusion of movement, and of shots which declare their audiovisuality through the morphological correspondence of sound and image, not only derails the attempt by linguistic structures (such as the alphabet) to account for the non-linguistic, but perhaps more importantly in the context of this study, signals qualities that are fundamentally unknowable within significative regimes. In demonstrating this 'elusive liquidity', the audiovisuality of film and video signals an 'outside' of the significatory, a region removed from its influence.

Rankin repeatedly pitches the material against the linguistic, creating a zone of disjuncture and turbulence around the significative. This same sequence also employs a rapidity of editing that does not allow one to reflect on the possible linguistic connections that might serve to link sound and image. Rather, these seem to rebuff one another, and the linguistic framework of equivalence that we seek to impose on the flow of sounds and images collapses, with the result that we are confronted by movement, shift and by differences that cannot be resolved. The result is a material feeling of flow, in relation to which the 'linguistic turn' appears to be fighting a losing battle. John Smith's film *Associations* (1975) produces a similar effect, albeit in a different manner. Here images from magazines and colour supplements are edited to 'illustrate' text taken from an article on linguistic theory, heard in voice-over. As with Smith's other films, the polysemic nature of signifiers is revealed in the disjuncture between actual and intended or sanctioned meaning. In *Associations* this takes the form of a visual illustration of the words of the text that is governed by association and latitude of meaning. For example, the word 'associations' is represented visually by four images – an ass, a sewing machine, the sea and a group of Asian women – producing the rebus 'ass-sew-sea-asians'. However, the stream of images which accompanies the spoken words is so rapid and indigestible that, as A. L. Rees suggests, what is revealed is the inadequacy of words as a means by which to represent visual objects (Rees, 2002: 17).

For Rankin, the importance of challenging linguistic structures relates to the problematic issue of the role played by difference in figuring identity. This is demonstrated in *This and That* by one of Rankin's most straightforward yet powerful uses of sound, which highlights the role of 'framing' in our categorisation and mapping of otherness. The sequence comprises a series of film clips that present the non-white, non-American 'other' in racial terms, bounded by an ornate gilded picture frame. As the sequence of shots develops, Rankin's point that framing (and hence representation) *creates* meaning becomes increasingly powerful. We see black and white footage of Vietnamese peasants, and a shot of Pacific island-ers playing bamboo flutes – a performance for tourists perhaps, or a TV news item. These are followed by clips from the 1938 movie *The Drum*, featuring the actor Sabu (why no surname?) dressed in turban and loin cloth, Buddhist monks praying, a white actor playing an 'Indian' chief in a Hollywood Western, Indian men (this time in India) carrying swords and rifles, a young child herding cattle in Ethiopia, a Thai woman selling gifts from a canoe pulling up to Rankin's tourist camera, and images of African famine culled from a fundraising telethon, superimposed over which are the numbers of telephone donation lines. Rankin comments on this thought-provoking montage, 'By inserting images of "others" into the frame, I wished to comment on the distancing, objectifica-tion and museumification of non-western peoples and culture.'[19] Running underneath the sequence, which has no sync sound, we simply hear a recording of an inauthentic, slightly over-produced tango being played with great energy. Rankin cuts to the quick with tremendous simplicity: music, which is often considered to be the most abstract of all art forms, and whose appeal seems to lie in the arrangement of non-representational sounds ('pure' and 'objec-tive' to borrow the terminology of the visual arts), is also marked by constructions of difference. The appeal of this slightly over-the-top tango music evidences an inscription of otherness, no less serious in its potential consequences than the laughable portrayal of the Native American leader by a white actor (Figure 2.19). The tango, as signifier of the exotic, conjures the other with as little sensitivity as Hollywood's portrayal of the Native American. Commenting on his choice of music, Rankin states:

> The tango did seem overly exoticist and flippant in juxtaposition with the 'others' inside the gilded frame and then later inside the museum displays. The ultimate that-ness is to be killed and then preserved . . . Also the accordion always seemed to me to be (at least in mid-20th century American music) a very inauthentic instrument, coming from a musak-like culture very alien to me and very solipsistic.[20]

2.19 *This and That (Part Two)*

Sounding the oceanic

In the process of deconstructing language, Rankin's work points to ways of thinking and of knowing that stand in contrast to the individuation and differentiation of linguistic modes. In this way, his work often refers us to the oceanic, and forms of embodied experience and perception, by way of both the representational and affective dimensions of cinesonic experience. Rankin's use of the sounds of sea and wind creates a feeling of embodied perception, a sensory envelopment of the audio-spectator. *This and That* opens with the image of the sea, superimposed over which the film's title ebbs and flows with the movement of the waves, presenting a dissolution of language enacted by the power of the ocean (Figure 2.20).

Shots of the sea and of the desert recur throughout the tape, images and sounds that offer the featurelessness of the ocean and the desert landscape, accompanied by location sound of gently lapping water and the rumble of wind, both of which also share the characteristics of being featureless and enveloping. Microphone noise and deep rolling sounds dominate Rankin's

2.20 *This and That (Part Two)*

soundscapes here. The rumbling sound of wind, which we first encounter against shots of the desert, is carried through to other sequences, foregrounding those protean, fluid, malleable qualities of sound which enable it to morph to the requirements of the images it accompanies. These are sounds that, in this respect, have no clear or fixed identity. Used in conjunction with the shot of an oppressive desert sky, the rumble of wind in the microphone suggests thunder (Figure 2.21); played against a point-of-view shot taken from a hospital trolley, it becomes the rumble of the trolley's wheels across the hospital's corridors (Figure 2.22). It also, perhaps, conjures the sound of blood circulating around our own bodies – the low-frequency sound that John Cage famously heard in an anechoic chamber at Harvard University. This is surely the most embodied of sounds, the sound that takes us deep within ourselves, a sound that is indistinguishable from our sense of self, our sense of being, our sense of identity.

Rankin's images also work to situate us at the centre of an enveloping audiovisuality. Rankin shoots the majority of *This and That* using a hand-held camcorder, and there is an attempt here, and in works such as *Central* (2001), *Path* (2003) and *Piccadilly* (2004),

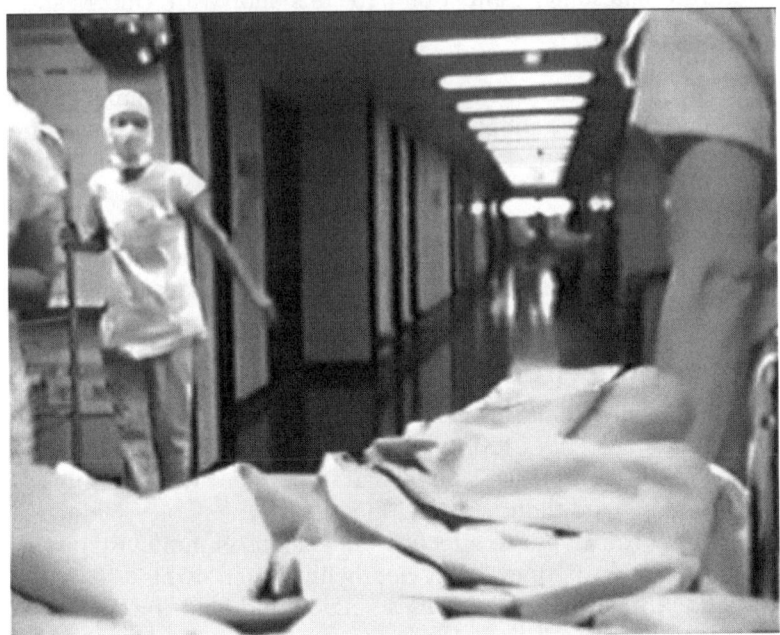

2.21–2.22 *This and That (Part Two)*

to place the audiospectator at the centre of the space presented on screen. In *This and That* Rankin's point-of-view shots are often those of the tourist, observing and recording their surroundings, shooting from ground level to look up at the ceilings of churches or at statues, standing behind other visitors in galleries, walking past museum exhibits. The microphone picks up the clunky sounds of the camera being handled, the rumble of wind, the buzz of every-day conversation. Some shots of the ocean are noticeably unstable, the horizon rocking from side to side, and thus appear to have been recorded at sea. The sound that accompanies this particular image features the slopping and lapping of water against the sides of an unseen boat, its timbers creaking as it flexes with the move-ment of the ocean. Point-of-view shots taken by Rankin walking in the rain or in the snow include the sounds of raindrops hitting the pavement, or snowflakes impacting gently on the micro-phone. In one notable point-of-view shot taken from a playground swing, we hear the sound of air rushing past the microphone with each successive movement backwards or forwards. This rhythmic sound echoes and suggests breathing, and thus works to create a sense of embodied intimacy that sutures us into, and envelops us in, the cinesonic event. Compare this shot with Tina Keane's tape *The Swing* (1978), in which classical music, superimposed text and objective, static camerawork create a sense of orderli-ness and intellectual distanciation rather than embodiment. The cinesonic strategies adopted by Rankin place us at the centre of a represented world, and simultaneously enfold us in an audiovisual experience. This relationship between listener and sound, in terms of the way in which the represented body and the audiospectator's body are impinged upon by the sonic, is a key aspect of Rankin's work. The rumbling sounds featured in Rankin's tapes have what he describes as a 'visceral quality';[21] they grab you bodily, pos-sessing and infecting the listener. And thus, in very simple terms, these sounds operate at the level of affect rather than by creating meaning. Evidence of this is given by the reaction of one audience to Rankin's tape *Path* (2003), which features extensive use of wind noise: 'My students said "I really like it, but get rid of that noise", because it bugged them' .[22]

The importance of the affective dimensions of audiovisuality to Rankin's work is perhaps most clearly illustrated by his 2001 vide-otape *Central*, which comprises a single hand-held track through a busy Hong Kong crowd. However, the shot is not played in its entirety until the end of the tape. Up until that point, we are offered only a small segment of the whole shot, played backwards and forwards repeatedly, but never exactly the same segment, since, with each play and rewind, Rankin takes us a little bit further on into the tape, and a little less further back. Thus we gradually progress from beginning to end via a series of overlapping play-rewind segments. Represented graphically, progress through the tape is thus:

The sound is that recorded by the video camera, laminated to the image and subjected to the same saw-like to-and-fro articulation as the image. While little snippets of conversation emerge as we progress temporally through the shot, and spatially through the crowd, the language heard is Cantonese, and so the opacity of the speech (to someone who does not speak this particular language), and the fractured nature of the general mix and flow of voices, work against the emergence of any clear linguistic meaning. At the same time, familiar sounds begin to emerge from the protean noise of the crowd, suggesting words that never actually materialise. Recognisable words seem to sprout from this swirling sonic soup, but then wither and die before they are fully realised, signalling perhaps our irresistible desire to invest the material with meaning, to translate the untranslatable. The repetition, coupled with reverse play, objectifies these sounds as we explore and inhabit their microsonic textures with each pass of the shifting loop. As we slowly advance through the tape, we become attuned to the complexity and flux of sounds that would normally pass us by unnoticed. Our sensitivity to this evolving micro-textural soundscape, this rich morphology of the everyday, connects with feelings of embodiment: we are subsumed, consumed, assimilated into this group of people, this moving image, the growling of the crowd. Rankin attributes the audiovisual experience created by *Central* to a form of transsensory affect: 'there's this sort of hurling thing that goes on there – moving, being catapulted forward, then you stop'.[23] What we witness in the audiovisuality of *Central* is

the blurring and mutual resonance of the senses that has been
described by Sartre in the following terms:

> the lemon is extended throughout its qualities, and each of its quali-
> ties is extended throughout each of the others. It is the sourness of
> the lemon which is yellow, it is the yellow of the lemon which is sour.
> We eat the colour of a cake, and the taste of this cake is the instru-
> ment which reveals its shape and colour to what we may call the
> alimentary intuition. Conversely if I poke my finger into a jar of jam,
> the sticky coldness of the jam is the revelation to my fingers of its
> sugary taste. The fluidity, the tepidity, the bluish colour, the undulat-
> ing restlessness of the water in a pool are given at one stroke, each
> quality through the others (Sartre, 1969: 186)

Central has a quality of back-and-forwardness that is seen and
heard and felt as the hurling action described by Rankin, and it
is the audiospectator that is 'hurled' just as much as the video
material being manipulated. Rankin's work foregrounds a bodily
experience of perception that seems to circumvent and challenge
significative modalities. Asking what this tape means is a pointless
question – it means nothing, it is non-sense. However, what the
tape *does* is to harness cinesonic experience in a way that gives a
sense of what it is to be in a crowd, what it is to be part of a multiplicity, what it is to be subsumed within a group of people, what
it means to come to terms with the oceanic as a way of knowing
and a way of being.

Refrain

The work of John Smith, Anthea Kennedy, Nick Burton and Scott
Rankin features points at which a destabilisation of signification
occurs in the field of the cinesonic. This destabilisation not only
takes the form of turbulence in relation to modes of signification,
but also begins to map a zone of sonic materiality that is 'untranslatable' within significatory regimes. To return to the example
of the concrete sound mirrors, when considered from the position of signification, it was the very *untranslatability* of the fluid,
dispersed, undifferentiated sounds of sea and wind that brought
about their failure, since this was a project founded upon an epis-
temology of isolation, individuation and differentiation. Like the
sound mirrors, the semiological project is simply unable to deal
with the temporal and spatial flow and flux of sonic phenomena,
unable to grasp their elusive liquidity. In its Saussurian formulation, the significatory modelling of sonic objects and events also

has the disadvantage of being based on linguistic paradigms, and consequently has few ways of considering the material in positive terms, founded as it is on notions of arbitrariness and negative differentiation. But even within Peirce's model of semiotics, although the trichotomy of signs gives some recognition to the sign's materiality, this is nevertheless processed by a concern with semiosis. Significatory modes of analysis are thus largely unable to deal with materiality that does not in some way seem to support the creation of meaning.

The fundamental limitations of the negative differentiation that lies at the heart of Saussurian linguistics are also revealed in oppositional and deconstructive formulations of film practice. The inherent weakness of this way of conceptualising the role played by film and video sound is that attention is inevitably deflected *from* the cinesonic *to* abstracted notions of absent, hegemonic models of audiovisual construction. The challenge then becomes to find ways of addressing the cinesonic that engage with its concrete particularity, and most specifically with the flow, flux, complexity and intersensoriality of film and video's audiovisuality.

At the same time, there is more at stake in working towards an alternative to significatory modes of analysis than simply finding more accurate and responsive ways of sounding the cinesonic. What Rankin's work shows is that the adoption of linguistic models, like those upon which semiology is founded, has consequences that go beyond the ability to map audiovisual phenomena more or less accurately, more or less convincingly. In *This and That* Rankin figures the relationship between perceptual experience, and the organisation of that experience, in terms of deictic forms which locate subject in relation to object:

> First 'pure' presence, perception 'This-ness', in the body, moving, seeing, reacting . . . Then cognition, discriminating (perceptually and cognitively) 'That-ness' from separating and naming, to categorising to taxonomies and collections to organising systems and languages and other symbolic systems [. . .] and representations . . . All these things build and layer in the head and the memory (in the mind and 'body'). They are compared and contrasted and parallel processed and emergent neural matrixes arise that we call thoughts and consciousness and metaphor.[24]

The problematic role of language and other representational modes in the construction of *that-ness* as otherness has already been touched upon briefly above, in reference to Rankin's exploration of framing. However, the artist's concern with the issue of difference also finds expression in other sequences in *This and That*, and in other works. In *This and That* Rankin presents us with a succession of shots featuring museum display cases filled with stuffed animals, his comment on this scene pithily summing up the real consequences of classifying, dividing and thinking about the world through the figure of difference: 'The ultimate That-ness is to be killed and preserved' .[25] In *The Pure* (1993), which takes as its subject the cultural attention and reverence given to notions of authenticity and purity, Rankin features a sequence dealing with the romanticisation of the 'native', the idea of the noble savage and western fantasies surrounding the notion of the lost paradise, offering the following reflection on colonial inscriptions of difference in his voice-over commentary:

> We are here now; they are there then. We are progress; they are developmentally arrested. We believe that they need our guidance in order to emerge into modernity, that modernity is what they desire, and that progress is a natural course of events. We are moved to civilise them. Of course, under certain circumstances, should they develop too quickly, we may be required to bomb them back into the Stone Age.

Thus, like Smith, Kennedy and Burton, Rankin recognises representation as the site of struggle – a political arena. What *This and That* proposes is that modes of thought founded on differentiation, individuation and notions of essence are highly problematic, and since we live our lives in a complex semiotic space, this issue has real political relevance.

If the untranslatable is inscribed within and against significatory modes as a destabilising form of turbulence, then this suggests that the notion of audiovisuality might also have a political dimension. Forms of audiovisuality that are unknowable within significatory regimes might indeed possess radical potential, and by exploring the cinesonic in ways that engage with its concrete particularity, and more specifically with its (non-significatory) flow, flux and transsensoriality, it becomes possible to figure cinesonic materiality in political terms. What we observe in the film and video work considered in this chapter are a number of strategies by which various forms of signification are destabilised, in the process of which cinesonic materiality begins to reveal itself. But what is at stake in cinesonic materiality is more than a simple refusal of signification, although this in itself has obvious radical potential. Rather, it is the potential *unknowability* of cinesonic materiality that constitutes its political dimension. Thus, unknowability within an established epistemological regime is not to be understood simply as a negation of that regime, but as a window onto another universe of possibilities. In this way we move from a radical poetics of refusal, to a materiality that opens a route to other ways of knowing, other ways of being and other ways of understanding what constitutes political aesthetics. In resisting signification, some sounds present a materiality that articulates itself in ways other than supporting the material difference required by linguistic formulations of meaning. The phenomena of ground noise and optical crackle, which form the focus of the next chapter, provide a particularly interesting example of sounds of this kind. These are sounds produced by the technology of film itself, which seem to lie outside of the complex of signification, text, meaning, semiotics and representation that has occupied the centre ground of film studies. These sounds escape the tripartite division of speech, sound effects and music that is commonly used to net the contents of the soundtrack. Yet paradoxically, these almost wholly ignored sounds are constantly present, in varying degrees, on all optical soundtracks of a certain age. The critical challenge this raises is to engage with something we do not usually attend to, and to do so in a positive terms; that is, to audition this sound not simply as noise which resists signification, but as a material manifestation of the technology of film itself.

Notes

1 The history, development and construction of the acoustic mirrors is documented in Richard N. Scarth's *Echoes from the Sky* (1999).

2 The term 'structural film' has been contested throughout its history, resulting in a number of reformulations designed to account more accurately for the work under consideration. The term was coined by P. Adams Sitney in the article 'Structural Film' to describe the work of Tony Conrad, George Landow, Michael Snow, Hollis Frampton, Joyce Wieland, Ernie Gehr and Paul Sharits; Sitney writes, 'Theirs is a cinema of structure wherein the shape of the whole film is predetermined and simplified, and it is that shape that is the primal impression of the film' (Sitney, 1969: 1). This use of the term was contested at the time by George Maciunas, who complained that Sitney had employed the wrong terminology, given inappropriate examples, proposed an inaccurate chronology and cited the wrong sources as origins of this body of work (see Sitney, 1971: 349). A few years later, in his highly influential 1975 article *Theory and Definition of Structural/Materialist*

Film, Peter Gidal made the addition of the word 'materialist', partly in order to distinguish his concerns from those of Sitney and the American avant-garde, but also to signal a Marxist political position on film practice (an account of the relationship between British and American Structural film is given by A. L. Rees, 1999: 72–87). However, in 1989 Gidal dropped the term 'structural' from his previous formulation 'structural/materialist', referring simply to 'materialist' film. Throughout this book the term 'structural film' is used, and should be understood to embrace the various positions on film practice signalled by the historical sketch above.

3 John Smith, interviewed by author, Leytonstone, London, 5 March 2002.
4 Channel 4 telephone call log, 19 December 1988. Provided by John Smith.
5 John Smith, lecture given at Canterbury Christ Church University, Canterbury, 14 October 2005.
6 Nick Burton, interviewed by author, Canterbury Christ Church University, Canterbury, 21 September 2004.
7 See note 6, above.
8 See note 6, above.
9 Anthea Kennedy, email to author 'Re. Sound stuff', 30 October 2005.
10 See note 9, above.
11 See note 9, above.
12 Cage comments in his article *Experimental Music*: '[the composer] may give up the desire to control sound, clear his mind of music, and set about discovering means to let sounds be themselves rather than vehicles for man-made theories or expressions of human sentiments' (Cage, 1999: 10).
13 See note 6, above.
14 See note 3, above.
15 See Wollen (1972).
16 See note 6, above.
17 Scott Rankin, email to author 'Re: Questions, questions', 8 October 2004.
18 Scott Rankin, interviewed by author, 26 March 2004, Canterbury, Kent.
19 Taken from unpublished *Artist's Statement*, provided by Scott Rankin.
20 Scott Rankin, email to author 'Re: None', 5 January 2005.
21 Scott Rankin, lecture given at Canterbury Christ Church University, Canterbury, 26 March 2004.
22 See note 18, above.
23 See note 18, above.
24 See note 20, above.
25 See note 20, above.

3 The sound of technology

Ground noise and optical crackle: the sound of film

There are a number of important cinesonic elements that escape the traditional tripartite division of the film soundtrack into speech, music and effects: one is noise, another silence and the third the sound of the technology of film itself. This last sound is almost completely neglected in studies of cinema, unless conceived in terms of noise or inadequacy. How, then, are we to describe, approach and, most importantly, map this material sound in positive terms; how are we to engage critically with this form of noise other than by situating it in relation to signification in terms of failure or refusal?

Noise, silence and the sound of technology come together in the figure of ground noise, the term used to refer to any undesirable noise inherent in reproduced sound. In the case of optical film sound, which forms the primary case study in this chapter, ground noise is in part created by the grain of the film stock on which the soundtrack is printed – a result of the play of silver halide particles through the beam of light cast by the projector's exciter lamp. As such, ground noise can simply be understood as the sound produced by film's material substrate as it passes across a sound reproducer. On magnetic recordings, including all the various analogue video formats, the equivalent of this sound is the hiss produced by the oxides of the recording tape. But even without film running through a projector, sound is still produced by projection and sound reproduction equipment, as a result of the electrical resistance inherent in the technology of film exhibition. Referred to as system noise, this quiet buzz of electrical circuitry combines with the hiss of the optical soundtrack in a sounding of film technology that is also a sounding of film's materiality. In addition to these sounds, optical crackle might also be considered a constituent of film's sonic materiality. This is the sound created by millions of tiny scratches that gradually mark a film print over time. Sometimes this latter sound is light and clear, sometimes heard as a rumble, reminiscent of the sound of wind in a microphone.

Together, the grain and scratch of the optical soundtrack comprise one aspect of what might be thought of as the sound of film itself: the sound produced by an unmodulated sound track, a sounding of film's material and the technological bases. It is a sound that is continually present in films with an optical soundtrack, although revealing itself most clearly in the 'silences' that surround and separate words, music and effects. For this reason it is present perhaps most noticeably in those films whose soundtracks tend towards dispersion and emptiness, rather than those aiming to create a continuum of sound. Although sometimes masked by music or other continuous sounds, this particular sound of film technology is always playing in and through the soundtrack, always there as the 'ground' against which other sounds are 'foregrounded'.

When framed within the context of noise, this sound presents a materiality that is understood to threaten the representational by interference, disruption and distraction. Thus, technical discourse on film sound constructs ground noise as a problem to be solved, a sound that needs to be minimised even if it can never be removed entirely. In the American Academy of Motion Picture Arts and Sciences' 1931 publication *Recording Sound for Motion Pictures*, Donald MacKenzie situates this sound in relation to a recording's fidelity. He states that, '[in order to] render the film as nearly perfect as possible . . . no frequencies other than those in the original sound source, should appear in the reproduced record, and there should be no static or noise – ground noise on the film or surface noise on the disc' (MacKenzie, 1931: 88–89).[1] This form

NOISELESS *Western Electric* RECORDING

3.1 Western Electric's Noiseless Recording logo c. 1934

of noise is figured elsewhere in terms of interference with the semantic substance of film, as in Stanley R. Alten's contemporary text *Audio in Media*: 'Because noise is an ever-present annoyance, the value of noise reduction cannot be overemphasised, especially in relation to dialogue and field recording, particularly with analog audio' (Alten, 2005: 232). Written almost three-quarters of a century after MacKenzie, Alten's comments introduce a historical dimension into the issue of noise. In suggesting that noise is a problem associated particularly with analogue audio, he implies that it becomes less of an issue with the arrival of digital technology. It is worth remembering, however, that the promise of noiseless recording, implicit in Alten's positioning of digital technology, has been with us since the very beginnings of commercial film sound technology; back in 1930 Western Electric was marketing its latest sound system as 'Noiseless' (Figure 3.1).[2]

Film studies and ground noise

Film studies is almost totally deaf to this sound of film technology, considered within technical histories only as a troubling presence to be reduced and ultimately removed by successive waves of technical innovation. For example, David Bordwell very briefly frames the reduction of ground noise, along with developments in directional microphones and an increase in the frequency and volume ranges of film recording, as part of the American film industry's drive to solve 'particular problems' between 1932 and 1935 (Bordwell, Staiger and Thompson, 1985: 300–1).[3] Generally, however, in a position that in some way parallels the conceptualisation of ground noise that emerges from the commercial film industry, film studies has constructed this sound (by neglect) as external to the film text, rather than embracing it as part of film's cinesonic textuality. As something which seems to lack apparent meaning, it finds no place in approaches derived from film-as-text traditions. Moreover, this particular sound is doubly neglected, doubly difficult to approach with existing critical resources, since it also presents the challenge of addressing a phenomenon that we simply don't attend to. The assumption is that the sound of technology is something that is listened *through* rather than listened *to*.

In terms of the film soundtrack, the audible materiality of this sound of technology will always represent a departure from one of two idealised norms: firstly silence, and secondly fidelity to the pro-filmic sound event. Motivated by the desire to reduce noise to zero, in one sense the technological development of commercial film sound aspires towards the condition of silence, thereby achieving a final and complete erasure of the technology of film itself, resulting in absolute fidelity. This aim is clearly stated by MacKenzie, who writes, 'The object of all recording is to furnish a sound which will be indistinguishable from the sound one would get from the real source if it were there' (MacKenzie, 1931: 84). Understood with this goal in mind, developments in film stock and in printing can be seen as an attempt to repress the medium's sonic materiality, an attempt to eradicate traces of its material base. A number of the developments in the manufacture of film stock that took place in the 1930s were undertaken by RCA and Western Electric's subsidiary, Electrical Research Products Incorporated (ERPI), to increase the frequency and volume ranges of film recording, and to reduce the ground noise created by the granularity of the film stock. These technical developments were a response to the fact that the optical film soundtrack records sound graphically in a strip alongside the picture area of the film print. The ability of this small area of the film print to encode sound rests in part on the capacity of the film stock to render photographic detail: coarse-grain stock encodes sound information with less resolution and with less precision than fine-grain stock. Therefore the grain structure of film not only creates a certain amount of ground noise itself, but also has a direct influence on the amount of information that can be recorded on the soundtrack, and thus on the fidelity of the recording. One of the perceived problems of early sound film stocks was that the frequency and volume range of recordings was quite limited; very low or high frequencies either could not be recorded or were distorted. According to Stephen Handzo, 'The graininess of the emulsion degraded the upper frequencies and read on the reproducer as noise' (Handzo, 1985: 389–390). Similarly, the dynamic range of early sound film recordings was compressed within a relatively narrow band, and consequently quiet sounds did not register well (if at all), while louder sounds distorted. A number of developments in film stocks were therefore specifically aimed at increasing fidelity: for example, the introduction of ultraviolet light in recording in 1936, the development of RCA's 'High-range' process for greater volume range and the use of fine-grain stock for better recording in 1939 (Bordwell, Staiger and Thompson, 1985: 301). Elsewhere, experiments carried out by Eastman and Du Pont resulted in the production of fine-grain film stocks such as Eastman No. 1302 and Du Pont No. 222 (Altman, 1985: 47). The result of these developments, and of others relating to microphones and to amplification and relay systems, was an expansion of the frequency range of recorded sound. According to Belton, the frequency range of sound film in 1928–30 was approximately 100Hz–4Khz, but by 1938 this range had increased to 30Hz–10Khz (Belton, 1985: 67). However, it should be remembered that the frequency range audible to the human ear is approximately 16Hz–20Khz, and thus the expansion of frequency range in film sound recording and reproduction still resulted in the production of a compressed and limited frequency spectrum, audible to the listener as such. It is in part this compression that gives film sound its sonic signature, differentiating the cinematic from the profilmic auditory event. In the same way that the technology of the telephone inhabits telephonic speech, so the technology of film resides as a trace in even the most seemingly faithful recordings.

What the history of technical developments in sound indicates is that film's sonic signature has changed over time. The significance of this simple observation should not be underestimated, as the historical dimension of cinesonic materiality provides the means to engage critically with the neglected sounds of film technology.

The audibility and inaudibility of noise

An alternative way of considering the attempts made by the film industry to improve fidelity is to view technical development in terms of the repression of materiality. This is not simply a critical viewpoint, but an avowed goal of classical film technique. In 1931 Carl Dreher, Director of the Sound Department at RKO Studios, wrote in his foreword to the Academy of Motion Picture Arts and Sciences' *Recording Sound for Motion Pictures,* 'In this field we are dealing not merely with a branch of engineering, but with engineering placed at the service of an art. We are dealing with a division of engineering which must produce physical realities, not in accordance with a rigid and inflexible technique, but for the purpose of arousing emotion in an unobtrusive and self-effacing manner' (Cowan, 1931: xv). The desire for self-erasure expressed by Dreher informs many aspects of sound production and post-production in classical cinema. In production this includes the prohibition against revealing the presence of film sound equipment, hence the ruse in the early days of sound film of concealing the microphone in a vase of flowers or hanging it just out of shot, from a walkway or boom. In post-production, editing practices that seek to achieve their own effacement include the use of fades and dissolves in preference to cuts, and the practice of cutting *to* sound rather than cutting *on* a sound in order to avoid the creation of audible sonic montage. Heard within this context, the reduction of ground noise is simply another means by which the film industry has sought to reduce the presence of cinema's material base.

Attempts to silence cinema's materiality direct us to the historical dynamic informing notions of audibility and inaudibility. Michel Chion makes the point that in the 1930s many films tried to create a continuum of dialogue, music and effects; for example, in musicals, where all sounds were designed to belong to a 'single universe'. He adds, 'They were helped by the fact that the background noise in films of the period, more or less consciously audible to the spectators, acted as a "basso continuo"' (Chion, 2003: 153). This *basso continuo*, in itself a sounding of film's technology, is largely absent from the modern screening of 35mm prints, due to the advent of Dolby noise reduction. Introduced in the mid-1970s, Dolby processes have had the effect of broadening the soundtrack's frequency range, improving dynamics, enabling greater intensity contrasts and, of course, reducing background noise – the purpose for which the system was originally developed.[4] Chion suggests that these technical changes have been accompanied by a change in the audiospectator's perceptual responses to the cinesonic event:

> Dolby cinema thus introduces a new expressive element: the silence of the loudspeakers, accompanied by its reflection, the attentive silence of the audience. Any silence makes us feel exposed, as if it were laying bare our own listening, but also as if we were in the presence of a giant ear, tuned to our own slightest noises. We are no longer merely listening to the film, we are as it were being listened to by it as well. (Chion, 2003: 151)

In the absence of audible ground noise, what Chion identifies as the audience's 'attentive silence' represents a change in perceptual activity that parallels film sound's shifting sonic signature. Thus, classical sound cinema's technical evolution, motivated by an aspiration to total self-effacement, has meant that the quality of the unmodulated soundtrack has changed over time. What both the *basso continuo* silence of the 1930s and the 'implosive' silence of the Dolby era reveal are the historical dimensions of this particular sound of film technology. Perhaps less obviously, but equally importantly, the expansion of frequency and dynamic range brought about by Dolby also marks a departure from previous incarnations of the audible announcement of film's technology. The changing nature of the unmodulated 'silent' soundtrack, and of film sound's broader sonic signature, signal the fact that the temporality of the sound of technology features important textual, spectatorial and perceptual dimensions, and that, furthermore, these are linked inextricably with shifting notions of audibility and inaudibility.

The currency of sound recordings, and by extension sound recording technology, seems not to announce itself, as each generation labours towards higher fidelity and finds itself marvelling at the latest rendition of recorded sound. The cinesonic, as we have seen, can be a slippery entity, lost in that easy act of elision that takes place when we move from sound to source, from material to meaning. A consequence of this is that we easily neglect film's sonic signature, preferring instead to engage with sound's semantic and representational content. However, the historical dimension of materiality renders this elision and slippage audible. Auditioned through the ear trumpet of history (why a more unlikely metaphor than 'seen through the lens of history'?) the sound of film technology materialises. Listening to recordings of the past, the listener is struck by the presence of a technology inscribed within and upon recorded sound. This sound of technology, when situated within a historical frame, presents itself as the inaudibility of the contemporary and the audibility of the past. While the listener can hear and perhaps identify the sonic signature of films made in the 1930s, we are hard pressed to hear what defines the precise quality of film sound today: hence, post Dolby, Chion can hear *nothing*, and in the apparent absence of sound, the audience's ears turn inside out in the attempt to hear *something*. We can observe similar phenomena in many other aspects of cinema; for example, the stuttering and mumblings of Marlon Brando's performance in *On the Waterfront* present a style of acting celebrated at the time for its unequalled realism, its unsurpassed fidelity. Viewed today, this style of performance reveals itself as style. What was once considered natural now appears mannered, its former transparency rendered opaque by the passage of time. Conversely, current film stocks, current televisual images and current sound recordings all seem to announce themselves less than those of the past. Yet it is surely a mistake to suppose that inaudibility is a unique feature of twenty-first-century technology, and that with the recent developments in digital media we are somehow finally approaching a point of complete technological inaudibility. Rather, inaudibility should be thought of as an effect of currency, and it is therefore temporal *displacement* rather than a specific historical moment that determines the sound of *pastness*.

Although the various media industries have always sought to repress the audibility of technology, there is a sense in which audiences in any case listen *through* certain sounds, relegating them to the background of conscious perception. Chion suggests that in the 1930s audiences were 'more or less' aware of ground noise, and that this *basso continuo* was 'more or less consciously audible to the spectators'. This more-or-lessness is a significant factor when considering the ways in which the sounds of past technologies affect the listener. While at some point, when listening to a film, we might consciously acknowledge the presence of ground noise, we nonetheless listen through it, usually becoming less aware of the sound as it gradually migrates to the borderline of conscious perception. Similarly, while we recognise the limitations of early sound film's reproduction of speech, the extreme compression it imposes on the human voice is nevertheless soon forgotten as we attend to the semantic content of a film's recorded dialogue.

A significant corollary of the perceived inaudibility of the present is the fact that audible materiality announces pastness. It is this observation that provides us with a means by which we can explore the sound of technology beyond the established formulations of noise that have dominated its consideration within film studies – formulations which construct this sound, in relation to the dominant significatory registers of film, in terms of interference and failure. Clustering around the notion of the sound of technology are a number of interconnected ideas relating to materiality, audibility, inaudibility and the historical. Thus, the cinesonic materiality we encounter in the phenomenon of ground noise can be considered in positive terms if we think about its relationship to the sense of pastness we experience when watching old films. A non-specific but yet very definite sense of the past accompanies the phenomenon of ground noise, and the many particular and subtle renderings of speech, music and effects that constitute the broader sonic signature we associate with it.

One thing that is striking about the sound of technology's pastness is the fact that we are immediately sensitive to the temporal displacement created by a vintage recording. While, unlike the expert archivist, we may not be able to associate the sounds we hear with a specific decade, nevertheless, old sound recordings do *sound old*. But what exactly is it that we hear in these recordings? What is the difference between recorded sounds that present themselves as 'old' and those that do not, and what determines that difference? In order to consider how pastness and cinesonic materiality are connected, it is necessary to listen more closely to the sounds that make up the historical sound of technology.

Sounding the past

The sonic field encompassed by this historical sound of technology can be usefully divided into four interrelated areas, each of which makes a contribution to the sounding of the past.

Rendering

The technology of film sound is not only heard as a background to other sounds, but inhabits each and every element of the soundtrack. Every sound heard in a film bears the trace of technology's sonic signature. If we were to analogise the soundtrack of a film in terms of voice, then the sound of film technology also resides in what Roland Barthes describes as the 'grain' of that voice. When, in his analysis of singers' voices, Barthes writes about this grain in terms of 'the very friction between the music and something else, which something else is the particular language' (Barthes, 1977: 185), his use of the word 'friction' describes a relationship between two elements that cannot be divorced. Binary formulations seem to fail us when thinking about the relationship between sounds and the qualities attributable to the bodies (or technologies) that generate them, for in the very act of naming constituent elements, we separate what we know and hear to be inseparable. Barthes works towards solving this problem by a choice of simile that stresses connectivity. Thus, writing on the voice of the Russian bass, he describes its sound 'as though a single skin lined the inner flesh of the performer and the music he sings' (Barthes, 1977: 181–182). The relational aspect of this formulation is directly relevant to understanding the notion of the sound of film, for permeating every sound announced by a film is the audible trace of a meeting of technology and sound; to rephrase Barthes, as though a single skin lined the technology of film and the sounds it produces.

The way in which a sound is rendered by a technology is in some respects akin to musical timbre, while a visual parallel might be the differences in film stock that serve to define a historical period, irrespective of the degree to which scratching and other signs of wear and tear might indicate a print's age. There are several aspects of production that have a bearing on this element of film's sonic signature, but most significant are the nature of the microphone, and the recording medium itself. Different microphone technologies respond in different ways to sound, emphasising certain frequencies, reducing or removing others. For example, all microphones produce a simple gating effect, since they are not responsive to all frequencies or all levels of amplitude. Microphones work by translating sound vibrations, registered on a diaphragm or metallic ribbon, into electrical impulses. Thus the sensitivity of a microphone is determined by the ability of the diaphragm or ribbon to be set in motion by sound vibrations and to respond sympathetically to them, as well as its capacity to transform these vibrations into an electrical current. The earliest microphones used in film lacked sensitivity, in the sense that they were not responsive to lower amplitudes or to a wide range of frequencies. The fall-off below a certain level of amplitude, and a relatively narrow frequency response, created a gating effect, and a consequent 'bundling' of sound within particular frequency and amplitude ranges, audible as the tinny, strident quality of early sound film. This amplitude gating is one factor that creates what sounds like a rapid attack and decay of sound on some older film soundtracks. In a number of films made in the late 1920s and early 1930s, the words of the actors seem to erupt out of the audible ground noise that cocoons them, and then just as quickly disappear back into it. The effect is a feeling that the sounds overcome some kind of inertia in tearing themselves from the soupy silence of Chion's *basso continuo* ground noise. This particular effect is also a result of the mastering process, in which the final soundtrack is encoded on the film print. The fact that only a certain amount of information can be registered optically on the film print – a factor discussed earlier in terms of the developments in film stock grain – also has an impact on the volume and frequency range of the soundtrack.

Being in part a product of mastering and the nature of the

optical soundtrack, the sonic signature associated with early sound cinema is not limited to those films recorded with the very earliest of microphones. The slightly explosive quality of speech which seems to tear itself from the background of ground noise is heard on a disparate range of film soundtracks, from classical Hollywood films such as *White Zombie* (Victor Halperin, 1932) and *My Favourite Wife* (Garson Kanin, 1940), to later independent and avant-garde productions such as *Vivre sa vie* (Jean-Luc Godard, 1962) and *The Chelsea Girls* (Paul Morrisey and Andy Warhol, 1966). Low-level background and ambient sounds rarely register on these soundtracks, and so there are moments of quiet in which we hear the hiss of ground noise and optical crackle and almost nothing else. In addition, the speech recorded in these films seems insulated from a wider sonic environment, as the rapid attack and decay characteristic of these recordings serves to differentiate and isolate dialogue from other elements of the soundtrack. The use of dubbing also contributes to this effect; in the film *My Favourite Wife*, an example of classic 1940s Hollywood screwball comedy, the process of post-synching dialogue results in the removal of the ambient background sound heard on production sound record- ings, helping to create the feeling that the performers' words are dropped like pebbles into a pool of still water.

In some films, the recorded elements of the soundtrack seem to liberate other lurking, viral sounds, revealing a distinct textural presence that is absent when the soundtrack falls silent. This tex- turing of sound, absent from the silences occupied by ground noise and optical crackle, also serves to isolate and differentiate sounds from the sonic continuum of ground noise, giving the soundtrack a ghostly, disengaged feeling. This particular quality of sound is a form of system noise, relating to one or more of the various stages of amplification that take place in production, post-production and exhibition; in this instance, the recorded elements of the sound- track become a kind of window, opened and closed onto the film's system noise.

Another consequence of the combined effects produced by microphone technology and the mastering process is a density and continuity of sound that results from having very little con- trast between recorded sound events. The dynamic range of any soundtrack is necessarily limited, but in some films this becomes clearly audible, especially in scenes in which more than one person is talking – in crowd scenes, for example – or where music and speech are combined. This compression produces a dense fusion of sonic elements, a relatively homogenous continuum of sound squeezed within a narrow bandwidth. The effect is heard in *The Chelsea Girls* and *Vivre sa vie*, both of which feature the use of direct sound. In Morrisey and Warhol's film this sonic density is particularly evident when their performers argue or shout, resulting in a heavy distortion that works to create a homogenising effect on the soundtrack. What is important to note in relation to the sonic qualities discussed so far is that this small sample of films covers a 30-year period, which suggests that these sounds create a general sense of the past, rather than directing the listener to a specific historical era. In the case of *The Chelsea Girls*, the sound also locates itself within a particular cultural milieu, since many independent films of this period featured 'low-fi' sound of this type.

Sound archivists refer to the recording medium as the 'carrier', and although a separation between medium and signal seems implicit in this term, it might nevertheless also be used to challenge this simple binary formulation. If we rethink the notion of carrier as being that of one infected by a virus, we come closer to a satisfactory formulation of rendering, by framing the relationship between medium and signal in terms of their fundamental connectedness. A virus cannot survive independently of its host, and in a sense becomes part of that host, inseparable from it. In the same way, recorded sound cannot be entirely divorced from the 'carrier' that brings it into being. Any medium will record and reproduce sound in a particular way, imprinting it with its own sonic signature. In the case of disc recording, for example, the groove itself can only accommodate certain ranges of amplitude and frequency. Above the upper limit of this amplitude range (very loud sounds) and below a certain frequency (very 'low' tones), the vibrations of the cutting stylus become so great that cutting may extend laterally beyond the parameters of the groove. The consequence of this is that two adjacent grooves may cut into each other, rendering the recording unplayable. Thus the sonic signature of disc recordings must necessarily be marked by a particular limitation of volume and frequency range. Similarly, very high frequencies could not be reproduced on early coarse groove discs, firstly because the recording equipment employed was not responsive to these frequencies, and secondly because the shellac material from which the records were finally pressed was not able to support the minute micromorphological features of the groove necessary to reproduce high frequency sound. In this way, the restricted ranges of amplitude and frequency heard in early sound-on-disc films – common also to sound-on-film productions – are audible to the modern listener as compression and limitation.

However, there are also more subtle effects that film technology can have on recorded sound. Competing with the sound-on-disc systems of the late 1920s and early 1930s were a number of sound-on-film systems. One of these, RCA's Photophone system, transcribed sound by means of a tiny mirror that moved in response to the variable electric current generated by a microphone. This mirror reflected a beam of light, and as it deflected in direct response to the modulating sound source, it caused the light to flicker. The resultant variable pattern of light was then recorded on a strip of film to produce a 'variable area' optical sound track.[5] However, the mirror itself had a degree of inertia, and the system therefore not only lacked sensitivity to faint sounds, but also over-modulated loud sounds (Bernds, 1999: 68). This produced what is referred to as 'volume expansion', the effect of which is to produce a slightly explosive quality of sound, and a cut-off below a certain level of amplitude. Volume expansion is another factor that contributes to a feeling of audible compression, distinctive of films produced using the system. Since Photophone remained in use until it was replaced by magnetic tape recording in the 1950s, once again, the specific rendering of sound it produced must therefore convey a general rather than a specific sense of the past.

Ground noise and system noise

Mention has already been made, in relation to the sound produced by electrical circuits, of the fact that the hardware of film production and reproduction generates system noise. To this can be added the sounds made by the camera or the projector's shutter, and those made by drive belts, motors and so on. Film production hardware can therefore produce sounds which may be inscribed into a recording, and traditionally measures have been taken to reduce this possibility, such as the introduction of the soundproofed 'icebox' and the camera blimp. Mechanical sounds produced by the camera are constructed as problematic in film-making practices, like those developed by the Hollywood studio system, which prioritise the concepts of flow and continuity. In classical cinema, sounds produced by the camera are prohibited not simply because they signal the means of production, but also because sound edits might be rendered audible by the varying levels and qualities of camera noise heard in a recording (resulting from changes in camera position within and between locations).

Audible sonic montage would, of course, be directly opposed to the basic tenets of the continuity style of filmmaking, potentially drawing attention to the film's construction and its own materiality, and thus disrupting audience engagement with the film's narrative. During post-production, filtering is used to remove as much camera noise as possible, and commonly a music track or other continuous atmos track is laid down to disguise sound cuts, thereby maintaining flow and repressing difference.[6]

Both the hardware and software of film production and exhibition play their part in creating ground noise. In the disc-based playback systems of early sound cinema, the crackle and hiss we associate with vintage recordings (referred to as surface noise) is the sound produced by the contact between the surface of the disc and the needle of the reproducer as it works its way along the groove. On the optical soundtrack, ground noise is the sound produced by the grain of film stock and the scratches that mark negatives and prints. All these sounds are central to the impact made by sound artist Jonty Semper's *Kenotaphion* project, which presents archive sound recordings of the two-minute silences held on Armistice Day and Remembrance Sunday at the Cenotaph in London. Semper collected all available recordings of the event from newsreels, radio and television broadcasts made between 1929 and 2000. What we hear in the assembled silences are not only the environmental sounds captured in the recordings, but also the sounds of the various technologies being employed to document these silences. In the case of recordings taken from the earlier newsreels, the sheer intensity of ground noise is quite striking to the modern listener, occupying the foreground of our conscious attention as we listen to these recorded moments of 'silence'.

As signifiers of a historical period, ground noise and system noise can easily be added to a contemporary sound mix to create a sense of pastness. However, if this is done, the result is only suggestive of vintage sound. To convincingly create the sense of pastness, in addition to the presence of ground noise and system noise, the signal part of the recording would need to be rendered in a particular way. The embeddedness of the sound of the past is demonstrated by the unconvincing nature of attempts to suggest pastness by mixing crackle and hiss taken from old films or discs with contemporary sound recordings. In this approach to the recreation of vintage sound, the appropriated ground noise seems to sit on the 'surface' of the recording, in the same way that the synthesised scratches added to contemporary video footage seem somehow divorced from the material substrate of the image. The crackle heard on old discs is created when the needle encounters the damaged wall of a record groove or particles of dirt. In the case of shellac discs, this sound is in part due to the coarse texture of the surface itself; that is, microscopic holes and fissures form part of the fabric of the material, registering as the pops, hiss and crackle of surface noise. In addition, hardwearing abrasive materials such as emery powder were added to the shellac to make the discs more resistant to wear and tear, resulting in an increased level of surface noise (one of the reasons why shellac was replaced by vinyl as a playback medium in the late 1940s). At each point where the needle encounters one of these fissures, holes or particles of dirt, there is a loss of recorded sound – a gap filled by a microsonic click. This may happen with more or less serious consequences, sometimes many hundreds of times per second. What modern recreations of vintage sound often do is merely superimpose the sounds of surface noise over a modern recording, which thus runs unbroken and unaffected below the appropriated noise of the past. This superimposition is not equal to the viral nature of true surface noise, which by contrast is fundamentally connected to the recorded sound it interacts with, and forms part of.

Content

In 1973, R. Murray Schafer famously declared, 'the soundscape of the world is changing'.[7] Particularly concerned with the threat to natural and traditional sounds posed by urbanisation and industrialisation in the late twentieth century, Schafer's work on the soundscape reminds us that our sonic environment is in a constant state of flux. Thus the specific sounds that are documented in recordings help to situate those recordings within a historical frame. Sounds that have all but disappeared from the contemporary soundscape (horses' hooves in urban areas, whistling paperboys, steam trains, etc.), and those that have changed over time (telephone 'ringtones', police sirens) all help to situate a recording in the past. Similarly, the way in which people speak, the way they interact with the medium and their accents and figures of speech all contribute to a sounding of the past, as do instrumentation and arrangement within the field of music. Prior to the introduction of electrical recording in 1925, music had been recorded acoustically, with players arranged around a recording horn that transferred sound vibrations directly to a cutting stylus. Unfortunately, stringed instruments did not record well under these conditions, so a tuba might take the parts originally written for double bass. In this way, the orchestration of a musical recording contributes to the sounding of pastness. Thus, while never divorced from the rendering that takes place as a result of recorded sound's technological existence, the actual content of a sound recording nevertheless has the potential to signal the past.

Playback

Different technologies of recording and transmission reproduce sounds in very different ways. There is a distinct difference between the quality of sound reproduced by a wind-up gramophone and a cinema set up for Dolby Digital Surround, as there is between the telephone and television. In this way, the resonant sound produced by a gramophone horn comes to signify the sound of the past just as much as the content and specific sonic signature of the recording being played. However, the qualities of sound associated with playback are only in part attributable to the hardware being used. Since sonic events occur in both space and time, the acoustics of the environment in which playback *takes place* also influences the specific signature of any reproduced sound.

Microsound and the drone

Having sketched some of the factors that contribute to a sounding of pastness, we must now consider the way in which the materiality of these sounds connects to a sense of the past, and how the listener's perceptual activity figures in this relationship. Is it the case that these sounds, and qualities of sound, simply signify the past by convention, by the inscription of difference that serves to distinguish historical periods, or are there other ways in which our perceptual responses to the material cinesonic event might figure in this sense of pastness? In what follows, I will focus on optical crackle and ground noise as sounds which signal just such a sense of the past, and on the quality of compression that contributes to the sonic signature of older film soundtracks. Central to the discussion that follows are two key observations that emerge from the analysis above: firstly, that ground noise is constant, and secondly, that film sound is compressed in terms of both its dynamic range and frequency range.

Despite not being continuous *tones*, the sounds produced by ground noise and optical crackle possess certain drone-like qualities. These work to disturb the normal temporal frames of reference that we bring to our experience of cinema. To understand this more fully, we might usefully draw upon Curtis Roads's work on microsound. The focus of Roads's work is on sounds of very short duration and how they are perceived when auditioned en masse. Although Roads is specifically concerned with the notion of microsound as it relates to musical composition and listening experience, his findings are nevertheless relevant to this discussion of film sound. Roads divides musical time into a series of domains (Roads, 2001: 3) which can be usefully transposed to a cinematic context to help us understand the temporal effects created by ground noise and optical crackle. The *supra*temporal domain is that which lies beyond individual compositions (or films), usually measured in terms of months, years, decades and centuries. The *macro*temporal is the timescale relating to overall musical form; transposed into filmic terms, this corresponds to the running time of a film. The *meso*temporal domain relates to divisions of form: groupings of sound objects into phrase structures; in film, this would relate to scenes, shots and moments within shots. Roads then identifies the *sound object* itself, and here we might think of the individual sounds that make up the film soundtrack. Below this level lies the *micro*temporal domain, which embraces sound particles down to the threshold of auditory perception; a temporal domain in which sound elements are measured in thousandths of a second.

Roads makes the point that although we may not notice microsounds individually, we can nevertheless hear them en masse. It is this interaction of hundreds or thousands or millions of microsounds that we hear in the sound of rain, in the roar of the ocean, in the movement of wind through the leaves of a tree and in the crackle of fire. If these individual sound events occur quickly in succession, then one sound begins to mask the next, and this contributes to the illusion of a continuous tone (Roads, 2001: 22).[8] Thus, no longer heard as discrete sound events, the microsounds that make up film's ground noise produce a continuous *unpitched* tone. To this are added the sounds produced by the scratches on the print itself, referred to so far as optical crackle. This latter sound does not have the density of ground noise, since it is made up of fewer discrete sound events per second. The amount and severity of scratching will vary from print to print, but a significant determining factor is age, since the longer a print remains in circulation, and the more times it has been screened, the more its surface will be marked by both visible and invisible scratches. The effect of this wear and tear is described by Saskia Baron in her account of a screening of a widely circulated print of Robert Frank and Alfred Leslie's *Pull My Daisy* (1959): 'Last time it played at the Scala the celebrated Kerouac rap was hard to follow, and the film was beginning to acquire that "patina" which makes itself more conspicuous than the film beneath it (Baron, 1986: 39).

The sound of optical crackle is certainly less consistent than ground noise, comprising short bursts of sound, random in terms of both duration and amplitude. Not only will certain parts of a print feature it more than others – those parts handled most frequently, normally the beginning and end of reels – but also there is no discernible pattern to the sound, which comprises a combination of light clicks and heavy thuds. However, the rate at which these individual events occur will produce different sonic effects, often including forms of continuity. Karlheinz Stockhausen explains the relationship between the frequency with which we hear a sound and the effect it creates in the article . . . . .*How Time Passes*. . . . ., in which he explores the connection between periodicity and pitch:

> Our sense-perception divides acoustically-perceptible phases into two groups; we speak of *durations* and *pitches*. This becomes clear if we steadily shorten the length of a phase (e.g., that between two impulses) from 1″ to 1/2″, to 1/4″, 1/16″, 1/32″, 1/64″, etc. Until a phase-duration of approx. 1/16″, we can still just hear impulses separately; until then, we speak of 'duration' . . . Shorten the phase-duration gradually to 1/32″, and the impulses are no longer separately perceptible . . . The latter process becomes perceptible, rather, in a different way: one perceives the phase-duration as the 'pitch' of the sound. 1/32″ phase-duration makes us, say, 'a "low" note.' (Stockhausen, 1959: 10)

The number of times a sound is repeated per second, and the length of the gaps between each repetition, are factors that determine a repeated sound's place within the continuity that exists between rhythm and pitch. According to Stockhausen, at about sixteen repetitions per second we lose the sense of individual sound events, and begin to hear forms of continuity.[9] In this way, the microscopic scratches that mark the surface of a film print can create a continuous, light, unpitched tone. It is unlikely that more severe scratches would be this frequent, but even when heard at around sixteen times per second, we begin to enter the area of continuous sound, where optical crackle hovers between a localised and global phenomenon. This observation is supported by Roads's experiments with sound 'grains' of 25 milliseconds in length. Using 15 grains per second, Roads observes rhythm; at 15–25 grains per second, fluttering and a sensation of rhythm; at 25–30 grains per second the grain order disappears; between 50 and 100 grains per second we hear what Roads calls 'texture'; and at over 100 grains per second a continuous sound mass is produced (Roads, 2001: 106). Thus, the observations made by both Roads and Stockhausen suggest that the individual microsounds that constitute optical crackle may also be sounded as a continuous unpitched tone. This sound, when combined with the ground noise created by film's grain structure, constitutes a sound of technology that is also the sound of pastness.

Dismantling time

The drone-like quality of this sound of technology sets in motion Roads's subdivision of time into various domains, erasing some of the distinctions he draws between them. The continuous tone challenges our usual conception of the discrete sound object: this sound has little or no internal development, and is morphologically featureless, having no rhythm, pulse, narrative, sense of progression or climax. When listening to sounds situated within an extended temporal framework we tend, in any case, to lose a sense of patterning. According to Roads, the sense of rhythm is lost below 0.12Hz, which means that if a sound repeats only once every eight seconds or more, we may no longer be able to perceive it in terms of rhythm. Thus, while the density of the combined sound of ground noise and optical crackle may vary over the course of a film, the length of time taken for these changes to occur means that it is unlikely that we would be able to impose any sense of order or patterning upon the sound, or perceive any kind of development. Furthermore, the listener tends to displace continuous sounds from the foreground of perception. As Roads observes, 'The ear's sensitivity to sound is limited in duration. Long continuous noises or regular sounds in the environment tend to disappear from consciousness and are noticed again only when they change abruptly or terminate' (Roads, 2001: 12); and since the sound of optical crackle may not always be particularly loud, it is unlikely to draw our *conscious* attention. All these factors would therefore seem to work against the perception of this sound as a discrete sonic object.

It might be argued that the fact that this sound of technology must have a beginning and an end gives it some status as a defined, isolated, morphologically distinct entity, especially when it seems to emerge most clearly in the gaps between speech, sound effects and music. But this is not the case, since, although this sound might seem to reside in the spaces left between other sounds, it actually runs continuously through a film. Rather, our attention is only consciously drawn to this sound in the extended absence of the sound objects that form what is commonly understood to be 'the soundtrack'. Consequently, this sound also resists Roads's conception of the mesotemporal: the grouping of sound objects into phrase structures. There are no phrases, no groupings, no patterning or memorable variations within the duration occupied by the sound. In the sound of ground noise and optical crackle, the mesotemporal, the macrotemporal, the sound object and the microsonic domains therefore merge to become one sonic experience, thus setting in motion the dominant temporal frames of reference we bring to bear on our engagement with the film text. The sound is homogeneous, lacking the memorable short-term morphological differences that mark development or progression of any kind. This sound of technology is non-directional, and non-narrative, in the sense that it neither supports narrative nor demonstrates any internal development. Such sounds might therefore be thought of in terms of stasis and suspension. Sustained tones of long duration produce a temporal slipperiness that casts the listener adrift, since there is no way of carving up duration in a sonic experience in which there is complete continuity between microtemporal and macrotemporal domains.

As a composite sound created by millions of microsounds, optical crackle is actually highly textured, and thus differs from the constant tones we would associate with musical drones. There are unpredictable, non-rhythmic micro-variations in the sound, and in this sense it shares similarities with the sounds of wind, water and fire. But nevertheless, because of its temporal duration and sonic consistency, we can say that it is drone like, as is the hum of distant traffic or the sound of air conditioning. This sound is perhaps best conceptualised as a borderline drone experience, since optical crackle injects individual, localised sound events into the global sound of ground noise. However, the mere fact that there are so many of these localised sound events means that their repetition, although not rhythmic, works to remove them from the foreground of conscious consideration. Thus, as Chion suggests, we are only 'more or less' aware of this sound.

The temporal and perceptual slipperiness of continuous sound is demonstrated by Michael Snow's 1967 film *Wavelength*. For thirty-seven of its forty-five minutes, the film's soundtrack consists only of a sine-wave tone that slowly rises in pitch from 50Hz to 12,000 Hz. This gradual change in frequency roughly parallels the visual structure of the film, described by Gene Youngblood as 'a forty-five minute zoom from one end of a room to the other' (Youngblood, 1970: 122). The sine wave that dominates the film's soundtrack hovers between being a sound in which development can be clearly perceived, and one in which that same development escapes audition at any given moment. When we listen to this film, although at certain points we 'feel' or 'sense' that the sine-wave tone is rising, it is difficult to hear this change within our normal mesotemporal frames of reference. One of the great strengths of Snow's film is the way in which it forces the listener to become aware of their acts of auditory perception, and yet not be able to come to terms with that act fully, in the sense that the percept itself seems fugitive. When listening to this sine wave, the 'content' of our perception is not easily grasped, not easily objectified, not easily separated from our awareness of the act of listening. In this respect, the image offers little help to the audiospectator, being at times a barely perceptible (although jerky) slow zoom into the wall opposite the camera. The sine wave presents a slippery surface in a barren landscape, forcing us towards a 'direct' experience of duration. Snow gives the audiospectator a tantalising taste of time, stripped of those events that would otherwise simply render it a container for film's narrative and representational elements. As Snow suggests in an interview with Michael Hartog, *Wavelength* is 'A time monument' (Hartog, 1978: 36); it is a prism through which time is seen and heard in both its vertical and horizontal dimensions.

Might it be possible, therefore, that the continuous sounds of ground noise and optical crackle share something of *Wavelength*'s power to destabilise the dominant temporal and perceptual frames of reference we associate, for example, with cinema's narrative function? Of course, in many films which feature audible ground noise and optical scratch, the audiospectator's attention is tuned to the visual actions on screen, and in this way duration is divided up into a series of events. It is for this reason, perhaps, that this sound may work at a subconscious level to produce a form of turbulence in which the stasis of the soundtrack is heard in tension with the narrative progression and visual movement of the image track; a dual-stream flow of sound and image that generates feelings of displacement, alienation and distanciation. In terms of sound-to-sound relations, this turbulence is heard when 'isolated' speech is dropped into and onto the ground noise of optical film. This is particularly evident in the dream-like, distanced voice-overs of film noir, when atmos sounds and music are removed, and the speech is suspended in the 'silence' of film's ground noise. The effect created here also relies on a certain calmness in the voice – even a tendency towards monotony – and a slowing of speech that has the effect of introducing silence into the narration. The resulting estrangement or atemporality created is that of the aquarium, and although in part this results from the separation of sound and image, the static, suspended sound of ground noise and optical crackle also contribute to the creation of this effect.[10]

The phenomenon of temporal suspension may explain why some of the most powerful moments of this static sound are those in which the image works less to mark time, when the stillness of the image comes close to matching that of the soundtrack. This is particularly noticeable, for example, during screenings of Antonioni's films. In *L'eclisse* (1962), we see the film's central character Vittoria assist her friends in a night-time search for a lost pet. She finds herself alone, and her attention is caught by a row of metal flagpoles (Figures 3.2–3.4). Their ropes, caught perhaps by a gentle breeze, tap against the poles, and Vittoria, like the viewer, is suspended in this simple, almost static image, as these gentle sounds float quietly in the warm oceanic crackle and hiss of the barely modulated soundtrack – the 'silence' that serves as background to every film's 'quiet' moments.

Antonioni often includes drone-like elements in the soundtracks of his films, although these are heard at much higher levels than the unintended sounds produced by ground noise and optical crackle. In *L'avventura* (1960) a similar moment of suspension occurs when the film's central characters, and again the audience, are confronted with the sounds of the sea and wind as they search a barren Mediterranean island for their missing friend, Anna. *Il Deserto Rosso* (1964) features several moments in which the very film itself seems transfixed in a scene made strange by the sound of steam escaping from a pipe, or the industrial noise of a power station. In all these instances, the shots are static and of extended duration, factors that serve to further reduce the attention we would otherwise place on movement and progression, and thus

3.2–3.4 *L'eclisse*

freeing us to respond to other dimensions of cinematic experience. Like ground noise and optical crackle, the sounds of wind, waves and industrial noise featured in Antonioni's work hover between continuity and change, stasis and movement. This temporal disturbance complements those narrative moments in which Antonioni's characters gaze out of frame with the look described by US Marines as the 'thousand yard stare' – a look that indicates psychological disconnection from the immediate environment. In a military context, this occurs as a reaction to the stress of prolonged combat, a removal of self from the horror of the moment. In Antonioni's work, although we are rarely afforded access to the interior motivations of his protagonists, there is always a sense in which this look indicates a character's temporary disconnection from the moment, or alternatively, their suspension within it. These are films in which sound and image work together to create the sense that time itself seems to be momentarily suspended, for both the film's characters and its viewers. If this is in part due to the drone-like qualities of continuous sounds, how then might other artistic uses of sustained sounds help to develop an understanding of the temporal and perceptual effects created by ground noise and optical crackle?

'There is the "dream chord", which I used to hear in the telephone poles'[11]

The work of La Monte Young, perhaps more than that of any other composer, has been concerned with the potential of static, continuous sound. Since 1958 Young has been best known for creating music that features the use of long sustained tones within extended time structures. The score for Young's *Composition 1960 #7* consists simply of a chord (B and F#) and the instruction 'To be held for a long time', while the score for *Composition 1960 #9* takes the form of a straight line drawn on a three-by-five inch file card, performed by Young as one single sustained pitch (Young and Zazeela, 1969: 32). In 1964 Young initiated his composition *The Tortoise, His Dreams and Journeys*, conceived as open-ended piece of potentially infinite duration, and of which he writes, 'This music may play without stopping for thousands of years, just as the Tortoise has continued for millions of years past' (Young and Zazeela, 1969: 16). Since the piece is still ongoing, any performances given since its initiation are considered by Young to be excerpts of the total work. A number of sound elements may constitute the piece at any given time, and performances have included chanted vocal tones, and sustained tones and drones produced by string instruments. However, the use of electronic tones has been a consistent element in the work, produced in the first performances by an audio frequency generator and a small electrical motor taken from an aquarium filter pump. These compositions were always conceived as part of a mixed media 'theatre' piece, or sound and light installation, the visual elements of which have been provided by Marian Zazeela in the form of light projections and neon sculptures. Young and Zazeela planned that these performances or environments should run continuously in what they referred to as 'Dream Houses'. The first continuous Dream House presentation ran from 1979 to 1985 in a building on Harrison Street, New York, while the second has been running as a continuous sound and light environment since 1993, under the auspices of the MELA Foundation, also in New York.

What is interesting about Young's work in relation to my attempt to sound ground noise and optical crackle in positive terms, is the way in which it serves as the meeting point of a number of interrelated ideas pertaining to temporal and perceptual experience. These ideas are sometimes discussed explicitly by the composer in relation to the sounds used in his music, but also weave through a personal mythology expressed in composition titles and in recalled experiences and influences. The choice of the term 'Dream House' serves to make an overt connection between the music played in it and a particular state of consciousness, thereby suggesting that the experience of listening to continuous sounds of extended duration may disrupt the dominant perceptual and temporal frames of reference we draw upon in our everyday 'waking' lives. Although working now with continuous tones generated by purpose-built electronic synthesisers, Young nevertheless perceives a connection between the musical drone and the sounds of wind, fire and water. Describing his early experiences of listening to the wind blowing through the cracks of the log cabin in which he was brought up, he comments:

> It sounded great coming in like that – very calm, very peaceful, very meditative. During my childhood there were four different sound experiences of constant frequency that have influenced my musical ideas and development: the sounds of insects; the sounds of telephone poles and motors; sounds produced by steam escaping from such as my mother's tea-kettle or train whistles; and resonation from the natural characteristics of particular geographic areas such as valleys, lakes, and plains. Actually, the first sustained single note at

a constant pitch, without a beginning or end, that I heard as a child that did not have a beginning or ending was the sound of telephone poles – the hum of the wires . . . I'm also very fond of power plants. (Young and Zazeela, 1969: 33)

Young refers to the sound he heard in the telephone poles as the 'dream chord', reconstructed in *Trio for Strings* (1958) as G, C, C-sharp and D. This particular chord also forms the basis of *The Second Dream of the High-Tension Line Step-Down Transformer* (1962), where it is expressed by the composer in terms of the ratio 12, 16, 17, 18 (Young and Zazeela, 1969: 47). While the sound heard by Young in telephone poles has been transposed into a musical form, the sound of fire features directly in his Fluxus piece, *Composition 1960 #2*, which may be of any duration and begins with the carefree instruction, 'Build a fire in front of the audience' (Mertens, 1988: 23).

The natural and man-made continuous sounds observed by Young during his childhood possess a number of important temporal and perceptual dimensions that his musical compositions seek to explore and exploit. Unlike the sound of ground noise and optical crackle, many of the continuous sounds used in the works that make up *The Tortoise, His Dreams and Journeys* are amplified to the point of physical pain (Young and Zazeela, 1969: 18). This level of amplification would seem, in part, to be a means by which Young enables the listener to experience aspects of sonic materiality that might otherwise not figure prominently in a musical performance:

> There are several ways you can approach it. One is that someone concentrates so heavily upon a given sound – he gives himself over to it to such a degree – that what's happening is the sound. Even though I could be sitting here, all I am is an element of the sound. Another approach is to walk into an area in which the sound is so abundant that you actually are in a physical sound environment. This happens when someone walks into one of my concerts. (Young and Zazeela, 1969: 35)

In this sense, Young proposes that the music engenders a kind of dissolution of self, either as a result of the act of concentrated listening, or through a kind of physical envelopment by the music.[12] At the same time, according to Young, this use of sound also works to materialise its own spatiality. Thus, listening to this particular use of continuous sound may foreground and make concrete one's own perceptual encounter with the space occupied by the music:

When a continuous frequency is sounded in an enclosed space such as a room, the air in the room is arranged into high and low pressure areas. In the high pressure areas the sound is louder, and in the low pressure areas the sound is softer. Since a sine wave has only one frequency component, the pattern of high and low pressure areas is easy to locate in space. Further, concurrently sounding sine waves of different frequencies will provide an environment in which the loudness of each frequency will vary audibly at different points in the room, given sufficient amplification. This phenomenon can rarely be appreciated in most musical situations and makes the listener's position and movement in the space an integral part of the sound composition. (Young and Zazeela, 1969: 11)

The conceptualisation of continuous sound offered by Young in commentaries on his compositional work recasts and reorients the temporal aspects of musical listening. In focusing on the physical and perceptual experience of being in a sound environment, Young displaces the linear, horizontal temporality that underpins the normative conception of music as an unwinding succession of individual sounds. As a dominant dimension of music, development over time is thus displaced by the physical experience of listening, of being inside a sound, and thus of being in the present. This mode of conceptualising sonic experience is further demonstrated by the fact that Young's work makes extensive use of chords as one of its central foundations, usually expressed in terms of simple mathematical ratios; Young comments, 'I noticed about 1956 that I really seemed more interested in listening to chords than in listening to melodies. In other words, I was more interested in concurrency or simultaneity than in sequence' (Young and Zazeela, 1969: 32). In their use of continuous chords of extended duration, Young's compositions work to downgrade the place of developmental progression in music, proving instead a perceptual experience that is expressed by the title of another of his works, *Vertical Hearing or Hearing in the Present Tense* (1966). When asked about the kind of time his *Tortoise* piece created, Young replied, 'Its own time, which is determined by and measured in terms of the frequencies we are sustaining' (Young and Zazeela, 1969: 63).

Young's conceptualisation of the drone as a sonic experience that locates us in the present suggests that particular forms of continuous sound may disrupt our normal conception of temporal flow as regular, measured and normally comprehensible in terms of a succession of events. While we may become more acutely aware of duration when listening to the drone, this experience is one of slippage, and of a dissolution that provides a mild parallel to the effects of sensory deprivation. What we witness when listening in this way is a non-linear sense of the present. But this is not a well-behaved present, taking its place neatly between the future and the past. Rather, this is a present that expands in all directions to disrupt our usual temporal frames of reference. Certainly the experience of listening to Young's work at high amplitude is very different to our experience of listening to the crackle and hiss of optical film, not least because the latter is a sound that we are not always consciously aware of, with the consequence that our own perceptual responses to it are not necessarily foregrounded. But the connections Young makes between the sounds of wind, water and fire, temporal experience, and the dream, all begin to provide a framework for thinking through the way in which the sounds of optical crackle and ground noise may affect the audiospectator. In this respect it is significant that in the work of video artist Bill Viola, the imagery of fire and water, and the dense oceanic rumblings of his soundtracks, are often coupled with the temporal expansion and suspension created by the use of slow motion. In Viola's videotape *The Passing* (1991), these elements are sutured into an engagement with, and representation of, forms of consciousness associated with dreaming and the recollection of memory. Furthermore, Viola's work clearly seeks to situate the transcendental in relation to temporal manipulation. The use of slow motion, and the oceanic soundtracks of the videotapes, are part of Viola's strategy to represent or create altered states of consciousness, and to signal the transcendental dimensions of both the material sign and what it signifies. Viola's work reminds us that chants and drones have traditionally been used in religious ceremonies to represent and to create a sense of the transcendental. And in Scott Rankin's tapes *This and That* (1990) and *Path* (2003), the rumble of wind hitting a microphone produces a low-frequency drone that, like Viola's uterine soundscapes, works to displace narrative temporality in favour of alternative temporal and perceptual registers.

All these audiovisual examples connect with our own everyday experiences of staring into an open fire, looking at the sea or staring out of a train window. Experiences such as these present a globalised visual field that is in many respects similar to the sonic field of ground noise and optical crackle. In both we face a multiplicity of elements and events that cannot be tracked individually. Our attention might alight from time to time on an individual

flame, a wave or an element of the passing landscape, just as a particularly loud scratch on an optical soundtrack may occasionally
catch our attention. However, we also experience this multiplicity
as a host, a mass: our vision may blur, and our conscious awareness of the sonic and visual environment seems to recede, exactly
as in the phenomenon of the thousand-yard stare. In this state we
enter an internal world of thoughts and memories. Paradoxically,
what this suggests is that the 'vertical' listening proposed by
Young, which situates us in the present by removing the horizontal
dimension of development over time, may also connect us with
the past through memory. In Young's case, amplification to the
point of pain would probably militate against the kind of reflective
experience prompted by other manifestations of continuous, stable
sounds heard at lower levels, such as ground noise and optical
crackle. But at these lower levels of amplitude, when the monotone becomes monotonous, we disengage from the environment
in which we find ourselves, and enter a state of consciousness that
proves fertile for the recollection of memory.

1946. *Crack-Up*. Tagline: Could I KILL . . . and not remember?

The connection between present and past, monotony and memory
is articulated in audiovisual terms by the Hollywood thriller
Crack-Up (Irving Reis, 1946), whose tagline neatly summarises
the centrality of unstable memory to the film's narrative. Early
in the film George Steele, an art curator recently returned from
active military service in World War Two, receives a telephone
call informing him that his mother has been taken ill. He makes a
night-time train journey to visit her, but mysteriously never arrives.
After what may have been a train crash, or the mental breakdown
suggested by the film's title, he turns up later that night at the Art
Museum in a bewildered state, having no memory of what has
happened to him. In an attempt to piece together the events that
took place that night, he makes the same journey the following day
in the hope that he will discover some clue as to what transpired.
The film thus shows the same approximate sequence of narrative
events twice: Steele queuing to buy a ticket at the railway station,
having his ticket checked (Figure 3.5), boarding the train, buying
cigarettes, looking out of the train window, checking his watch and
so on. However, in the second version of the scene, Steele is trying
to remember, attempting to crystallise into reliable memories the
vague feelings he has about the events of the previous evening.

pp

3.5 *Crack-Up*   **3.6** Monotone figure from
                                                    Crack-Up

Crack-Up offers a rare opportunity to observe the differences that variations in a soundtrack contribute to two scenes that feature the same narrative elements. In the second sequence, Leigh Harline's score is dominated by the use of sustained string and woodwind tones, structured around a single note played on the violin. This single, sustained note is repeated, producing a paired monotone figure that itself repeats throughout the sequence (Figure 3.6), and which is played over a slowly changing melodic woodwind accompaniment. We hear this theme as Steele stares into the eyes of the train conductor, when he surveys the other passengers in the carriage, and when he looks out of the train window into the darkness outside – that is, at every moment he attempts to recall the events of the previous evening.

Heard outside the context of this film, Harline's composition might be considered quite radical, particularly because of its use of monotony. But perhaps what is most striking about this piece of music is the connection it creates, within a cinesonic context, between the contemplative aspects of sustained, consistent sounds and the recollection of memory – or more accurately in this case, failures of memory expressed as the vague, uncertain, non-specific feelings that haunt Steele. These unstable personal recollections contrast with the memory of war that hangs over the whole film. The script makes many references to World War Two, which had ended just one year before *Crack-Up* was released; at one point Steele compares the chaotic scene of his apartment, which appears to have been burgled, to the recently bombed city of Nagasaki. But while the war is a definite presence, a dark shadow hovering over the film, Steele's attempts to remember the events of the previous evening struggle with something that *resists* recollection. In both versions of the scene taking place on the train, Steele is shown gazing through the window, his face reflected in the glass as he looks out into darkness. These images are accompanied in the first version by the rhythmic sounds of the train, as shots of Steele are intercut with close-ups of the train wheels and the track. At the end of both versions of the sequence, Steele becomes mesmerised by the lights of what appears to be an oncoming train, like an animal caught in a car's headlights. The sense of stasis and suspension that the film creates in its exploration of inactive states of uncertainty fundamentally challenges the narrative basis of Hollywood film, driven as it is by a cause-and-effect logic that demands action, movement and resolution. It is significant therefore that the first version of this scene ends climatically, with an implied crash or collapse, since classical Hollywood cinema cannot sustain the intense sense of gaseous undefinability that has been set up here. The diffusive atmosphere of this scene is punctured by the sudden insertion of kinetic energy, provided by a rapid Soviet-style montage of shots of the lights of the oncoming train, close-ups of the transfixed Steele, and the interior of the carriage, each of which is only a few frames in length. However, in the second version of the sequence, this dramatic climax is replaced by rapid intercutting between close-ups of Steele looking once more out of the window, becoming ever more fearful as the lights of the oncoming train approach, and over-the-shoulder shots silhouetting Steele against the lights of the approaching train (Figures 3.7 and 3.8).

At what might have been the moment of impact – suggested in the first sequence by the Soviet-style montage – the music is interrupted by the harsh, violently rhythmic sounds of the oncoming train rushing past the window. And thus the drone of memory, expressed by Harline's *misterioso* use of repetition and monotony, is displaced by the concrete and kinetic sounds of movement: an interruption of stasis by the flow of linear montage, signalling that time is back on track, violently separating past from present, matter from memory.

If La Monte Young's work demonstrates the ways in which drones may destabilise and suspend our normal sense of temporal progression, then the use of monotony and repetition featured in *Crack-Up* suggests that memory may figure as an important element in the specific forms of temporal experience engendered by the use of continuous sounds. In this instance, it is the character Steele who experiences feelings of memory

3.7–3.8 *Crack-Up*

failure, rather than the audience being drawn into a state of consciousness suitable for the recollection of memory. By the same token, temporal suspension is only suggested by the music – just enough so that Steele's condition and situation can be represented. Thus, what we hear in *Crack-Up* is a domestication of the drone, and what we feel is just the slightest suggestion of its power to affect temporal and perceptual experience. Although in the work of Antonioni, Snow and Viola there are modes of audiovisuality that may work in a more direct manner on the audioviewer to create greater intensities of temporal suspension, what *Crack-Up* suggests is the place occupied by memory in certain forms of temporal and perceptual experience set in motion by sustained sound. This connection between memory and the drone is central to understanding the ways in which the experience of listening to continuous sound relates to the sense of pastness. If in *Crack-Up* a sense of the past surfaces in a disturbed form when the use of the domesticated drone signals the failure of memory, then it is possible that memory might play some part in creating the sense of pastness that we experience when listening to the sounds of optical crackle and ground noise. If this is the case, how, then, might we understand the perceptual processes that connect drone, memory and the past, and thus the relationship between the materiality of the sound of technology and the sense of pastness?

A particularly useful resource that can be drawn draw upon to consider these questions is Gilles Deleuze's second *Cinema* book, *The Time-Image* (1989). The value of Deleuze's work to this study is that it is primarily concerned with the representation of time in film, and with the cinematic treatment of memory. As its subtitle suggests, Deleuze's book focuses on the visual aspects of cinema. However, the ideas contained within it can nevertheless be transposed to a consideration of the cinesonic. Drawing in particular on Deleuze's ideas about the relationship of memory to the way in which we experience time, I hope to show that while convention plays its part in making the listener associate the sound of a particular technology with a broad historical period, our response to that sound is not just a Pavlovian, learned response to an arbitrary signifier. In the case of optical crackle and ground noise, I propose that convention operates within a complex of perceptual and cognitive processes set in motion by the drone-like qualities of the sound of technology.

Deleuze and the direct manifestation of time

In *Cinema 2* Deleuze proposes a cinema in which certain shots fuse the pastness of a recorded event with the presentness of viewing to disrupt cinema's dominant narrative temporality, thereby enabling the spectator to experience time in other ways. This is witnessed, for example, in those moments of suspension and strangeness found in the post-war European art movie. This proposition serves as a useful starting point to think about the way in which the sounds of optical crackle and ground noise might embody and articulate a sense of the past. When we watch an old film we are situated as spectators in the presentness of the perceptual experience, while in addition witnessing the presentness of the recorded profilmic event (in the sense that film, as the photographic registration of the present, is said to be always in the present tense[13]). However, something else intervenes, and the sounds of ground noise and optical crackle introduce a sense of past tense into this experience.

Drawing on Henri Bergson's work on memory, Deleuze makes a distinction between *actual* images and sounds, and *virtual* images and sounds. Thus, an image stored in the memory is *virtual*, until the point at which it is recalled, when it becomes an *actual* recollected image and enters the present tense, so to speak (see Figure 3.9 for a schematic representation of these relationships). But a recollected image, drawn from memory, bears no marks of the past from which it is drawn – all it can do is represent the present the past once was. Recalled memories do not play in black and white – they are not scratched or faded, or accompanied by crackle and hiss. How, then, can a sense of pastness adhere to a sound or image perceived in the present?

To explain this paradox, Deleuze distinguishes between the actuality of the present and the virtuality of the past. Time forks in two directions, as present moments join the past, becoming virtual images and sounds, stored away in memory. These virtual images and sounds can only become actual through recollection in the present. Once again drawing on Bergson's work, Deleuze proposes that the *feeling* of pastness is therefore connected only with this zone of unactualised or virtual memories, and is not a feature of recalled memories. According to Bergson, it is only the act of remembering, the act of searching memory, that gives a recollected image its pastness; in *Matter and Memory* he comments, 'the image pure and simple will not be referred to the past unless,

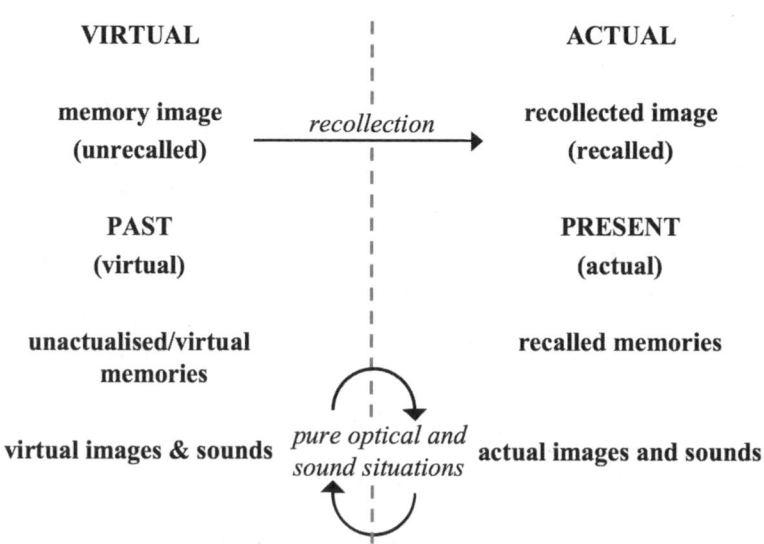

3.9 Relationships between virtual and actual images and sounds

indeed, it was in the past that I sought it' (Bergson, 1991: 135). Thus, pastness is not a quality of the recollected image itself: as stated above, recalled memories play only in the present tense. However, when an act of remembering fails, the presence of this zone of the virtual past is signalled, although its contents are never actualised in the present.

The virtuality of memory is central to Deleuze's explanation of cinematic temporality, since he proposes that certain moments in post-war art cinema have the power to make time itself perceptible, precisely because the actual image or sound perceived by the spectator in the cinema enters into relationship with some form of virtual image, whereby the two become indiscernible. It is this indiscernibility that produces what Deleuze terms 'pure optical and sound situations', which are those images and sounds that have the capacity to make time directly perceptible, and which therefore suspend and disrupt narrative temporality.

To understand this claim, we need to consider the role played by experience and memory in the processes of perception. Bergson states that when we recognise and identify objects, we rely on our accumulated experience of them: that is, when we perceive an object (and presumably a sound) we revive a past memory of it, noting the resemblance of the object that is present to similar objects we have encountered in the past. As stated above, Deleuze suggests that the images (and presumably sounds) stored in our memory are virtual until they are recollected, when they become actual. However, what we experience in 'pure optical and sound situations' – which are those moments when time itself becomes perceptible – is a disturbance to the normal perceptual process whereby an image perceived by the spectator enters into relationship with an image held in the memory, which is then recollected and becomes an actual memory image rather than remaining a virtual image. But Deleuze claims that what happens in pure optical and sound situations is that the image perceived by the spectator (or the sound heard by the listener) gets caught in a circuit with a memory image that remains virtual and unrecalled. The perceptual process is then disturbed, caught in a kind of unresolvable loop. This seems to be what happens when we experience feelings of *déjà vu*, for example, in which a perception triggers a failed attempt to recall a memory. What is significant about *déjà vu*, in relation to the temporal effects created by ground noise and optical crackle, is the fact that it is associated with a strong sense of temporal disruption, experienced in part as a feeling of pastness.

Tranposing Deleuze's ideas from a visual to a cinesonic context, it might be reasonable to suppose that the actual sounds of optical crackle that we hear in a film link up with some virtual image or sound located in memory. However, this virtual image or sound would need to remain virtual and unrecalled if it were to produce the effect that Deleuze describes, of making time itself perceptible – in this case, making the feeling of the past perceptible, despite the fact that we are listening in the present. What this means is that any memory or association potentially prompted by the sound of optical crackle would somehow need to remain repressed, unactualised and unrecalled if a sense of past tense were to be maintained by the sounds we hear. And it is in this respect that the materiality of the drone plays a key role in our perception of pastness. The drone-like sounds of optical crackle and ground noise offer the constant presence of the unactualised, the unresolved, the virtual, because this drone demands a constant listening that nevertheless never enters the foreground of consciousness, and which consequently never results in any form of resolution, significatory or otherwise. At an unconscious level, the spectator's perceptual processes are constantly ranging through possible ways in which this sound's identity might be resolved, both as a sound object and in relation to the cinesonic text. However, this sound represents nothing in narrative terms, nor does it become actualised in terms of unity with any perceived object source or visual event presented on screen – which is to say, the sound is assigned no identity through reference to an object-source presented on screen. Rather, it lurks at the borderline of consciousness, always ready to form a relationship with other elements of the film text that might switch on its potential to participate in the film's representational and significatory networks, without ever actually doing so.

At every moment the film is haunted by the shadowy, nebulous presence of this region of the unactualised. Crucially, this shadow is also the presence of every other film that features optical crackle. By convention, we associate each individual manifesta-tion of optical crackle with vintage film, with the film 'archive' in its broadest sense. In cinema, this region of the unactualised extends beyond the personal memory of the spectator, into the transpersonal memory space of the archive. This archive, the totality of all 'old' film, stands as a vast storeroom and dumping ground for moments of the past captured on film. The shadowy presence of the unactualised of optical crackle and ground noise opens out onto this ungraspable, uncontainable expanse of old film. All old films, at least for the audiospectator, belong to this nebulous region. When we are not watching or recalling specific films, all 'old' films dissolve into the virtuality of the past. The sounds of optical crackle and ground noise mark a specific but broad region or layer of this virtual past. This region is that of the unactualised film, the region of the genuinely virtual film. What defines this region, which is ungraspable in its multiplicity of indi-vidual films, is the sound of optical crackle, black-and-whiteness and scratchedness. Optical crackle is a trace or imprint that links this amorphous body together, and it is the sign that something has been recovered from this space of transpersonal memory – a sign of pastness, like the dust on a document retrieved from an archive.

Is this in the end to suggest simply that the sound of optical crackle and ground noise is an indexical signifier of pastness? Of course, this is true, but this presents a special case of signification that is in some senses also the failure of signification. What this sound directs us to is not a specific memory of a particular film: when I unconsciously audition this sound, searching to confirm its identity, I do not recall memories of *White Zombie*, *The Chelsea Girls* or *My Favourite Wife*. Rather, I am directed by the drone of optical crackle and ground noise to a region of virtual films:

unnamed, unrecalled in their specificity, unremembered in their individuality, but whose presence is sensed as that ungraspable multiplicity residing as a nebulous, shadowy presence haunting every old film I watch. The drone of the sound of technology does not direct the listener to specific recollections, but rather aligns them with the virtual. It is this alignment in itself that imprints a sound or an image with the mark of the past. And it is the constancy of the drone that not only disturbs our normal experience of the passage and ordering of time, but also sustains alignment with this virtual past, thereby creating the feelings of pastness we experience when listening to the sounds of optical crackle and ground noise.

Refrain

The sounds immanent to past technologies of film, such as ground noise and optical crackle, have been almost completely ignored by studies of film sound. Conceptualised as meaningless noise, such sounds are neglected by the dominant critical notions of what constitutes the cinesonic text, whereby exclusive attention is placed upon speech, music and effects. However, noise is not the one-dimensional phenomenon it is often taken to be, and can be explored in positive terms through a consideration of its historical, temporal and affective dimensions.

Noise has been persistently valorised in the arts for its violent, shocking, disruptive potential, but as the case of ground noise illustrates, noise can also be quietly invasive. The political dimensions of representation, discussed in Chapter 2, provide one context in which noise may take on radical potential; in its failure or refusal to signify, noise seems to present an untranslatable, turbulent materiality. If this materiality has historical dimensions, as illustrated by the case of ground noise's shifting audibility, then perhaps the radical potential of other forms of noise might also be affected by historical considerations. This issue is explored in the following chapter, in an examination of the cinesonic deployment of electronic sounds. These sounds, once strange and shocking, have become increasingly familiar and conventional with the passage of time; how, then, might this passage of time impact upon their radical potential? And if, as Chapter 2 suggests, audiovisuality itself might have a radical dimension, where might electronica be situated within the context of the cinesonic?

Notes

1 MacKenzie's reference to disc technology points to the fact that at this time there were two alternative sound systems in use: one in which sound was recorded on and reproduced from disc, and another in which sound was recorded using photographic film, and reproduced from the film print itself.

2 The innovation of Western Electric's 'Noiseless Recording' was to use black rather than clear film for the unmodulated (and hence silent) optical sound track on release prints. Previously the use of clear film meant that dust and scratches were registered by the optical sound reader as noise. By using black as the unmodulated sound track, dust did not register, and only scratches severe enough to remove the film emulsion might produce unwanted sound.

3 Parallel developments took place in other countries, and an account of the European response to the transition to sound is given by Neale (1985). However, reference is only made in my own study to the specific sound systems that emerged from Hollywood's transition to sound. These are used to illustrate the technical background to the issues discussed.

4 Dolby noise reduction works by dividing an audio signal into four discrete frequency bands. The signal of each band is boosted and then compressed to remove low-level noise, and then expanded again. The four frequency bands are then recombined, producing an audio signal with less ground noise.

5 Before the introduction of digital technology, there were two ways of encoding sound optically on film, referred to as the variable area and variable density methods. The variable area soundtrack encodes sound as a waveform, while the variable density soundtrack encodes sound as a series of parallel striations of varying densities of black or clear film. The Fox Movietone system and the Western Electric system both recorded variable density soundtracks. In the former, the light source activated by the variable current was a gas-filled tube (the Aeolight), while the latter used a variable slit (the Light Valve) through which light passed onto the recording film.

6 Mike Figgis describes using this technique during the production of *Internal Affairs* (1990). Reshoots for the film were shot on a noisy Arriflex camera. Figgis considered the location sound unusable, but found it difficult to secure the cooperation of his lead actor to rere-cord the dialogue: 'So, I found out the key of the sound of the camera magazine, and I scored the music for that scene in the same key. So the score eats up the sound of the magazine and it ends up as a piece of music' (Figgis, 2003: 13).

7 Schafer's declaration originally appeared in the 1973 pamphlet *The Music of the Environment* (reprinted in Cox, 2004: 29–39). The ideas presented here were elaborated by Schafer in *The Tuning of the World*

(1977), reprinted as *The Soundscape: Our Sonic Environment and the Tuning of the World* (1994).

8 Roads states that a gap of less than 200 milliseconds between two microsounds will produce this kind of forward masking.

9 Citing work on rhythm and tempo by Paul Fraisse (1982), Roads suggests that we sense pulse or meter between approximately 8Hz and 0.12Hz (Roads, 2001: 17). Above this range we no longer perceive rhythm, but forms of continuous sound. Below this range the gaps between individual sounds become too great for the listener to be able to situate the sounds within a perceived rhythm.

10 Adorno briefly mentions a similar phenomenon in relation to radio broadcasts of music, in a theoretical formulation that provides support for the idea that sounds located in relation to ground noise are somehow distanced. In the 1941 essay *The Radio Symphony*, he describes the ground noise of radio as a 'hear-stripe' upon which the music being broadcast is placed, and suggests that while it may or may not attract the attention of the listener, as an objective characteristic of the sound being auditioned, it plays a part in our perception of the total sonic event. He writes: 'One might venture to suggest that the psychological effect of the hear-stripe is somewhat similar to the awareness of the screen in the movies: music appearing upon such a hear-stripe may bear a certain image-like character of its own' (Adorno, 2002: 251). Although this formulation is not developed any further in the essay itself, comments in the unpublished 'Memorandum: Music in Radio' help to explain this simile (cited by Richard Leppert in his commentary on Adorno's essays on music. See Adorno, 2002: 218–19). Here Adorno comments that music 'appears to be projected upon the stripe and is only, so to speak, like a picture upon that stripe' (Adorno, 2002: 219). His formulation of the hear-stripe foregrounds a sense of distanciation, attributing to the music what Leppert terms a 'second-order presence' (Adorno, 2002: 219). Adorno explains the effect of this in terms of the positioning of the listener in relation to the music: 'The listener has the feeling, not that he is being confronted with the music itself, but that he is being told something about the music, or being introduced to music by radio. It does not sound like Beethoven's music itself, but like "now you will hear something about Beethoven"' (Adorno, 2002: 219).

11 La Monte Young (Young and Zazeela, 1969: 47).

12 John Cage recorded his experience of hearing Young's work in precisely these terms: 'In the lobby after La Monte Young's music stopped, [Henry] Geldzahler said: It's like being in a womb; now that I'm out, I want to get back in. I felt differently and so did Jasper Johns: we were relieved to be released' (Cage, 1985: 16).

13 Pasolini argues, 'Reality seen and heard as it happens *is always in the*

present tense. The long take, the schematic and primordial element of cinema, is thus in the present. Cinema therefore "reproduces the present" [. . .] but as soon as montage intervenes, when we pass from cinema to film . . . the present becomes past: a past that, for cinematographic and not aesthetic reasons, is always in the present mode (*that is, it is a historic present*)' (Pasolini, 1980: 3–5).

4 Strange sounds

Theremin Cellos Win Music Public in "Electric Concert"

Members of the Theremin Electric Symphony Orchestra making their debut at Carnegie Hall, New York. The electric cellos, seen in the center, reproduce woodwind and brass music, tone and volume being regulated by levers and coils.

Like the sounds of ground noise and optical crackle discussed in the previous chapter, electronic sounds have also been figured as noise. In part, electronica has been framed in this way because of its status as a *strange* sound. As the cultural theorist Jacques Attali states in his seminal work on noise, 'In music, the instrument often predates the expression it authorises, which explains why a new invention has the nature of noise' (Attali, 1985: 35). As relative newcomers to the musical soundscape, electronic sounds seem to announce emergency and change, and the disruptive non-conformity that results from their unfamiliarity locates these sounds within the field of noise. When inscribed within certain aesthetic systems, it is this disruptive non-conformity that attributes radical potential to those sounds deemed to be 'noise'; and in the case of electronic sound, this noise value has enabled it to take on a radical aspect within works in which it is used to challenge, disrupt and disorient.

However, within a cinesonic context, the use of electronic sounds has become almost entirely conventional. These once strange sounds – which are no longer strange, but familiar – have become nostalgic *signifiers* of the strange. The sounds of the theremin, the trautonium and numerous other electronic instruments with creaky names, have been commonly used in classical cinema to suggest a dystopian future in which robots go bad, or alternatively to signify madness and the monstrous. Within this cinematic context the mobilisation of electronica does indeed seem to confer on its sounds something of the status of noise, their presence sonically signifying a disruption to the normal, a challenge to existing models of social organisation, a breakdown of the accepted norms of behaviour, a monstrous threat to paradigms of the natural. But this could be thought of as simply the representation of noise, since these strange sounds are domesticated and stripped of their disruptive power through submission to narrative and musical codes. In mainstream cinema the alterity of noise, for which it has been valorised within the arts, is thus resolved in terms of the *signification* of otherness: the alien, the mad, the broken, the monstrous, the aberrant.

This significatory potential of electronica raises a number of fundamental questions that need to be addressed if we are to understand the ways in which noise is articulated within a cinesonic context, and the impact this context may have on its presumed radical potential. If we formulate noise as sound that does not signify, how does its 'non-identity' relate to the significatory dimensions of cinema? And if the radical potential of electronica rests with its sonic status as noise, how then might its sounds figure within a radical *audiovisual* poetics – that is to say, within *audiovisual* modes that seek to challenge the dominant creative and conceptual formulations of sound–image relations in cinema? Can electronica still retain the radical potential it once possessed, even though its sounds are no longer strange?

Electronica noise theory

In theoretical terms the refusal of noise to signify, which is fundamental to both its status and its power, is a refusal to be translated, a refusal to be equated with anything other than itself. In its concrete particularity, noise presents a sonic materiality that finds no equivalent; noise demands to be heard in the here and now, grabbing the listener by the ear rather than evaporating in processes of signification and directing attention elsewhere. This refusal to submit to a code, musical, linguistic or otherwise, marks the *non-identity* of noise, and signals its potential to transgress, resist and disrupt the codes by which art forms and systems of meaning are organised. And in the sense that control over meaning is an attribute of power, and thus an inherently political issue, so noise challenges the power structures inherent in both regimes and acts of signification. In this way, the materiality of noise resists processing by the abstract structures that would otherwise locate sounds within networks of meaning.

The problematic allure of abstract structures, observed so far in relation to Saussurian linguistics, is articulated in political terms in Theodor Adorno's critique of identity thinking. Adorno coins this term to refer to a mode of thought that subsumes the specificity of phenomena within abstract classificatory frameworks, thereby reducing any individual concrete phenomenon to an expression of an abstract paradigm. According to Adorno, this act of slippage or redirection misrepresents any concrete phenomenon that we attempt to come to terms with. Transposed to the consideration of sonic materiality, Adorno's critique suggests that, in the same way Saussurian linguistics reduces individual concrete speech events to the abstract structures of language, so identity thinking reduces materiality (amongst other things) by equivalence; Adorno writes, 'Bourgeois society is ruled by equivalence. It makes the dissimilar comparable by reducing it to abstract qualities . . . that which does not reduce to numbers, and ultimately to the one, becomes an illusion' (Adorno and Horkheimer, 1997: 7). Considered within the context of political economy, identity thinking proves highly problematic, since according to Adorno everything in bourgeois society becomes reduced, and reducible, to an exchange value, processed by the monetary code through which equivalence is ensured. Issues of political economy are indeed relevant to a discussion of electronica, since this is the dominant theoretical context in which cultural theorists such as Attali have situated noise, and within which the study of noise has been primarily positioned in relation to political discourse. Furthermore, issues of political economy are also raised by the fact that most audiences are familiar with the sounds of electronic instruments like the theremin precisely because they have been inscribed into the world of exchange, their sounds having both meaning and value in commercial cinema. However, of more immediate relevance to a consideration of the relationship between the materiality of noise and the abstract structures of meaning is the (false) notion, proposed by identity thinking, that concepts adequately deal with phenomena; this is the notion that objects and events can be fully known and contained by concepts, and therefore reduced to examples of an abstract paradigm. As Adorno puts it so succinctly in his Introduction to *Negative Dialectics*, 'Conceptual schematas self-contentedly push aside what thinking wants to comprehend' (Adorno, 1997: 4). This is exactly the problem we face when sound is situated exclusively within the abstract structures of significatory regimes, causing us to neglect the materiality of the sonic in favour of what a sound means or represents. In cinema, the dominant illustrative model of sound–image relations ensures that we often understand sound as simply the attribute of an object source.

In its refusal to signify, noise resists the conceptual frameworks that would otherwise direct our attention from a sound's concrete materiality, placing it instead on the sound's relationship to an abstract paradigm. Auditioned within the context provided by Adorno's concept of identity thinking, noise is thus marked by its non-identity, its non-equivalence – a refusal to be known, to be contained – and a resistance to subjugation by the codes and structures it therefore seems to threaten. The concrete particularity of noise cannot be known by these codes, and thus noise seems to propose itself as raw, material sound, before and beyond meaning, matter liberated from all forms of construction. In the language of information theory, noise is entropic: it is unpredictable, unconventional, formless, stochastic. But as the example of electronica demonstrates, within a cinesonic context this is not necessarily the case, since here some forms of noise may become almost entirely domesticated and conventional, whether signalling the other, or offering resistance to signifying regimes. Yet it is precisely the presumed alterity and non-identity of noise that has been championed in the arts, and consistently celebrated in relation to its oppositional and disruptive potential. This formulation is a direct legacy of the futurist/avant-gardist tradition, which conceptualises and celebrates noise as shocking, violent and war-like. It remains the dominant model of noise within the arts, and the primary channel through which the radical potential of the phenomenon is articulated within a broadly political context; thus, Attali states 'Noise is a weapon' (Attali, 1985: 24), and that 'To make a noise is to interrupt a transmission, to disconnect, to kill' (Attali, 1985: 26).

Within a cinesonic context, a tension therefore emerges between the identity and non-identity of noise, and between the radical potential of noise and its domestication by narrative, musical and other cinesonic codes. As Attali suggests in relation to music, although a new instrument may predate the expression it authorises – hence creating a sound's strangeness – new codes will almost inevitably emerge that make this sound knowable, and thus new musical expressions can and will be authorised:

> In music, the instrument often predates the expression it authorises, which explains why a new invention has the nature of noise . . . it contributes, through the possibilities it offers, to the birth of a new music, a renewed syntax. It makes possible a new system of combination, creating an open field for a whole new exploration of the possible expressions of musical language. (Attali, 1985: 35)

What Attali signals here, and is also illustrated by the case of ground noise, is that the way in which we audition a sound changes over time, and thus the quality of its audibility may alter. Sounds that once presented an untranslatable materiality, like those of electronica, now evoke feelings of nostalgia, while sounds that were once neglected, and listened *through* rather than listened *to*, begin to reveal their materiality, as in the case of ground noise. Attali offers this change in positive terms, as a form of renewal whereby noise provides an open field of potential and opportunity. However, when considered in a slightly different way, his observations suggest that what we hear in the changes taking place over time are processes of normalisation and containment, shifts from non-identity to identity, and from materiality to signification.

Noise's shock of the new situates the radical strangeness of electronica within a historical context, thereby offering a critical framework within which we might sound its potentially radical materiality. That is, the materiality of the strange sounds of electronica can be sounded by considering the ways in which tensions between the radical potential of noise, cinesonic codes, and the processes of history weave through the cinesonic text. To explore these issues, I will draw upon three bodies of work, each of which is located within a different historical moment or cultural tradition. The first of these is the experimental film work of John and James Whitney undertaken in the early 1940s, in which optical sound synthesis was employed with the explicit aim of creating electronic sounds with no historical precedent. Described by the critic William Moritz as 'one of the most radically original audio-visual manifestations ever devised' (Moritz, 1979: 65), the Whitney Brothers' *Five Film Exercises* (1943–44) are of particular relevance to a study of the cinesonic because they represent an attempt by their makers to combine the sonic and the visual in ways that seek to explore their complementarity, and thus offer an alternative to the dominant significatory models of sound–image relations proposed by classical cinema. The second body of work I draw upon in this chapter are classical Hollywood films produced in the 1940s and 1950s, in which the noise of electronica has been deployed within a significatory context to represent various forms of otherness. Finally, to consider a more contemporary use of electronica, I turn my attention to Tina Keane's 1996 film *Deviant Beauty*, which features an almost entirely electronic soundtrack. Situated within the traditions of avant-garde film practice and its associated discourses, Keane's film enables us to consider the ways in which the radical potential of electronica might be reconfigured within a contemporary context, and how this in turn might impact on our understanding of audiovisuality more generally.

Electronica and optical sound synthesis

Since the widespread introduction of optical sound recording and playback in the early 1930s, a number of filmmakers had experimented with ways of synthesising sound by painting, drawing or printing directly on the optical soundtrack; among these were the American filmmakers John and James Whitney. Although rarely acknowledged in histories of music, the technology of optical film sound opened two parallel and related strands of sonic practice that were to have a profound influence on the soundscape of twentieth-century western art: the first of these was sound editing (dealt with in Chapter 6), the second, sound synthesis. As has already been demonstrated by the example of ground noise, film technology generates as well as reproduces sound. The significance of the conceptual shift from reproduction to generation represented by experiments in optical sound synthesis should not be underestimated, since this fundamentally challenges the ontological basis of the dominant model of cinema as a medium of record and reproduction. A good deal of the attention given to the production of film sound centres on the ways in which sounds are recorded for a soundtrack, and the subsequent arrangement and

treatment of those sounds in post-production. Within a technological context, the conception of the microphone as a mechanical
equivalent of the ear prioritises a notion of sound as an external
phenomenon – as being 'out there'. What subsequently happens to
these sounds in post-production is then conceptualised in terms
of orchestration. Recorded sounds may be edited and mixed, but
individually these sounds are still understood to belong to a milieu
essentially external to the technology in which they are actually situated. Even when subjected to various forms of cinesonic
processing (recording, cutting, mixing), recorded sounds maintain
an identity that marks them as external to the technology of film;
hence Barraud's dog, Nipper, *is*, at some level, listening to his
master's voice. This habit is yet another consequence of the dominant conceptualisation of sound that figures sonic phenomena
primarily in relation to an object source; thus, in sound editing or
sound design we may still think in terms of the sound *of* something
or other, rather than its recorded analogue. In contrast, sounds
internal to this technology are considered to be noise, and as such
they impose themselves between the profilmic auditory event and
its audition by the listener, thereby threatening the fidelity of a
recording.

This particular ontological model of film sound is, however,
challenged by the process of optical sound synthesis, in which
sound is created by the direct inscription of marks or patterns onto
the optical area of the film, rather than by the transcription of
sound originated from recordings. In the normal process of recording sound optically, sound vibrations collected by a microphone
are converted into a variable electric current which, in turn, excites
a light source in the recording device. The sound-modulated light
beam that results is then recorded photographically, inscribed on
the light-sensitive strip of film as a pattern of light. In each of the
three main optical systems developed by the American film industry, a different method was used to produce a sound-modulated
light source: in the Movietone Fox system the light source activated by the variable current was a gas-filled tube; in the RCA
Photophone system a tiny mirror turned in response to the modulating sound source, reflecting light onto or away from the unex-
posed sound film; and in the Western Electric system a variable slit
controlled the amount of light registered on the recording film. The
optical recording process thus results in the visible inscription of a
light pattern onto photographic film stock. This pattern can be one
of two types, either variable area (Figure 4.1) or variable density

4.1 Variable area optical soundtrack

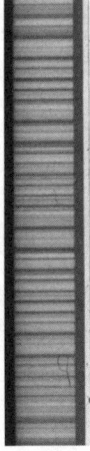

4.2 Variable density optical soundtrack

(Figure 4.2). These soundtracks are located along the edge of the film print, as indicated in Figures 4.3 and 4.4. During playback the process of inscription is essentially reversed, so that the patterns recorded on the film now create a modulated light source which, by means of a photoelectric cell, produces a variable current which is then amplified to drive loudspeakers. This technology therefore creates the possibility of generating sound by drawing, painting or printing directly onto the film's sound track, or alternatively

4.3 16mm film print with variable area optical soundtrack

4.4 16mm film print with variable density optical soundtrack

by printing images, shapes or patterns photographically onto this area of the film print. All these methods were employed during the 1930s by filmmakers and composers experimenting with the technology of optical film as a means to synthesise sound.[1]

The electronic sounds produced by these methods prove problematic in respect to cinema's dominant models of sound–image relationships, and the ways in which these relate to cinematic space. Central to the operation of classical cinema is the mapping of profilmic space, and the subsequent construction of fictive or narrative space; however, sound produced by optical synthesis has no source definable or identifiable in terms of either of these cinematic spaces. At the same time, optically synthesised sound is not easily located within the imaginary orchestra pit proposed by the classical film score, since it emanates from the technology of projection itself, rather than the reproduction of a musical performance. Thus, a journalist writing in 1932 on the experiments of one of the pioneers of optical synthesis remarked, 'Rudolph Pfenninger creates tones from nothing' (*Tönende Handschrift*, 1932; quoted in Levin, 2003: 58). Optical synthesis produces sound that issues from a space that cannot be registered in classical cinema, emerging as it does from the very apparatus that makes such an effort to erase its own presence. Situated within an understanding of sonic phenomena underpinned by the object-source model, this is indeed a sound that seems to come from nowhere – a ghost in the machine. Electronica produced by optical synthesis refuses to be inscribed into the dominant spaces of cinema; rather, it is a sound that deterritorialises the spaces constructed, mapped and represented by cinema. At a conceptual level, this sound challenges the common formulation that relates sounds to object sources located in what we might think of as stratified or gridded Cartesian space. The 'sourceless' sound produced by optical synthesis permeates cinema, collapsing represented and technological space into one another.

This indeterminacy provides a key to understanding some of the affective qualities of synthesised sound. The indeterminate spatial identity of this particular sound, which can also be understood as a total permeation of cinematic and technological space, attributes something of the magical power of Chion's acousmetre to optically synthesised electronica.[2] This is a sound that speaks to us without position, one whose source lies not on screen, nor in any instrument (electronic or otherwise) *recorded* for the soundtrack, and because we are so accustomed to conceptualising sound in terms of an object source, this spatial indeterminacy is potentially disturbing. Electronic sounds synthesised by optical or other means are often described as other-worldly, sounds to which we might appropriately apply the term 'uncanny', understood in the sense of the German word *unheimlich*. Literally translated as 'unhomely', the *unheimlich* would logically seem to refer to something from outside (or without) the home. Transposed into spatial terms, we might consider the homely as that which is anchored in known, striated space, while the *unheimlich* is that which is not. However, as Freud suggests in his essay *The Uncanny*, the *unheimlich* does not simply describe that from without: the other or the alien. He observes that its antonym, the word *heimlich*, can convey both a comforting sense of the homely and also a more negative sense of something that is hidden or secret. The corollary of this is a formulation of the uncanny that Freud expresses in the following terms:

> this uncanny is in reality nothing new or foreign, but something familiar and old-established in the mind that has been estranged only by the process of repression. This reference to the factor of repression enables us, furthermore, to understand [Friedrich] Schelling's definition of the uncanny as something which ought to have been kept concealed but which has nevertheless come to light. (Freud, 1958: 148)

What Freud sketches in this observation is a form of concurrence, a presence of the *unheimlich* within the *heimlich*, of the other and the excluded at the centre, and therefore a dissolution of that which demarcates internal from external. In this way we move from a striated or stratified state in which things are known and knowable in terms of spatial differentiation, and in which boundaries protect notions of essence, to a smooth space of co-presence or permeation. Returning to the noise of optical synthesis, the other-worldliness of electronica might indeed lie in its alterity, its unhomeliness, but this quality can also be understood in terms of the sound's rejection and transgression of the 'officially' demarcated spaces of classical cinema. Here is a sound that has no home, that cannot be enclosed within a territory marked by boundaries, and that refuses to adhere to the sonic-spatial categories inherent in dominant modes of film practice. This is a sound that haunts cinema, threatening the integrity of the division made between representational and technological space. In keeping with Freud's definition of the uncanny, what we hear in the sound of electronica is the resurfacing of that which is repressed – the unthinkable of cinema, the sound of technology itself.[3]

Sound synthesis and optical inscription

The figure of technology is foregrounded, rather than repressed, in the work of the Whitney Brothers and other filmmakers experimenting with optical sound synthesis. The sounds produced by this technique, such as those that comprise the soundtrack of John and James Whitney's *Five Film Exercises*, are the eerie, synthetic sounds we most commonly associate with electronic instrumentation. In the popular imagination all such sounds are labelled 'electronic', although synthetic sounds can also be generated by mechanical, optical and magnetic techniques. Similarly, within the field of music, all these various methods of synthesis are brought together under this single term. Thus the *musique concrete* composed by Pierre Schaeffer in the late 1940s, initially produced by the manipulation of recordings made on disc, has been celebrated as one of the origins of electronic music. As a label for a category of sound, 'electronica' is a convenient term, but one of the consequences of its usage is that writers too readily ascribe the eerie or machine-like quality of synthetic sound to the mysterious, otherworldly properties of electricity. Thus, Erik Davis writes, 'the revolutionary sonic media that followed in the wake of the telegraph – telephone, phonograph and radio, not to mention Theremins, Moogs and Roland 303s – [can] be regarded as creative transmutations of the new "elements" that would come to undergird the 20th century's cultural consciousness: electricity and electromagnetism' (Davis, 2002: 16). What Davis refers to as 'the electromagnetic imaginary' – 'the mythic, animistic and just plain weird cultural dimensions of electricity and electromagnetism' (Davis, 2002: 16) – is undoubtedly relevant to a discussion of the affective impact made by electronic sound on the listener; however, this cannot account entirely for the phenomenon of electronica, if only because the term embraces sounds generated by other than strictly electronic means. The problem with the general label 'electronic' is that, in focusing attention on the electrical aspects of these particular sounds, it neglects the more general issue of syntheticness. I would argue that one of the keys to opening up electronica to critical consideration is a discussion of the synthetic, of which the electrical/electronic is but one expression or manifestation. Syntheticness is a quality shared with sounds synthesised by other than electronic means, and approaching electronica by way of the synthetic provides for a much wider critical discussion than simply tracing electrical currents. Such confusion is perhaps understandable, since the development of sound synthesis in music was dominated by the work of pioneers in electronics, such as Leon Theremin and Raymond Scott. These figures have a much higher profile in popular consciousness than do artists like the Whitney Brothers, whose experiments in synthesis seem more properly located within the field of visual arts. The iconographic images of electronica feature musicians and composers struggling with unwieldy piles of valves and tangled leads, rather than film-makers stooped over an optical printer.

Trouble in utopia: synthesis and the Witney Brothers

In the 1930s and 1940s optical sound synthesis had a great appeal to those who wished to create their own direction in cinema or in music, and in the writings of the Whitney Brothers dating from this period the synthetic is constructed in fairly utopian terms, as a means by which to pursue new avenues of creativity. Throughout a career that encompassed musical composition, and pioneering work in animation and computer graphics, John Whitney's abiding interest lay in the complementarity of sound and image, and in the artistic possibilities of their synthesis – a term that should be understood, within the context of the Whitneys' project, to refer to both generation and fusion. In 1943 and 1944, John worked with his brother, the artist James Whitney, on a series of short experimental films known collectively as *Five Film Exercises*. In each of the five films, the Whitneys manipulated simple graphic forms (e.g. Figure 4.5) to produce animations that were accompanied by optically synthesised soundtracks. The optical system devised by the brothers to synthesise sound harnessed the movement of pendulums to control the inscription of light onto film. Using a series of connecting rods, the Whitneys' sound recorder de-magnified the movement of oscillating pendulums to make fine adjustments to a variable slit; the light that passed through this slit was then registered on film stock. The instrument had a selection of thirty pendulums that could be swung singly or in combination and, by adjusting the length of each pendulum, their frequencies could be arranged to form a scale. In this way the filmmakers were able to score synthetic music by controlling the number, length and frequency of the pendulums. Thus, no sounds were required to produce the patterns of light which, when inscribed on the optical soundtrack of a film print, and then run through a sound projector, would generate electronic tones.

4.5 *Film Exercise No. 4* (John and James Whitney, 1944)

The electronica synthesised for these films has a strange, unearthly quality, sounding at times like an electronic organ, at others reminiscent of a steamboat calliope, and ranging in frequency from low pulsing infrasonics to high-pitched tones. The sounds produced by the Whitneys' pendulum sound recorder could take the form either of single sine waves or, alternatively, of what the filmmakers referred to as 'vertical note mixtures' – their adoption of serial techniques, and a rejection of traditional forms of western art music, meant that they discarded the term 'chord' (Whitney, 1980: 153). At other times the sounds created for these films remind the listener of the sharp tap of a woodblock, or sometimes of dripping water. It is a vocabulary of sounds that became more familiar a decade later through the work of the animator Norman McLaren, most particularly perhaps in his film *Neighbours* (1952).[4] This synthetic soundscape was also to be heard a decade later in mainstream cinema, in the 'electronic tonalities' produced by Bebe and Louis Barron for the science-fiction film *Forbidden Planet* (1956), although in this case the Barrons produced sound by electronic rather than optical means.

Despite their simple visual vocabulary, the animations that

comprise *Five Film Exercises* are nevertheless quite complex, since the abstract forms of the image track provide a profusion of permutational variations in colour, colour intensity, shape, scale, position, horizontal and vertical movement, and movement in perceived spatial depth. In addition, all of these elements are controlled in terms of speed of movement or change. A further level of complexity is then added by the relationships forged between these images and the soundtrack, which sometimes work in parallel, sometimes in counterpoint. The permutational logic of the films owes much to Arnold Schoenberg's influential twelve-tone technique, which John Whitney had first encountered in 1939 while studying in Paris. The acknowledged influence of serial music on the Whitneys' work can not only be seen, but also heard, since the soundtracks employ explicit structural devices. *Film Exercise No. 1* (1943) is structured around a three-beat figure that is increasingly condensed with each new return, then used in reverse to conclude the film, while *Film Exercise No. 5* (1944) employs a canonical form with sound counterpart also in canon (Whitney, 1947a: 60).

But even before the Whitneys constructed their pendulum sound recorder, music had served as a temporal model for their early silent film work. Writing in 1959 for Karlheinz Stockhausen and Herbert Einert's serial music journal *Die Reihe*,[5] Whitney recalled, 'Our activities were not alone musical since our first interest had been to compose abstract graphic compositions with a time structure as in music' (Whitney, 1980: 154). The article describes how their early 8mm film, the silent *Twenty Four Variations* (1939–40), comprised permutations of a simple graphic matrix composed of a rectangle and a circle.[6] The matrix (Figure 4.6) was broken down to produce both positive and negative shapes, which could then be animated in phases and moved around the screen. Another level of visual complexity was added by the method of printing devised by the Whitneys, again directly influenced by Schoenberg's twelve-tone technique. Having produced a short animated sequence, they then reprinted it to produce other serial permutations: 'We devised an optical printer in which this film strip could be rephotographed onto colour film using colour filters, either in normal direction or retrogression, right side up or inverted, or mirrored. Graphically, here was a parallel to the transpositions and inversions and retrogressions of the twelve-tone technique' (Whitney, 1980: 155). The relationships between sound and image observed in the *Film Exercises* are clearly influenced by the permutational logic first explored by the Whitneys in *Twenty Four Variations*.

4.6 Graphic matrix for John and James Whitney's *Twenty Four Variations* (1939–40). Original German edition ©. Copyright 1960 by Universal Edition A.G. Wien. English edition ©. Copyright 1965 by Theodore Presser Co., Pennsylvania

In *Film Exercise No. 4*, for example, graphic forms are sometimes accompanied by sounds that in some way parallel an aspect of the image; for example, at certain points during this film a flickering rectangular form is accompanied by an intermittent sound that mirrors the image's rhythmic changes. Elsewhere in the same film the appearance of other visual forms is marked by a synchronous 'woodblock' sound, while at other times there is a delay between sound and image that is 'in a proportional relationship to the depth or distance of its corresponding image in the screen space' (Whitney, 1947a: 60–61).

The eerie, synthetic sounds produced by the pendulum recorder might justifiably be described as 'futuristic', and while today this term creaks under the weight of ironic nostalgia, it is not wholly inappropriate. During the 1940s the writing of the Whitneys is often utopian in tone, and particularly so when referring to the possibilities offered by technology, constructing their own relationship with the machine in wholly positive terms. For a previous generation of artists, the utopian notion of a universal language turned around the figure of visual abstraction;[7] for the Whitneys, however, universality was guaranteed by the machine. This position on technology is stated clearly in their 1947 essay 'Audio-Visual Music', in which they write, 'Our very realm of creative action is implicit in the machine. Emphasis is necessarily upon a more objective approach to creative activity. More universal. Less particular. More so by virtue of the inherent impersonal attribute of the machine' (Whitney, 1947b: 34). Furthermore, the Whitneys saw in the machine a means by which new fields of creative activity might be opened to the artist, that would in some way offer an appropriate response to the condition of modernity: 'But the machine is yet a poorly integrated, clumsily handled invention else man would not be face to face with his destiny by it today. Personal contact with new creative fields by way of the machine would hardly be worth struggling after were it not for the tremendous variety of new clay to be found there, its universality and its close relationship with modern experience' (Whitney, 1947b: 34). By linking technology, creativity and modernity in this way, the Whitney Brothers also articulate a rejection of tradition. The machine was seen to make a fundamental and radical break with past forms of cultural practice, thereby proposing itself as the means by which to generate entirely new forms of artistic activity and creative expression: 'The introduction of the machine in such proportions as has taken place only in this century constitutes a quantitative change effecting a distinct qualitative revolution. The motion picture camera is no more an improved paint brush than our sound track device is an improved musical instrument' (Whitney, 1947b: 34). In this way the Whitneys purposefully disassociate the camera and the pendulum sound recorder from past technologies of the visual and sonic arts, and their associated modes of expression. In keeping with the desire to explore modes of construction suitable for a truly modern art form, one of the main objectives of *Five Film Exercises* was to create a synthesis of the sonic and the visual in ways that realised their complementarity. In relation to this, the filmmakers figure

the development of the pendulum sound recorder as the solution
to a problem, encountered when attempting to forge an 'appropriate' relationship between sound and image:

> It is common place to note that film and sound today have become
> a permanent unity. We are attracted by the prospects of an idiom
> as unified, bi-sensorially, as the sound film can be. Naturally, we
> have wanted to avoid weakening that unity, which would be the
> very essence of an abstract film medium. It occurred to us that an
> audience would bring with it its own disunifying distractions in the
> form of numerous past associations and preconceptions were we
> to use previously composed music in relation to our own abstract
> image compositions. We, therefore, tried the simplest, least common,
> primitive music we could find. But another source of disunity became
> apparent. In this case, the dominant source of distraction was a con-
> tradiction between the origins (the players, instruments, time, place,
> etc.) of this kind of music and our animated image. Thereafter, little
> thought was given to any other consideration than to search for a
> method of creating our own sound by some means near as possible
> to the image animation process, technically and in spirit. (Whitney,
> 1947b: 32)

The way in which the Whitney Bothers perceive the complementarity of the sonic and the visual in the passage above raises
a number of issues about the nature of this relationship, and the
cultural context within which it is articulated. Here the writers
conceive sound and image in terms of unity, and the actual possibility of achieving audiovisual synthesis is never questioned.
It is telling that the essay is entitled 'Audio-Visual Music', since
historically music has served as the primary cultural arena within
which parallels between sound and image have been explored,
both conceptually and creatively, in the reflection on synaesthetic experience undertaken within painting, and in the various
experiments with colour organs. It is significant, therefore, that in
anchoring their audiovisual experiments within the field of music,
the Whitneys do not view abstract film as an extension of painting. In this sense their work is distinguished from that of the first
generation of abstract animators, like Hans Richter and Viking
Eggeling, who saw film initially as a means by which to develop
painterly concerns, enabling them to introduce a further temporal dimension into fine-art practice. The unification of sensations
achieved by the sound film is constructed by the Whitneys as the
essence of an abstract film medium, and while this places their
work within the mainstream of modernism, their position differs

from that of those artists and theorists who seem to have been preoccupied by the need to differentiate and isolate one medium from another. Thus, we see in Soviet cinema of the 1920s and 1930s a resistance to theatrical influences on the art of cinema, and an initially problematic relationship with sound, since film was considered to be a purely visual art form. Similarly Bertolt Brecht, whose work was so much concerned with the specificity of his chosen medium, considered the combination of art forms to be highly problematic:

> so long as the arts are supposed to be 'fused' together, the various elements will all be equally degraded, and each will act as a mere 'feed' to the rest. The process of fusion extends to the spectator, who gets thrown into the melting pot too and becomes a passive (suffering) part of the total work of art. Witchcraft of this sort must of course be fought against. Whatever is intended to produce hypnosis is likely to induce sordid intoxication, or creates fog, has to be given up. *Words, music and setting must become independent of one another.* (Brecht, 1964: 37–38)

When so much of the discourse relating to the visual arts during this period revolves around notions of purity, abstraction and essence, it is significant that in the Whitneys' work the notion of audiovisual synthesis radically challenges the boundaries established between different art forms.

And yet, at the same time, the Whitneys strive to isolate and disassociate by avoiding representational images, and the sounds of recognisable instrumentation (what might be termed 'the sound of music'). Their decision to build the pendulum sound recorder, rather than use existing forms of instrumentation, is inspired in part by the very sourcelessness of electronica. This is sound that seems to be without mimetic or significative potential, and is generated not by plucking, striking or blowing, but by the play of light. The Whitneys not only wished to avoid the 'disunifying distractions' created by the associations of existing pieces of music, but also required a playerless, instrumentless, timeless, placeless sound – a music that aspires to nothingness. The solution of using 'the simplest, least common, primitive' music they could find was thought unsatisfactory because its 'origins (the players, instruments, time, place, etc)' created a similar disunity with their imagery (Whitney, 1947b: 32); thus, they were in search of a sound that did not signify. Expressed in other terms, the material sound they required was *noise*: sound without identity, sound marked by non-identity.

Their position on the unsuitability of certain sounds for use in these films produces an interesting reversal of the normal conception of noise. In a system which strives not to signify, the 'sound of music' becomes noise. Attali certainly recognises this as a theoretical possibility when he writes, 'noise is the term for a signal that interferes with the reception of a message by a receiver, even if the interfering signal itself has a meaning for that receiver' (Attali, 1985: 27). According to this formulation of noise, based on a model drawn from C. E. Shannon's *A Mathematical Theory of Communication* (see Figure 4.21),[8] within certain contexts the recognisable and the representational may possess the power to disturb and disrupt. Paradoxically, noise potential may therefore be attributed to sounds that are familiar and wholly known, as demonstrated in Montreal in 1998, when recordings of opera were successfully used to rid railway stations of undesirable loiterers.[9] As will be shown later, this establishes the possibility that the now conventional sounds of electronica may yet regain their original power to disturb.

The tension between the abstract and the representational that we observe in the films and writing of the Whitneys points to a broader sonic force that their work seeks to hold in check. The Whitneys make the observation that, had they employed previously composed music to accompany their abstract images, their audience might have brought its own 'disunifying distractions' to their work, in the form of past associations and preconceptions (Whitney, 1947b: 32). The controlling and somewhat disapproving attitude taken by the filmmakers to their audience might be seen as a response to the perceived threat that the 'sound of music' posed to the isolation and purity of their abstract image compositions. However, what lies behind this is perhaps a deeper anxiety about the power that sound itself may have to threaten the utopian perfection of their synthetic world. The Whitneys' vision of modernity is articulated in terms of abstraction and essence, realised in the geometric purity of their visual universe. This rigorous simplicity is mirrored in the choice of structural approach employed to organise the films: firstly the visual matrix, whose limited constituent elements parallel the notes of Schoenberg's tone row, and secondly the permutational articulation of sound and image, also inspired by serial techniques. In its abstract purity, the imagery of these films represents a utopian vision of noiseless modernity, paralleling the empty, expansive whiteness of the International Style. For the Whitneys, the visual world becomes an arena over which they have absolute command. This desire for authorial control is apparent in their writing, where it is expressed in terms of artistic freedom: 'there is for us perhaps more personal freedom than is possible in any other motion picture field today. Our sound and image technique provide a complete means accessible to one creator. We believe in the future of the abstract film medium as one differing from the others in that it demands none of the large scale collaboration typical in present motion picture fields' (Whitney, 1947b: 33). Thus, in addition to the conflict between the abstract and the representational that runs through this work, tensions between freedom and control, order and expression can also be observed. The way in which the filmmakers conceptualise sound–image relationships, and the way in which they corral their own electronica to meet their desired goals suggest, perhaps, that it is not simply the 'sound of music' that represents an uncontrollable threat to their new utopia, but rather that sound itself may potentially disrupt their hermetic vision of modernity. It is important to remember that the Whitney's visual world and its structuring logic had already been established in *Twenty Four Variations*. Therefore, in *Five Film Exercises*, the sonic is allowed into an already established project, but on condition that it is shaped, driven and contained by the visual. The films undoubtedly work to create an audiovisual synthesis, but it is one in which the sonic is absorbed by the primary term of the audiovisual contract – namely the visual.

The relationship established between sound and image in *Five Film Exercises* is not a fixed constant. Sometimes the sonic and the visual are tightly synchronised, sometimes they are arranged in counterpoint. However, what both types of relationship demonstrate is that the sonic is consistently situated *in relation to* the visual. Notwithstanding the Whitneys' claims to be working towards audiovisual synthesis, accompaniment might seem to be a more appropriate term to describe sound's relation to the image in these films. In the following statement, for example, the closing sentence suggests that the filmmakers position the visual as the primary term of the audiovisual relationship:

> In composing the sound, we seek to exploit a spatial quality characteristic of the instrument which reinforces that effect of movement in space which we seek to achieve in the image. Since both image and sound can be time scored to fractions of a single motion picture frame, there is opened a new field of audio-visual rhythmic possibilities. The quality of sound evokes no strong image distraction such

as was observed in other music. Consequently, the sound is easily integrated with the image. (Whitney, 1947b: 33)

The Whitneys' concern with control, and the centrality of structure to their work, both point to the desire to contain and shape the materials that constitute these films. Certainly John's later career indicated his strong attraction to and appreciation of structure, demonstrated in a 1970 interview given to Gene Youngblood, in which he comments on the contemporary audiovisual scene of the time, 'The light show people are doing something like an infant pounding on the keys of a piano. Sometimes it can be very creative and terribly exciting. But in the long run, looking at it as an adult, it's just banging away at the piano without training' (Youngblood, 1970: 214). However, while framed in positive terms as a way of opening new areas of creativity, the Whitneys' desire to control their optically produced sound to 'fractions of a motion picture frame' is telling. Running through the Whitneys' writing is the undeclared notion that sound is the dionysian term of the audiovisual relationship, and must consequently be controlled. Thus, not only did the sound of music need be managed, but, somewhat paradoxically, the disruptive potential of their own electronic noise had also to be carefully contained. In the *Five Film Exercises*, it appears that electronica simply could not be left to do its own thing.

But in what sense could the Whitneys' own electronica pose a noisy threat to the audiovisual world they had themselves created? Almost seventy years after these films were made, the Whitneys' electronic soundtracks remain powerfully noisy. The morphological unpredictability of their electronica, the sudden changes in tone and amplitude, and the sheer intensity of volume all retain the power to disturb, even if, for the modern listener, the sounds no longer possess the strangeness they once had. But while this electronica must have one kind of noise potential – that is, it must lie outside of signification – it is nevertheless highly controlled. Hence, this is not noise that is in any sense beyond construction, but is in fact decidedly constructed. What ultimately controls these sounds is their submission to a visual code; sounds which fail to obey the visual lead, which refuse to be subsumed by audiovisual synthesis, and which therefore maintain some form of independence from the image, run the risk of becoming noise *in relation to the visual*, setting up the kind of distraction the Whitneys worked so hard to avoid. It is for this reason that it was not only the sound of music that needed to be controlled by the Whitneys; in addition, the audiovisual *turbulence* potentially created by their own electronic noise also required containment. It is this turbulence that the Whitneys seek to control by their careful scoring to fractions of a single motion picture frame, and by the move towards combinatory audiovisual synthesis. In *Five Film Exercises* the potential turbulence of electronica is contained by a particular formulation of sound–image relationships: an audiovisuality that entrains the sonic through complementarity. From this it is possible to make the observation that *sound can be noise not only in relation to other sounds, but also in relation to the image.* This form of audiovisual turbulence is not to be understood in terms of counterpoint, the largely art-cinematic model of sound–image relationships proposed in 1928 by the Soviet filmmakers Eisenstein, Pudovkin and Alexandrov in the famous article *The Sound Film: A Statement from the USSR*. In any case, this Soviet modelling of sound–image relationships does not apply to *Five Film Exercises*, since the films are largely informed by John Whitney's concern with the complementarity of sound and image, and thus employ audiovisual parallelism as well as contrapuntality. Rather, this potential audiovisual turbulence identifies an aspect of noise not covered by any existing theorisation, one that builds on a notion of cinema as *transsensory* or *intersensory*.

In *Five Film Exercises* the visual is always prioritised above the sonic, and it is the sonic that needs to be explained, contained, resisted and reinvented. The Whitneys' solution to this was the creation of science-fiction music: pure and synthetic, that in its rejection of the past comes to represent a voice from the future, free of associations of any kind save those of the filmmakers' carefully controlled synthetic universe itself. The Whitneys' sci-fi electronica is thus a sign of repression, a form of censorship, implicit in which is an acknowledgement of the power it seeks to repress. The paradoxical absence of noise in the purity of the Whitneys' synthetic universe signals its repression, and thus returns us to notions of the uncanny. While the noise-free might be in some senses comforting, it may also produce a sense of disquiet, as with the automata and dolls mentioned by Freud, or in the situation signalled by the B-movie cliché, 'It's quiet . . . maybe too quiet'. The academic and VJ Charles Kriel has suggested that the noise-free is uncanny because it signals, and hence returns to our attention, that which is repressed (in this case noise).[10] His argument, based on Freud's proposition that a repressed thing returned is uncanny, suggests that our unconscious desire to fill blank space leads us to an encounter with that which has been repressed in order to create this same noiseless blank space; alternatively, as Attali neatly puts it, 'There is no order that does not contain disorder within itself' (Attali, 1985: 34). Electronica, as the sound of utopia, therefore carries within itself the dystopian seeds of its own undoing. In eradicating disruptive noise from their utopian abstract universe, the Whitneys' sci-fi electronica returns us to that which has been repressed.

Drawing on the work of Kriel and Attali, it could be argued that the freedom and alterity of noise might paradoxically signal the repression and control that is central to any system in which noise is inscribed. All systems or codes must necessarily repress a host of elements to function and define themselves as such, to draw themselves out from the swirl and mix of elements and milieus. More radically perhaps, Michel Serres proposes that *everything* emerges from noise, when he states in the book *Genesis*, 'The raucous, anarchic, noisy, variegated, tiger-striped, zebra-streaked, jumbled-up, mixed-up multiple, criss-crossed by myriad colours and myriad shades, is possibility itself. It is a set of possible things, it may be *the* set of possible things' (Serres, 1995: 22). If this is so, then in order for systems to emerge, things must be excluded from the total set of all possibilities, all milieus, all elements. And if Kriel's formulation of the uncanny suggests that the absence of noise is disturbing, then it follows that what does not disturb – that which we perceive as 'normal' – is paradoxically marked by the presence of noise, not as its constitutive outside, but as somehow immanent to it. The Whitneys' carefully controlled synthetic universe is therefore haunted by the shadow of the chaos and noise it seeks to repress. In this way the return of the repressed is sounded in the uncanny quality of the Whitneys' electronica.

Noise and the monstrous

While the synthetic soundtracks of the Whitney Brothers' films were designed to break with existing forms of musical sound, the filmmakers' strict modelling of sonic phenomena points to a desire to domesticate some potentially problematic element of electronica itself. But what is it about electronica in particular that demanded it be contained by audiovisual synthesis, and what would have been the consequences had the Whitneys not controlled it in this way? An answer to these questions is provided by a consideration of the way in which electronica has been deployed in classical cinema, and in particular the way in which narrative films have translated the non-identity of noise into significatory potential.

The Whitneys were consciously creating machine sounds that had no historical precedent; but synthetic sound, chosen for its very unfamiliarity, brings with it a dynamic of unknowability. This dynamic permits electronica to assume a series of meanings over which the Whitneys could have had no control. Yet, ironically, it is this same series of potential meanings that *domesticates* the synthetic within the milieu of classical cinema. The very newness and non-identity of synthetic sound – sourceless, playerless, timeless, placeless, unrecorded – presents a problem of categorisation and conceptualisation in relation to existing cultural codes and structures, and it is this that brings strange sounds within the field of noise. As previously stated, sound is most commonly conceptualised in terms of those objects perceived as its source; in this way the material sonic signifier directs the listener to an object referent. However, when this simple link with an object source is lacking, as must logically be the case with 'new' and unfamiliar sounds, a sound may present the material attributes of a sign, but fail to signify. The problematic nature of this undigested materiality is evidenced by asking the simple question, 'what is the synthetic the sound of?'

Sounds that elude this simple classificatory framework are, of course, deemed to be noises. In this way, the category of noise becomes a catch-all, a means by which the problematic nature of non-identity and non-significative materiality may be dismissed and forgotten. In the context of significatory regimes, that which does not adhere to the codes and structures which make phenomena knowable must necessarily be excluded, since failure to do so would threaten the very existence of those regimes. This material 'stuff' has to be labelled 'noise', and conceptualised as deformed or unformed entropic nonsense/non-signs that demonstrates only the qualities of deformity or entropy. This makes noise threatening, since it is composed of the discarded detritus that cannot be contained by regimes of signification. In this sense the materiality of noise is monstrous, defying the notions of essence and identity that are central to the codes and structures of significatory regimes, while simultaneously signalling the repression that is central to any system in which noise is inscribed. Within these regimes, noise represents a collapse of stratification, a monstrous permeability that threatens the very classifications that guarantee stable and coherent identity. Thus, as in the classic formulation of the horror film, it is the monster that threatens normality.

The alterity of noise is most often formulated as subversion, interference, disruption, disconnection and turbulence in relation to a dominant code or power. Accordingly, Attali writes, 'Noise, then, does not exist in itself, but only in relation to the system within which it is inscribed: emitter, transmitter, receiver' (Attali, 1985: 26). But what Attali does not acknowledge is that what he refers to as 'the terror of noise' lies not only in violence, but also in its undecidability, indeterminacy, unknowability, unmasterability, in its lack of essence; noise 'does not exist in itself'. Thus the terror of noise lies in part in its monstrosity. What Attali recognises in the definition quoted above, but does not address in his own analysis, is the fluidity, the mutability, the absolute lack of essence of noise. Noise becomes the slipperiest of sounds – it appears before us with its insistent particularity, yet evades adequate conceptualisation, since it can only ever be assigned the non-identity of 'noise'. And if, as Attali states, 'noise is the term for a signal that interferes with the reception of a message by a receiver' (Attali, 1985: 27), then noise must necessarily be that which is carried along with the message, infecting and inhabiting it, but yet can never be part of that message. It is thus always the other, always outside, unwelcome and beyond or outside understanding, at least in the terms proposed by the dominant code it infects. However, noise problematises any simple binary, dyadic formulations of isolated, individuated and differentiated essence proposed by noise/signal and noise/order models. Part of the indeterminacy of noise rests in the fact that it is both internal (received along with the signal) and external (not part of the signal), neither fully one nor the other.

This uncertain status of noise is illustrated by the case of the electronic score created by Bebe and Louis Barron for the 1956 MGM science-fiction film *Forbidden Planet*. Anxieties were expressed at an institutional level about the electronic sounds created by the two avant-garde composers, whose previous work had included spending one year working for John Cage, editing quarter-inch tapes to realise the 500-page score of his composition *Williams Mix* (1952). In the first instance, the Musicians Union would not allow MGM to hire the two composers under normal terms and conditions. According to Bebe Barron, at least one objection to their involvement in the film's production was the familiar concern that musicians would be put out of business by electronic music

(Barron, 1997: 262) – a sharp contrast to the Whitneys' approval of the liberating capacities of the machine. But beyond the production context, this dispute signals deeper anxieties regarding the uncertain identity of electronica. As a result of the problem with the union, the Barrons were forbidden to refer to their work as 'music', and so it was described by the studio as 'electronic tonalities'. When it came to Oscar nominations there was confusion over whether the soundtrack should be judged as music or sound effects. As Barron observes, 'that's why our Academy nomination got screwed up. They didn't know who to give it to; they had no set categories for it' (Barron, 1997: 261).

Electronica and classical cinema

Notions of the terror of noise have been consistently articulated in classical cinema through the deployment of electronic sound, particularly in Hollywood films of the 1940s and 1950s, where electronica was commonly used to signal the monstrous. Thus Bebe Barron fittingly describes the electronic sounds she produced with her husband Louis for *Forbidden Planet* as 'end-of-the-world-type' sounds (Barron, 1997: 256). However, on occasion the composers were also required by the film's producer to create 'love music'. According to Bebe Barron, this proved to be quite a challenge: 'we went through absolute hell to get something that didn't sound awful, like monsters or war. So it was a tough assignment. I found some stuff that was legato notes, almost like viola sounds, although we would usually dump things if they resembled existing instruments' (Barron, 1997: 261). Like the Whitneys, the Barrons were in pursuit of a new soundscape, and by their own admission MGM was interested in this experimental work because the electronica they produced connoted monstrosity. The fact that a sound resembling a traditional instrument, and therefore familiar, should have been used for a comforting love theme suggests, perhaps, that there is a fundamental link between the unknown, the unfamiliar and the monstrous, thus explaining why the strange sounds of electronica have been so effectively employed within the genre of horror.

At the same time that *Forbidden Planet* articulates the relationship between noise and the monstrous through its representational deployment of electronica, the film's narrative and thematic concerns draw upon, and illustrate, other aspects of noise. The notion that noise is located within a system, posing an internal rather than an external threat, and may erupt to destroy that system if not repressed, is articulated by the dominant source of destruction and terror in the film, the Monster from the Id. The monster is at once insubstantial and yet powerfully destructive, remaining invisible until it attempts to breach the protective force field erected by the crew of the United Planets Space Cruiser around its base on the planet Altair IV. The monster's overt Freudian significance as the primitive, instinctual unconscious articulates the idea of a disruptive presence located within, and thus one that must be contained and repressed. In narrative terms, the monster appears to be unconsciously conjured by Dr Morbius when the intimate relationship with his daughter, Altaira, and his control over her, is threatened by the arrival of visitors to his planet. This tension between repression and the turbulent forces of the Id was also expressed at the level of film production, when the monstrosity of the Id seemed to threaten the dominant normality of the film's diegesis, thus necessitating further narrative containment. According to Bebe Barron, most of the 'Freudian stuff', which she personally found so fascinating, was edited out the final film, in particular the scenes concerning dreams, and those between Dr Morbius and his daughter which had clear sexual undertones (Barron, 1997: 257). In this way the narrative and thematic concerns of *Forbidden Planet* provide the context in which the noise of electronica finds significative resonance. In sounding Freud's notion of the Id, the Barrons' electronica signals not only the disruptive power of noise, but also its refusal to be located as a wholly external phenomenon. Noise parallels the Id in the sense that, at one level, it is conceived in terms of otherness, yet is located within. Noise might thus be figured as a monstrous viral presence, infecting and threatening the systems and structures that seek to contain or remove it.

The relationship between synthetic sound and themes of monstrosity, infection and repression signalled by the soundtrack of *Forbidden Planet* is consistently articulated by the use of electronic instrumentation in classical cinema. This is illustrated by Hollywood's use of the theremin, one of the first electronic instruments to be heard on film soundtracks. Resembling a large radio cabinet with two protruding antennae, the theremin has no keys, strings or pedals, but is played by the movement of the performer's hands through an invisible electromagnetic field, producing vibrato and portamento electronic sounds that are often described as 'other-worldly'. In films of the 1940s and 1950s, this sound is frequently called upon to signify madness, fear and emotional distress. In Hitchcock's 1945 film *Spellbound*, whose tagline 'The maddest love that ever possessed a woman' indicates the centrality of unstable mental states to its storyline, Miklos Rozsa's orchestral score employs the theremin artistry of Dr Samuel Hoffman to suggest the paranoid amnesia of the film's central protagonist (Figures 4.7–4.9).

The storyline of *Spellbound* revolves around issues of identity and memory as the amnesiac John Ballantine, played by Gregory Peck, attempts to recover his forgotten past. When Ballantine first appears in the film, he has assumed the identity of the psychiatrist Dr Anthony Edwardes. However, he is revealed to be an impostor after suffering the first of a series of paranoiac breakdowns, each of which is signalled on the film's soundtrack by the sound of the theremin. The key to Ballantine's mental problems lies in his own repression of memory, and thus once again the noise of electronic sound is articulated within a significatory context through association with repression and breakdown. Furthermore, in common with *Forbidden Planet*, the threat to stability and normality that disturbs the narrative equilibrium of *Spellbound* is posed not by an exterior force, but from within.

Samuel Hoffman, the thereminist who played on the soundtrack of *Spellbound*, was often billed as Dr Samuel Hoffman. Although he was in fact a chiropodist by profession, his title serves to locate both the theremin and his mastery of it somewhat outside the world of music, positioning it instead within the realms of science and technology. The theremin itself thus seems to have an indeterminate identity, located somewhere between musical instrument and scientific equipment. The instrument's otherness within a musical context is also sounded in its lack of adherence to a tempered scale. Although operating over three octaves, the theremin is capable of infinite divisions of tone, and, because of the way in which it is played, thereminists tend to produce portamento-like transitions rather than single, distinct, isolated notes. This continuous pitch variation places the theremin into the category of what the musicologists Siegmund Levarie and Ernst Levy (1983) have referred to as the 'barbarian', defined by them as any music that 'deliberately returns to a precivilised, premusical state in which the unformed, the undistilled, the inarticulate are placed on the throne as supreme values' (Levarie and Levy, 1983: 73). According to Levarie and Levy, such sounds are only ever used in classical music to invoke the barbarian, as, for example, in the use of cymbals by Mozart and Haydn. Distinguishing barbarianism

4.7–4.9 *Spellbound*

from normative modes of musical practice, Levarie and Levy make the observation that, in classical music, portamenti – the smooth transitions from one note to another – are never prescribed, but left to the player's own taste (Levarie and Levy, 1983: 73). This is perhaps because, within a musical tradition based on prescribed tonal values, such notation becomes impossible. The portamento cannot be fully known within the tone-based, text-based system of western art music, and must therefore remain essentially external to it. If not excluded in this way, the presence of sounds defying neat tonal organisation would challenge the whole foundation of a tempered musical system.[11] In this regard, the sounds of the theremin parallel the unstable and problematic identity of *Spellbound*'s male protagonist. John Ballantine/Anthony Edwardes' shifts in identity, marked by paranoiac breakdown, point to a lack of subject clarity, definition and essence that finds its counterpart in the 'barbaric' portamenti of Hoffman's theremin. Through the use of the theremin, the film's music signals what is normal (stable identity) and permissible (sanity), and what is forbidden and monstrous (mental illness).[12]

While it is not unreasonable to suppose that, as time went on, audiences must have become increasingly familiar with synthetic sound, its power to connote the strange seems not to have diminished with the passage of time. Almost twenty years after the release of *Spellbound*, Antonioni's 1964 *Il Deserto Rosso* employed electronic music composed by Vittorio Gelmetti to signal the mental breakdown of the film's central protagonist; similarly, Oskar Sala's electronic contribution to the soundtrack of Hitchcock's *The Birds* (1963) is used to signal both breakdown and monstrosity. Unlike *Spellbound*, *The Birds* has no traditional orchestral score, but uses electronica to create effects suggestive of bird-song, the cries of gulls and the flapping of birds' wings. In the final climactic scene of the film, in which Melanie Daniels is attacked by gulls, the electronic nature of these sound effects becomes increasingly audible as the attack intensifies in ferocity. In this way the noise value of the electronica intensifies as the sounds become less naturalistic. Like other films in which electronic sounds figure as noise, in *The Birds* there is a sense in which the threat to normality, signalled on the soundtrack by electronica, comes from both outside *and* within. The normally stable ecosystem in which humans and birds coexist (albeit on human terms), appears to be upset by the arrival of the active, self-confident Melanie Daniels, who also disturbs the existing Oedipal stability of the relationship between her lover,

Mitch Brenner, and his mother, Lydia. The disturbance to patriarchal, phallic order is thus expressed in the unexplained upset of
the *natural* order of the ecosystem. The chaos that erupts when
the birds attack, while triggered by an external force, is in fact
an internal collapse of an existing order. The destructive power
unleashed by the arrival of Melanie Daniels is already located
within existing social and ecological structures, but has until this
point been controlled and repressed. What the electronic sound
effects featured in *The Birds* articulate is the noise inherent in any
system or structure – noise that is both created and repressed by
regimes of order and control.

The domestication of noise

Despite the potentially problematic nature of electronic sound,
what the Hollywood movies *Forbidden Planet*, *Spellbound* and *The
Birds* demonstrate is the power that classical cinema has to absorb
the shock of the new, and disarm what might otherwise be radical
modernist noise. Narrative cinema's domestication of electronica
is undertaken primarily through its articulation by musical codes,
but the noise value of electronic sounds may also be contained
by the cinesonic construction of sound effects. In addition to sup-
plying what was essentially film music – despite being described
otherwise – the Barron's electronica also provided sound effects for
the film's futuristic technology, including, for example, the weaponry used by the film's main protagonists in their battles against
the 'Monster from the Id' (Figure 4.10). In its deployment as a
sound effect, the Barrons' modernist noise is completely domesticated through the synchronisation of sound and image, rendering
it thoroughly convincing as the sound of futuristic weaponry. In
this way the material opacity of noise is made transparent through
electronica's cinesonic deployment within a narrative context.

However, the synthetic sounds used in cinema are domesticated
in the first instance through articulation within existing musical
frameworks. As Attali claims, the disruptive power of noise can be
contained by music: 'Noise is a weapon and music, primordially, is
the formation, domestication and ritualization of that weapon as
a simulacrum of ritual order' (Attali, 1985: 24). Music's containment of noise is evidenced by the Whitneys' strict modelling of
sonic phenomena, inspired originally by Schoenberg's twelve-tone
technique. The move to contain electronica through submission to
musical codes is also illustrated by the career of the thereminist

4.10 *Forbidden Planet*

Clara Rockmore, who mastered the instrument in order to play the work of composers such as Rachmaninov, Ravel and Tchaikovsky. By playing well-known pieces from an established and respected musical tradition, and by teaching herself to sound individual tones rather playing in a wholly portamento style, Rockmore reduced the opacity of the theremin's electronic noise, thereby subsuming its materiality within systems of musical meaning.

The interplay between codes of control and the noise of the synthetic creates what might be termed 'controlled panic'. Attali has argued that codes such as music, in their domestication of noise, make its sounds knowable to the listener, and thereby reduce the anxiety associated with it. In this way harmony has been seen as a means by which music resolves the anxiety created by dissonance. In working through the balance between dissonance and harmony, music can therefore be seen as the organisation of controlled panic (Attali, 1985: 27). However, even though music may be a means by which noise is contained, it may also represent a form of noise in itself. Potentially destructive to existing systems of order, noise presents a challenge to established power relationships; not only can new types of music represent a form of noise in relation to established musical traditions, but also music itself may become a source of cultural noise within the wider social sphere. Attali argues that, for this latter reason, music has been repressed and controlled in Europe since the thirteenth century, first by the church, and later by capitalist political economy. Some of these various forms and processes of containment are demonstrated by both the work and careers of John and James Whitney. While the noise potential of the Whitneys' electronica was absorbed through the musical context provided by Schoenberg's twelve-tone system, John Whitney himself was 'contained' through inscription into the world of exchange. After his initial period of collaboration with James, John continued the project he had established in the early experimental films, pursuing his investigations into the complementarity of music and visual art through computer technology. In the late 1950s, after a decade working in commercial film and television, John's experimental work led to the development of an analogue computer, which he constructed from the mechanism used to guide anti-aircraft guns. In 1960 he established Motion Graphics Incorporated, using the computer to produce graphics and title sequences for film and television.[13] In 1966 he became IBM's first artist in residence, and was awarded a three-year research grant to explore graphic motion using the IBM 360 Digital Computer. The corporation then provided further sponsorship for his work in 1971, demonstrating its faith in the commercial value of artistic experiment. His brother James, however, chose not to be inscribed into the world of exchange, effectively 'dropping out' to pursue his interests in eastern philosophy and to work in ceramics and painting. He continued to make films, however, producing animations concerned with mystical, spiritual and speculative-scientific issues. His interest in cosmology informs the imagery of his best-known films, *Yantra* (1950–58) and *Lapis* (1963–66), two of only five films he made following his collaborative work with John in the 1940s, and which were painstakingly produced from hand-drawn patterns of dots. In this respect it is James who works through the logic of the noise of music. If, as Attali suggests, the musician is a marginal figure whose job it is to repress noise, yet who remains forever at its edge, then James is the heroic outcast whose outsider status is made manifest in his resistance to the world of exchange.

The processes of containment observed in the relationship between music and noise can also be seen and heard in cinema. Within a cinesonic context, the noise of electronica may be domesticated by its entrainment within narrative, as in the case of *Forbidden Planet*; or alternatively, by submission to the visual, or some other form structural logic, as in the case of *Five Film Exercises*. In both instances, to use Adorno's terminology, noise loses its non-identity, and becomes containable within the context of identity thinking. In the context of mainstream cinema, noise accepts commercial (exchange) value as it is absorbed into the significatory worlds of narrative film, while in the experimental work of the Whitney Brothers, noise loses its non-identity through submission to established musical structures expressed in visual terms, and hence through its submission to a visually led notion of audiovisual fusion.

As stated previously, one of the things that renders electronic sound monstrous is its ambiguity, its lack of essence. In a world where we conceive sounds in terms of their links with objects, the status of electronic sound can be problematic. This indeterminacy is a challenge to identity thinking, and what Deleuze and Guattari refer to as an arboreal system of knowledge, reliant as they are on structuring notions of differentiation and essence. The electronic may occasionally sound like a viola, but it will always be Bebe Barron's bastard, deformed viola, and the further that sound departs from a resemblance to a traditional instrument, the more deformed, freakish and monstrous it becomes. Since noise has no inherent meaning, it is tempting to think of the synthetic as always the other, always outside, unwelcome and beyond or outside understanding; but in the classical cinema, these sounds are stripped of their disruptive power by submission to narrative and musical codes. By means of this form of domestication, the film weaves meaning through noise, and in an art form dominated by narrative or visual structures, such domestication is clearly evident. But at the same time, in the films analysed here, there is enough controlled panic to demonstrate, in a significatory fashion, the noise potential of the synthetic. And this perhaps is why these sounds have been used so effectively to generate and signal horror and terror in classical cinema.

Deviant Beauty and the contemporary noisescape

From the analysis undertaken so far, three key observations can be made: firstly, sounds which are familiar and wholly known can have noise potential; secondly, sound can be considered noise not only in relation to other sounds, but also in relation to the image; and thirdly, this audiovisual turbulence is to be understood not only in terms of counterpoint (sound *not* illustrating image), but also as a possibility created by the transsensory or intersensory nature of cinema. Building on these ideas, consideration can now be given to the issue of how electronic sounds might maintain their radical potential in contemporary work; might there be some form of sonic sublation by which filmmakers could re-engage with the traditions and conventions of these sounds, but in ways that would give them contemporary resonance?

Tina Keane's 1996 film *Deviant Beauty* features what is in many ways a classical electronic score. Essentially musical in conception, it employs sampling, looping and various cut-up techniques to create synthetic sounds that entirely dominate the film's sound-track. Keane created this electronica from a number of recorded sound sources, including field recordings made at London's Victoria railway station, and the sounds of running water. Sounds from these recordings were then digitally processed and manipulated to produce the electronica we hear throughout the film. Standing in opposition to this monumental, wall-to-wall synthetica there is in fact only one shot in the whole of *Deviant Beauty* that features true sync sound. Keane's film thus breaks with dominant modes of audiovisual practice by eschewing the synchronous location sound that would normally accompany live-action footage, in favour of a through-composed music track. Nevertheless, sounds from the diegetic world do make an appearance in the film; in one scene we hear the footsteps and ragged breathing of the film's protagonist as she tries to escape the subterranean world in which she has become lost. However, because these sounds have been added during post-production, rather than recorded on location, and because they are not precisely synchronised with the action on screen, they are not rendered as entirely diegetic or naturalistic, but rather find their place as narratively situated sonic textures mixed and looped with the electronica.

To understand how the electronic sounds of Keane's soundtrack are articulated within a cinesonic context, it is first necessary to consider the ways in which the film's images are organised. The film has a loose narrative structure, outlined in Keane's description of *Deviant Beauty* as 'an androgynous woman's surreal journey through the carnivalesque' (Keane, 2009). This narrative arc is divided into four sections or movements, entitled The Spectacle, The Descent, The Pit and The Landscape.[14] In the first of these we are introduced to the film's androgynous protagonist, shown observing a trapeze artist performing in a circus tent. The film foregrounds notions of spectatorship, voyeurism and pleasure right from its opening moments, in a low-angle shot of the protagonist watching the circus performer through opera glasses (Figures 4.11 and 4.12). As Keane explains in her synopsis of the film, one of the project's main concerns is the potentially problematic nature

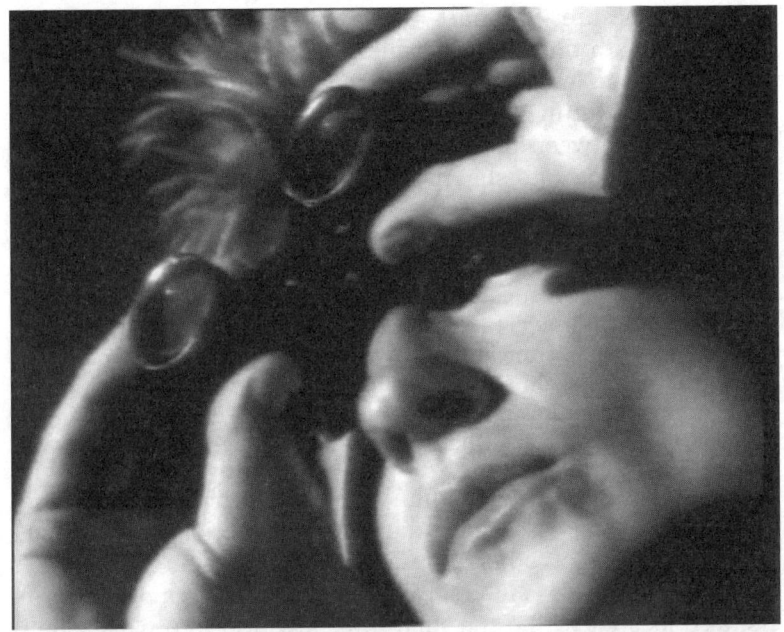

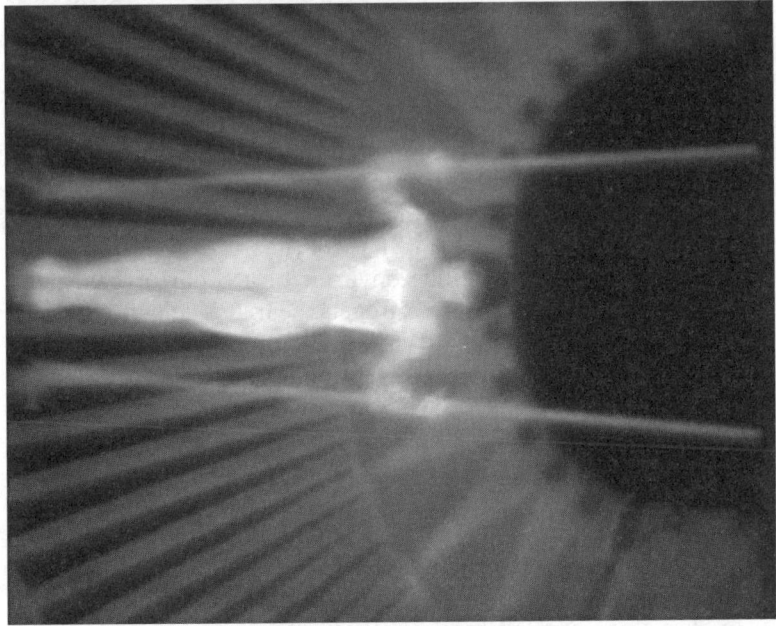

4.11–4.12 *Deviant Beauty*

of visual pleasure: '*Deviant Beauty* embodies spectator, erotica, sexuality, death and decay. It questions our expectation of, and pleasure in, the image, against the death and emptiness that lies beneath the alluring surface' (Keane, 2009). Keane explains the relationship between the film's opening images and her concern with issues of spectatorship in the following terms:

> it's all about this idea of pleasure . . . but . . . My work always has this edge: where there's all this pleasure, but there's always an edge to it. And so I thought that could be interesting to have the male-female person looking through these glasses at the trapeze artist, which then again takes you into the idea of voyeurism, which also takes you into cinema. So it is again about cinema. So constructing that in a way, and using the glasses . . . as x-ray eyes that go beyond the body, beyond the skin and see what's actually happening.[15]

The second section of the film shows the protagonist descending a series of staircases in the dark, shabby interior of what might be a warehouse or other industrial location (Figure 4.13). Her downward progress is intercut with images of two circus performers, also located within the subterranean world into which she is descending. The shift from circus tent to anonymous underground space is marked by changes in the trapeze artists' costumes. No longer dressed in circus garb, one performer is shown to be naked beneath her suit jacket as she spins by her neck from a rope, while the other is dressed only in underwear as she performs inelegant turns dangling from a loosely strung rope (Figure 4.14). Also marking the protagonist's descent is an encounter with a menacing clown, juggling fireballs in the darkness.

The third section of the film, 'The Pit', features the protagonist wandering the dark, maze-like environs of a cellar or basement. Driven by erotic, voyeuristic desire, she searches this increasingly nightmarish space, hoping to spy upon the performer she had observed previously in the circus tent. Finally she tracks down the trapeze artists, now naked, swinging in and out of the shadows of this subterranean world (Figure 4.15). After an uncomfortable encounter with her erotic target, the protagonist tries to escape from the Pit, running along the shadowy walls of the basement (Figure 4.16), while the two naked circus performers repeatedly try to lock hands as they swing towards each other on the trapeze.

In the final sequence of the film, the protagonist exits the Pit through a door opened by the clown, and runs across the landscape of the English South Downs as the clown's mocking laughter

4.13–4.14 *Deviant Beauty*

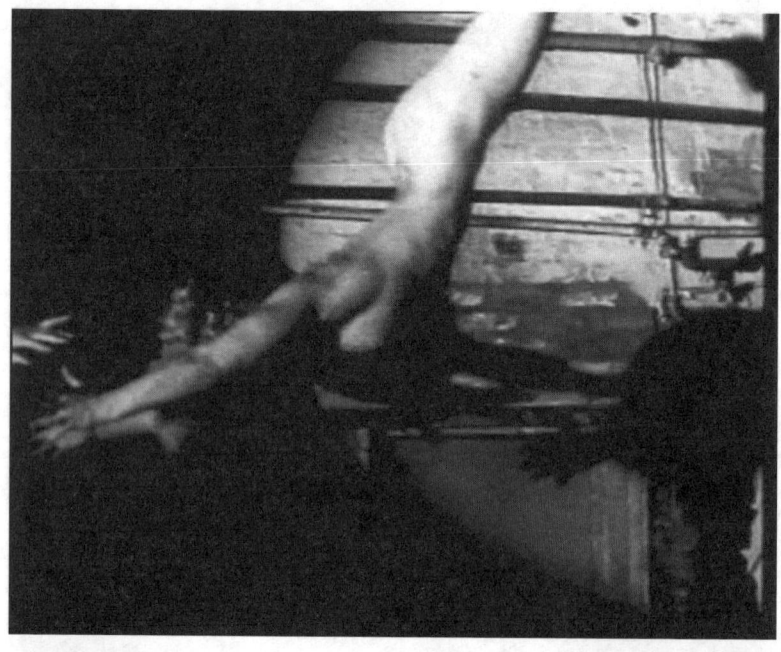

4.15–4.16 *Deviant Beauty*

echoes through the soundtrack. The film then concludes with vertiginous shots of waves crashing against the base of the white chalk cliffs at Beachy Head.

Sound and imagetrack

The visual and narrative strategies deployed by Keane in *Deviant Beauty* can be situated within the project to deconstruct visual and narrative pleasure that in Britain was first articulated in structural film practice, and later theorised along gender lines by Laura Mulvey in her seminal article *Visual Pleasure and Narrative Cinema* (1975). The film's use of negative (Figure 4.17), the tension it establishes between representation and abstraction (Figure 4.18), the use of long takes, and the mixture of image formats (Super 8, 16mm and Hi8 Video) all serve to establish a dialectic space between materiality and representation.

In *Deviant Beauty* this form of deconstructive materialist film practice runs in parallel with narrative strategies that work to problematise the relationships between visual pleasure, voyeurism and spectatorship. At a thematic level, the narrative deals with the tension between surface appearance and what lies beneath. Keane comments, 'It was very much about sense of loss, and also it was about the time of AIDS, and lots of people dying from AIDS at that time, and also quite a few women I'd known who'd died from breast cancer. It was very much about the idea . . . of the façade, in the sense of the idea of beauty: the façade in the way that people can look OK, but what's *actually* going on mentally and physically?'.[16] Both the narrative and the narrative space of the film are key elements through which these themes are developed and explored. At a narrative level, the protagonist's descent into the subterranean world draws on a mythical surface/underworld dualism, while the film's visual and narrative references to the carnivalesque and film noir are presented in such a way that their seductive allure is counterbalanced by a pervasive atmosphere of fear and menace. Thus the protagonist's pursuit of her erotic target results not in the fulfilment of her desire, but in rejection and humiliation: a rebuff that is signalled by the cold stare of the circus performer, who returns not only the protagonist's voyeuristic gaze, but also our own (Figure 4.19). This exchange of looks opens up to critical scrutiny not only every image in the film, and also our own spectatorial relationship with these images. Caught in the act of looking, the spectator is sutured into Keane's critical questioning

4.17–4.18 *Deviant Beauty*

of visual pleasure. The so-called 'fourth look', effectively forbidden in classical narrative cinema, confronts the spectator as voyeur, making us uncomfortably aware of our own scopic drives, our own pleasure in the spectacle the film presents us with, and our own affective reactions to the erotic charge of Keane's imagery. This self-reflexive gaze towards the camera thus serves to implicate the spectator in the voyeurism that the film foregrounds and problematises at a narrative and thematic level. Through its critical self-reflexivity, Keane's film works to deconstruct the relationship between particular modes of visual representation and erotic ways of looking.

Like the film's images, its cinesonic strategy can be contained and domesticated within the discourses of deconstruction. There are few sounds that intrude into the electronica without being used up by it, the laughter of the clown towards the end of the film being the only shot in *Deviant Beauty* to feature true sync sound (Figure 4.20). At one level, the absence of synchronous location sound means the electronic soundtrack is divorced or distanced from the film's images, existing within its own milieu. In this way, the film might be seen to deconstruct the illusionistic modes of audiovisuality that propose a naturalistic relationship between sound and image. But like most sonic constructions situated within an audiovisual context, the independence of Keane's electronica is limited: the sound here is never completely indifferent to the images presented on screen. What, then, is the precise nature of the relationship between Keane's electronic soundtrack, and the film's visual and narrative elements?

In *Deviant Beauty* the formulation of the electronic as noise works in two ways to suggest that a problem lurks beneath the surface of the visual. Firstly, the electronic soundtrack exhibits a glassy indifference to the visual world. Keane explains that electronica was chosen for the soundtrack precisely because the sounds are not naturalistic, and are therefore at some level disconnected from the images: 'the idea of actually having electronic-type music – and shifting that – is the fact is it moves you away from how we normally read these films. It takes us into another space'[17] There is, then, a purposeful disconnection between sound and image that serves to subvert the expectations set up by normative codes of audiovisual construction, and which provides an alternative to dominant modes of cinematic experience. The film creates an audiovisual dualism that suggests to the viewer that the two terms of its binary configuration are not in harmony – that is,

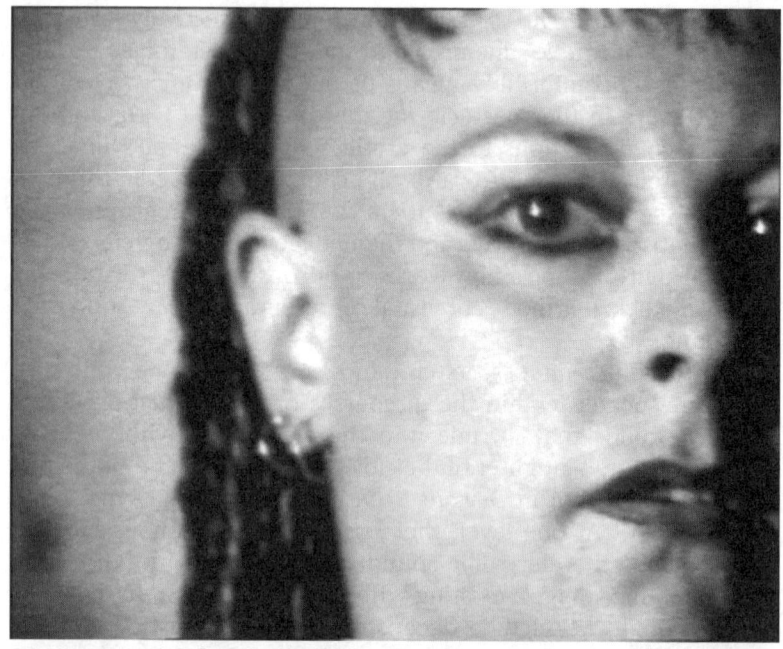

4.19–4.20 *Deviant Beauty*

sound and image are not in accord. This audiovisual detachment generates a distanced, aquarium-like atmosphere in the film, as if Keane's images constitute a world observed through glass. The cinematic result is to render sound and image as two separate streams, operating at different speeds: a disconcerting audiovisual dualism that at once submerges the viewer in this underwater world, while reflecting this estrangement back into the space between the viewer and events on screen.[18] The effect created by the disparity between sound and image is sometimes amplified by Keane's precise choice of electronic sound. For example, in the film's opening sequence, a low-angle shot of the trapeze artist performing in the circus (see Figure 4.12) is accompanied on the soundtrack by a repetitive bass line. The particular timbre of the low-frequency sound used here works to create a feeling of estrangement and distance from the image. In relation to the profilmic and fictive spaces of the film, this is a sound that seems marked by exteriority, which belongs in the background – the kind of sound that emanates from 'elsewhere'. The audiovisual dualism that results creates a sense of gentle turbulence, an eddying that serves to signal to the audiospectator that beneath the alluring surface of the visual, there is something amiss.

The second way in which Keane employs the soundtrack to signal the problematic nature of the visual is by harnessing the traditional, tried-and-tested power of the electronic to suggest an unsettling or even monstrous presence. In *Deviant Beauty*, electronica is used in a straightforward fashion to signify what Keane describes as 'the death and emptiness that lurk beneath the alluring surface'. During the film's opening sequence, as we watch the trapeze artist perform in the circus tent, the rhythmic bass line which constitutes the soundtrack until this point is disturbed by the addition of a descending electronic tone in a higher register. The discordant quality of this portamento sound, and the fact that it is out of sync with the rhythmic bass line, further enhance the status of Keane's electronica as a signifier of noise. Superimposed over a more conventionally musical sound, this electronic tone acts as a form of interference, suggesting the 'noise' that exists behind the seductive glamour of the visual world. By using electronica as a signifier of the monstrous, and by generating audiovisual turbulence through partial disconnection of sound and image, Keane's electronica works to destabilise and deconstruct the visual world encountered by the film's viewers.

In addition to the effect created by the separation of sound and image, moments of audiovisual synchronism work in a conventional way to suggest that some of the film's images should be subject to a particular reading. The first shots of both the protagonist and the menacing clown are marked on the soundtrack by the introduction of a bubbling, rapid electronic figure generated from recordings of running water which, after having been digitally processed, sound something like the tuning of a radio. In both instances, the correspondence of sound and image generated through editing serves to anchor the effect created by this sound at a narrative level. Using a very traditional cinematic device, Keane suggests to the spectator that the characters we are being introduced to are problematic in some way, and that appearances can be deceptive. Like the detuning tone that 'infects' the bass line soundtrack at the start of the film, this particular electronic figure is articulated as a form of noise in relation to the more traditionally musical elements of Keane's electronic soundscape. In synchronising the appearance of these characters with this particular sound, Keane draws upon the codes of classical cinema to construct character, and to signpost narrative and thematic development.

Deviant Beauty's electronic soundtrack works to suggest there are no innocent visual pleasures, and that more is at stake in the subject–object binary formulation of voyeurism that literally meets the eye. This reading of the film sits very comfortably with forty years of deconstructive film theory and practice. However, contrapuntal formulations, oppositional formulations and deconstructive formulations of film share one problem: they are all binary constructs whose worth rests upon the presence of the thing they seek to work against. The value of these formulations lies in their capacity to challenge existing models and structures, but their limitation is that they must always be haunted by these same models and structures, thus forever returning us to the very thing they try to resist. What the practice of deconstruction produces must always therefore be the secondary term in an axiological binarism. In this sense, deconstruction *constructs* nothing – it refers us only to the thing we seek to deconstruct. While allowing the exploration of existing values, the fundamental problem of deconstruction is that it has no way of escaping a locus determined by its target, has no horizon beyond that dictated by the object of deconstruction. As a cinematic practice, deconstruction can only ever be defined in negative terms, and can never escape the systems and codes it seeks to explore or challenge. The essential weakness of this approach is perhaps best summarised by Brecht's elegant teaser, 'What happens to the hole when the cheese is gone?'[19]

After forty years of intensive critical undoing, fuelled by structuralist and post-structuralist theory, how might it be possible to move on to think, and to produce culture, in another register? Within the context of a radical poetics of audiovisuality, how can we rethink the place and role of sound in film and video, and move beyond the deconstructive and oppositional rationales and practices that have dominated avant-garde film for so long?

By drawing on the conceptual resource of noise, it is possible to re-energise certain cinesonic practices that have become conventional, and to reconfigure those theoretical, critical and creative modes that have become trapped in the binary loop of deconstruction. A writerly appropriation of *Deviant Beauty* provides a means by which we might begin to re-engineer theoretical formulations of the cinesonic. As a creative conceptual resource, Keane's film not only allows us to think of ways in which electronic sound might be undomesticated and reradicalised, but also suggests broader alternatives to existing ways of modelling cinema's sound–image relations. It is in its defiance of binary structures that the figure of noise can be used to appropriate *Deviant Beauty*'s audiovisuality, resituating it within a range of cultural and political discourses beyond those implied by the comments of its creator, or proposed by deconstructive film theory. And it is the figure of noise that presents the possibility of reframing electronica, thereby restoring its radical potential within a cinematic context.

We can never return to the electronic its strangeness, and so it will never again be genuinely monstrous; other aspects of noise must therefore be identified and mobilised if the electronic is to be reframed and re-energised within a radical poetics of audiovisuality.

Communication theory formulates noise as that which interrupts a signal; thus, Attali states, 'A noise is a resonance that interferes with the audition of a message in the process of emission' (Attali, 1985: 26). The position on noise adopted by Attali's definition, which is also inherent in Shannon's model of communication (Figure 4.21), views the phenomenon from the perspective of signal, thereby situating noise as somehow secondary, external and separate to the primary element of the communication system. In relation to the signal, noise is therefore figured as the other, always outside, unwelcome and beyond understanding in the terms proposed by the codes that organise communication.

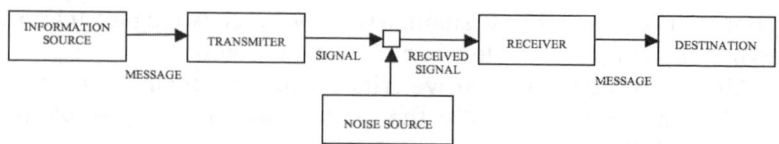

4.21 C. E. Shannon's model of a communication system (1948)

However, this separation of noise and signal is somewhat artificial, since within a communication system noise is carried along with a message, infecting and inhabiting it. So at the same time as being formulated in terms of externality, noise is in some sense also internal. Neither fully one nor the other, noise stands for the outside but is located within. In the terms proposed by the binary pair 'internal–external', noise is undecidable, indeterminate. In this way the model of noise inscribed within a communication system challenges conceptual formulations founded on isolation, individuation, differentiation and essence. It is in this respect that the noise of electronica might pose a radical challenge to simple binary formulations of sound–image relations. And it is in this respect, also, that electronica suggests radical aesthetic and political alternatives to the model of noise as violence, since in addition to being disruptive and violent, noise is also inescapable – it is an inherent part of every system.

The ineluctable modality of noise

In *Deviant Beauty* the continuous presence of the electronic challenges any simple binary formulation of sound–image relations. The film's electronica is insistent, inescapable, and occupies the sonic world of the film to the exclusion of almost all else. The soundtrack is a pervasive viral presence that haunts every image, fills every image, invading the audience's senses. In this way, the relentless electronic soundtrack becomes noise in relation to the image, realising the theoretical possibility considered earlier in relation to the work of John and James Whitney. Keane's electronica maintains a constant *transsensory* presence within the visual throughout the duration of the film. And so while allegiances with characters may change, and while our emotions may shift in response to events presented on screen, the soundtrack continues to infect the visual. In terms of audiovisual construction, *Deviant Beauty* employs a familiar cinesonic formulation, a counterpoint of sound and image, while also using electronica on an entirely conventional level to signify the monstrous. But by rethinking the continuous presence of wall-to-wall electronica in terms of the ineluctable modality of noise, we begin to loosen the grip of dyadic formulations over the film and our understanding of it.

The audiovisual noise generated by the film's soundtrack leads to a recognition and an acceptance of the inescapable turbulence that exists between sound and image. This turbulence is systemic, and is not simply the signifier of a problem that deconstruction invites us to oppose. Infecting the images like a virus, this noise will be forever present; it will sometimes be intimate, sometimes distant, but within the world of *Deviant Beauty*, this electronic sound is *inescapable*. Listened to in this way, the film's cinesonic strategy unlocks the radical potential of the formerly domesticated noise of electronica, letting it loose to inhabit and suffuse the visual experience of looking. It is therefore in relation to audio-visuality, rather than sonic status, that the electronic becomes delinquent once again.

We might now think afresh how the film's formal cinesonic strategy works in relation to Keane's problematisation of visual pleasure. *Deviant Beauty* unequivocally proposes that the specta-tor's scopic drives are not innocent; if we listen to the soundtrack as a contrapuntal or deconstructive device, it signals, in Keane's own words, 'the death and emptiness that lies beneath the alluring surface' (Keane, 2009). It is in this way that the soundtrack plays its part in the film's questioning of 'our expectation of, and pleas-ure in, the image' (Keane, 2009). But auditioned in this way, the film can go no further than constructing certain aspects of visual pleasure and erotic looking in negative terms. If, however, we approach the soundtrack as noise, considering sound–image rela-tions in terms of an audiovisuality of permeation, infiltration and invasion, then the film moves beyond a simple condemnation of visual pleasure to propose that the problematic aspects of specta-torship are continually present, unavoidable and inescapable. Just like noise in a communication system, our own personal desires and motivations are continually present and active, and cannot simply be eradicated by a move to censor or externalise. In this way the film's audiovisuality proposes a productive acceptance of the desires and pleasures that form our scopic drives, however painful such acceptance might be. In the same way that the image is host to the noise of electronica, and in the same way that the image is unable to resist the persistent presence of the elec-tronic, so we are host to those desires and drives that have been formulated as problematic by a particular strand of discourse relating to visual pleasure. Thus, when Keane describes the humiliating laughter of the clown, she might also be describing the way in which the rest of the soundtrack figures the problematics of visual pleasure: 'There's no escape from it. You go out to the landscape, you're running, and you're trying to move away from it, but there it is – it's following you'.[20]

The soundtrack of *Deviant Beauty* negotiates a position on visual pleasure that rejects any simplistic, formulaic stance of negation, contrasting perhaps with the work of Peter Gidal, whose concern with the repressive aspects of representation resulted in the effective exclusion of the human form from his work. In this respect the cinesonics of *Deviant Beauty* assume a position, and work through a logic, that has been identified in the visual aspects of Keane's work by the critic Jean Fisher:

> in the rather censorial climate against visual pleasure and the imaged female body that prevailed during the 1970s there was always something subversive in Keane's refusal to relinquish either; a recognition above all of the necessarily erotic essence of the image, quite distinct from any depictions of flesh, where a mutual seduction between the work's intensities and the gaze of the viewer is the enabling condition for realising a new perception of existence. (Dyer, Fisher and Wollen, 2004: 8–9)

What the electronica of Keane's film can offer is a means by which we can engage with the problematic issue of visual pleasure without simply thinking in terms of negation and opposition. *Deviant Beauty*'s formulation of sound–image relationships works through transsensory permeation rather than the isolation, individuation and differentiation of sound and vision normally encountered in deconstructive film practice. Make no mistake, the film is no celebration of visual pleasure: the protagonist is haunted by the laughter of the clown as she runs away from the Pit and across the landscape at the end of the film. The final images of *Deviant Beauty* are of the white chalk cliffs at Beachy Head, a landmark infamous as a suicide spot. But in the figure of noise, *Deviant Beauty* demonstrates Attali's claim that there is no order that does not contain disorder within itself. If the problematic aspects of visual pleasure are viewed as something that we as spectators must engage with, and work with, rather than something that we should *simply* recognise and oppose, then we place ourselves in a position in which movement replaces stasis, enabling us to think in terms other than those formulated according to the dynamics of the dialectic or binary opposition.

There has been a consistent tendency to think of noise in the arts in predominantly futurist/avant-gardist terms: a modernist conception of noise as shocking, violent and war-like; but the fact is that electronic sounds are no longer shocking. However, they do posses a morphological density that is difficult to resist or escape at a sensory level. The synthetic nature of these sounds gives them the potential of almost infinite duration, presenting a post-human/ inhuman musical sound that defies the familiar bodily narratives of plucking, hitting or blowing. In this sense, electronica exhibits an insistence that is rare in acoustic instrumentation, although heard, for example, in the extended solos of John Coltrane, in which the endless rescrambling of modal phrases creates a barrage of notes that refuses to release the listener from its grasp. Thus, electronica can draw upon its dense, drone-like saturated qualities, as well as its explosive, interruptive properties, to situate itself as a form of noise. What *Deviant Beauty* demonstrates is that if sound can dog us, bug us or perhaps even terrorise by saturation, then conventional cinesonic formulations may still have political power, and even the hackneyed sounds of electronica may find contemporary relevance by reconnecting with their noise potential.

This source of radical potential means it is no longer necessary to think of noise as political simply in terms of the discrete, combative attack (noise as warfare). Noise may also become political through an insistent attack on *identity*, figured in terms of permeation and internal dissolution (noise as terrorism), rather than external deconstruction. Articulated within the context of a radical audiovisual poetics, this reorientation of noise is essentially a move from montage to folding. What this in turn prompts is a conceptual reformulation of sound–image relationships, in which a potentially radical audiovisuality is framed in terms of permeation, rather than the binary differentiation inherent in the image-plus-sound formulations of deconstruction, or the vertical montage of contrapuntality. And herein lies the value of the figure of noise as a way of negotiating audiovisuality, in terms other than those proposed by existing models of sound–image relationships: the ineluctable modality of noise (ever-present within the signal, and constituting the materiality from which the signal temporarily emerges) presents a dyadic formulation that resists binary modalities reliant upon differentiation, mutual exclusivity or opposition. As such, this model of noise provides a way of critically negotiating sound–image relationships that truly engages with the notion of *audiovisuality*.

Refrain

The forms of audiovisuality considered in this chapter suggest that, rather than disentangling the sonic from the visual in both film theory and practice, we should perhaps look for ways in which they can become productively entangled. The relationship between noise and meaning is one of mutual inscription; however, the value attributed to meaning means that we tend to think of noise as being inscribed within and against a signal. But as Michel Serres suggests, and as Freud's formulation of the *unheimlich* proposes, noise is a constant presence. Just as noise is inscribed against meaning, so meaning is inscribed within and against noise. Thus, meaning emerges from noise, which is the total set of all possibilities, all milieus, all materialities. The essential connectedness of the relationship between signal and noise is not easily described – an indivisibility that is addressed by Michel Serres when he writes, 'As soon as a phenomenon appears, it leaves the noise; as soon as a form looms or pokes through, it reveals itself by veiling noise. So noise is not a matter of phenomenology, so it is a matter of being itself' (Serres, 1995: 13). However, Serres' conceptualisation still carries a sense of separation, positing noise as background, signal as foreground. What the notion of audiovisuality requires is a formulation of mutual inscription that describes a symbiotic relationship between image and sound. This relationship of mutual interaction and interdependence forms what Deleuze and Guattari might describe as a 'refrain' – a kind of counterpoint, but one in which its constituent elements can never be separated. As a conceptual formulation, this configuration engages with dyadic constructions (like sound–image relationships), but in a way that resists the binary separation of elements. As a way of figuring sound–image relationships, the refrain offers to the consideration of audiovisuality an engagement with forms of fusion and inseparability. In the next chapter, these notions are brought to bear on a consideration of the audiovisual practice of 'mickey-mousing' – the pejorative term used in the film industry to describe the musical illustration of visual events.

As a cinesonic modality, mickey-mousing has often been seen in negative terms within in classical film practice. However, within other cinesonic contexts, a critical engagement with this practice allows us to think about a form of audiovisuality that differs radically from the model proposed by hegemonic forms of dominant cinema. Here sound is not a significatory supplement to the image, but instead fuses with it, so that the two elements of the audiovisual begin to merge in such a way that they lose their individual identities. To quote Norman McLaren's definition of synaesthesia, the practice of mickey-mousing creates moments when 'the eye hears and the ear sees'.[21] As such, mickey-mousing provides a useful case study for a further examination of conceptual and creative modalities that embrace forms of fusion, and resist differentiation and deconstruction.

In addition to the use of mickey-mousing, the cartoon soundtrack is also marked by forms of audible sonic montage. This particular approach to the construction of the soundtrack violates the norms of classical cinema, which, as Doane (1985) and Altman (1985) suggest, tends to work towards inaudible sound editing through the use of fades and audio dissolves. The compositional practices of mickey-mousing and montage have been celebrated by a number of musicians and writers for their radical musical potential. However, this celebration raises the question of how the supposed radical potential of the cartoon soundtrack fares in the complex intersection of audiovisual relationships that define the cartoon genre, and in particular the correspondence of sound and image pejoratively termed mickey-mousing; how does the cartoon's supposedly radical soundtrack fare when heard within the context of a *Bugs Bunny* or *Road Runner* short?

Notes

1 Research into optical sound synthesis was undertaken both in the Soviet Union and in Western Europe during the 1930s. One of the first to consider the creative use of synthesised sound was the Bauhaus artist Lazlo Moholy-Nagy. In 1933 he produced the experimental film *The Sound ABC*, synthesising sound by printing letters of the alphabet, drawing people's profiles, and placing fingerprints and various other marks and symbols on the soundtrack area of a strip of film. The optical soundtrack was then rephotographed so that its 'images' could be projected simultaneously with the sounds they produced; thus sound and image were generated from the same visual patterns. Around the same time the animator Oskar Fischinger had been carrying out his own experiments in synthetic sound. Fischinger painted geometric shapes onto long scrolls of paper which were then transferred photographically onto an optical soundtrack; also working in Germany,

Rudolph Pfenninger pioneered a similar system of optical synthesis (see Levin, 2003). Comparable experiments were undertaken in the Soviet Union in the early 1930s; a detailed account of these is given by the animator Norman McLaren (see Manvell and Huntley, 1975: 185–193), who also describes his own work in synthetic sound in 'Notes on Animated Sound' (McLaren, 1953). In addition to the experimental work undertaken by filmmakers, a number of composers also became interested in the creative potential of optical sound synthesis. In 1933 the composer and film editor Jack Ellitt independently pioneered a system of synthesis, in which he drew directly onto celluloid to create an optical soundtrack. In the mid-1960s Daphne Oram, the British pioneer of electronic music and founder of the BBC Radiophonic Workshop, employed a similar graphic system for her Oramics machine. This made use of an optical sound reproducer taken from 35mm film equipment to generate sounds from patterns drawn on several strips of film; an overview of the Oramics machine and its use can be found in Oram's *An Individual Note of Music, Sound and Electronics* (1972). Curtis Roads (2001) is one of the few musicologists to acknowledge the role played by film technology in the development of electronic music, making reference to the work of Denis Gabor (the inventor of holography) and his Kinematical Frequency Converter; in the late 1940s Gabor used the optical recording system taken from 16mm film projectors for his own pitch-time experiments (Roads, 2001: 61).

2 Chion defines the acousmetre as 'A kind of voice-character specific to cinema that in most instances of cinematic narratives derives mysterious powers from being heard and not seen' (Chion, 1994: 221). The acousmetre plays an important role in films such as *The Invisible Man*, *The 1000 Eyes of Dr Mabuse* and *The Wizard of Oz*.

3 Brophy describes this sound of cinema in terms of the *electric*. Significantly, his own analysis figures this particular sound in terms of exclusion: 'In its amalgamation of the plastic arts, cinema never experiences a dilemma in foregrounding the painterly, the theatrical, the choreographic, the photographic or the acoustic. All these modes of depiction, their historical artistry and their specific disciplines are regarded as 'cinematic' when they are blended onto the screen. But what about the electric? Cinema shows its electrical circuitry is generally unwanted despite its revelation of its technical being' (Brophy, 2004: 10).

4 For this film McLaren created a library of cards, each bearing a graphic pattern. These were photographed, and printed on film to create an optical soundtrack. Each card had a specific tonal value, and in this way McLaren was able to score the film using a musical approach to composition. The soundtrack produced by McLaren follows the conventions of the animated cartoon genre, making extensive use of

short musical themes, and featuring musical sound effects created to synchronise with action on screen.

5 This article was first published in its original English version in Whitney (1980: 151–155).

6 The film is not currently in distribution, and according to William Moritz the only copy remains the original 8mm reel located in the Whitney vault. In addition to John Whitney's own description of the film, Moritz gives some idea of the experience of watching it in an article on the Whitney Brothers' early work (Moritz, 2006).

7 For example, the use of visual counterpoint in Viking Eggeling's seminal abstract animated film *Diagonal Symphony* (1923–25) can be seen as part of a utopian search for a universal language. The film grew out of Eggeling's collaboration with Hans Richter on the 'orchestration' of linear forms in developmental scroll painting. According to Richter's description, *Diagonal Symphony* is structured on 'the interplay of relationships between lines which he [Eggeling] had arranged . . . in contrapuntal pairs of opposites, within an all-embracing system based in the mutual attraction and repulsion of paired forms' (Richter, 1965: 63). Behind the film's use of spatial and temporal counterpoint lay Eggeling's concern to define a logic that would hold true for all forms of abstract art – a set of 'laws' that would not only be universally applicable, but, more importantly, would create a universally comprehensible visual language. Borrowing the term for the central structuring bass line used in Baroque music, Eggeling's 'thorough-bass of painting' (*Generalbass der Malerei*) was not just a contrapuntal compositional model, but also a utopian attempt to identify a language that transcended national boundaries. See Selwood (1981) for an analysis of the various cultural influences on the development of abstract animated films in Europe.

8 C. E. Shannon's highly influential paper *A Mathematical Theory of Communication* (1948) proposed a general model of communication systems in which noise is introduced *into* a signal as it is relayed from transmitter to receiver.

Although Shannon's model has been developed and revised by a number of theorists, his figuration of noise remains a powerful influence on the way in which the phenomenon is described and understood.

9 'Opera has become the latest weapon employed by Montreal's Metro system to chase off youthful toughs who loaf about downtown stations, demanding spare change from passersby, chain-puffing cigarettes under "No Smoking" signs, cussing, spitting, and generally making life unpleasant for real subway riders. The police can't seem to frighten them away. But Metro officials reckon the late diva Maria Callas or tenor Luciano Pavarotti might just do the trick. Montreal is already claiming success, saying that there are fewer young idlers

strutting about the city's busiest subway station and that regular riders are being hassled less since the opera started booming' (Nickerson, 1998).

10 'Noise and the Uncanny'. Conference paper given at *Cybersonica: International Festival of Music and Sound*, ICA, London, 5–7 June 2002.

11 Such sounds have rarely found their way into western orchestral music, an exception being Varèse s use of a siren in *Amériques* (1918–21); however, here the siren's worldly associations give the sound a programmatic value that reduces the difficulty of accepting it within a western art music tradition.

12 Notions of differentiation and essence are problematised by Bernard Herrmann's score for Hitchcock's *Psycho* (1960). In dressing as his dead mother, speaking in her voice and performing her actions, Norman Bates attempts to challenge and transcend notions of fixed gender, personal identity, the self, the living and the dead. Herrmann's music in the famous shower scene seems to convey what Philip Brophy has termed 'dissonant transsexuality' (Brophy, 2004: 10). But there is more at work here than dissonance; the screaming strings stand in for, and echo, Marion Crane's unheard screams as she is repeatedly stabbed by Bates. Thus Hermann's score disrupts the neat trichotomy of speech, music and effects by blurring the divisions between different types of sound.

13 The film *Catalog* (1961) includes the work Whitney produced during this period with the analogue computer.

14 The four sections are given in Keane's written description of the film, but do not appear in the film itself (see Keane, 2009).

15 T. Keane, interviewed by author, Hackney, London, 17 December 2003.

16 See note 15, above.

17 See note 15, above.

18 The device is memorably employed by Godard in *Alphaville* (1965). A film that operates wholly on dual speeds, Alphaville is set in an anodyne, emotionless future that also stands for the contemporary Paris of 1965. Out of synch with its numbed inhabitants, the private detective protagonist Lemmy Caution is bemused by the spaced-out, government-issue prostitute who appears to be provided with his hotel room. The potentially compromising situation turns out to be a set-up for an assassination attempt. As Caution violently beats his assailant in the bathroom (while the prostitute calmly takes a bath), the soundtrack changes from a high-profile direct sound aesthetic to a simple use of musak. The technique is also used to great effect by Jacques Tati in *M. Hulot's Holiday* (1953). Hulot's innocent enjoyment of jazz records played at high volume disturbs the guests of the hotel engaged in their various peaceful leisure pursuits, bringing them

to converge angrily on the source of the sonic disturbance. Hulot is shown with his back to the camera, peacefully puffing on his pipe as a 78 whizzes on the turntable by his chair, deafening the residents with fiercely up-tempo jazz. In both examples, differential flow of sound and image creates a strangely disconnected visual field. In *Alphaville*, music is truly *anempathetic* – Chion's term for sound that exhibits conspicuous indifference to what is happening in a film's plot (Chion 1994: 221). Thus, Godard's blank-faced musak stands in meaningful opposition to the ultra-violence of the images.

19 *Mother Courage*, scene VI.
20 See note 15, above.
21 McLaren used this phrase to describe his animated film *Synchromy* (1971). Here the graphic patterns created by McLaren on the optical soundtrack, which generate the electronic sounds we hear, are reprinted on the image track to create a synaesthetic audiovisual experience.

5   Mickey-mousing

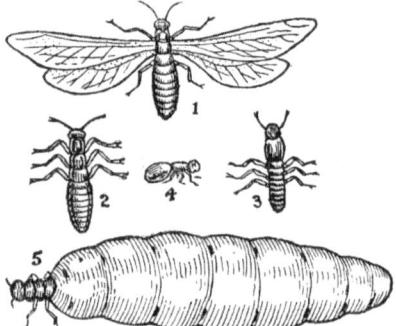

Fig. 1.   1, Winged termite ; 2, wing-
less termite ; 3, soldier ; 4, worker ;
5, female swollen with eggs.

The big stick

Cartoon sound begins with violence, or rather its threat. This
assertion is evidenced by the Warner Bros. cartoons of the 1940s
and 1950s, whose soundtracks are emblematic of the genre. In
tapes of a 1951 studio session recorded for the cartoon *Putty Tat
Trouble*, Warner Bros. arranger Milt Franklyn can be heard tapping
his conductor's baton on a music stand as he summons order from
chaos.[1] The conversation of the fifty or so people assembled in the
recording studio ceases. His rhythmic drumming refrain is a rally-
ing call, a point of focus before engagement with the enemy, or
amid the swirling violence of battle. Romantically, we imagine the
members of the Warner Bros. orchestra united by Franklyn's rhythmic refrain, called to work collaboratively for their art, for the
common good. But the military associations of the baton hint at
control by the threat of violence: nobody wants to be hit with a big

stick. Franklin's refrain is what Gilles Deleuze and Felix Guattari might refer to as a territorial assemblage – this sound marks his territory, declaring those falling within it his subjects, just as the refrain of bird-song marks territory in the natural world.

But these military associations surely run contrary to the cherished image of cartoons as minoritarian, free, anarchic, liberating, anti-establishment and all the rest of it. After all, the chat that Franklyn silences is one of excitement, of enthusiastic anticipation – these recording sessions represented a break from routine for the musicians involved:

> **Carl Stalling**: The musicians said they enjoyed the cartoons more than anything else. They looked forward to coming down to record the cartoons. It was screwy stuff, you know. (Barrier, 1971: 26)
>
> **Scott Bradley**: I hope Dr. Schoenberg will forgive me for using *his system* to produce funny music, but even the boys in the orchestra laughed when we were recording it. (Bradley, 2002a: 118)
>
> **Bob Clampett**: Many's the time that Carl [Stalling], Treg [Brown] and I waited while the fifty-piece Warner Bros. orchestra would finish recording the score for a Bogart or Bette Davis feature, and then bat out one of my *Bugs Bunny* or *Porky* shorts. When Leo Forbstein [the orchestra's director] told them to put our cartoon score on their stands, a wave of relief would spread through the entire orchestra. Suddenly, two violinists would pop up and begin duelling with their bows, or some such horseplay. Others would call out things in jest, and by the time Carl stepped to the podium, raised his baton and they broke into the unnaturally rapid tempo of our *Merrie Melodies* theme song ('*Merrily We Roll Along*'), or subtitle, or whatever, they would be in a completely different mood for Bugs than for Bogey. (Barrier, 1971: 26)

Although cartoons occupy a central and inescapable place in popular culture, they are nevertheless in some ways marginalised in relation to the classical Hollywood film text; the animated cartoon is undoubtedly a major minor form. This minor mode grants it a certain audiovisual licence, enabling the cartoon to resist the hegemonic and largely significative models of sound–image relations proposed by mainstream narrative fiction film. However, the cartoon's marginal status does not simply turn on its resistance to normative modes of audiovisual construction, but also finds expression in animation's position within an industrial context. At Warner Bros. during the 1930s and 1940s, animation represented a craft practice of a particularly labour-intensive

kind, a cottage industry resistant to mass production and mecha-
nisation, situated somewhat uncomfortably within an expanding
multinational corporation. Famously opposed to the demarcation
of labour demanded by industrial film production practices, the
Warner Bros. animator Tex Avery dispensed with a scriptwriter,
preferring instead to write his own stories, and insisted on maintaining control over as much of the laborious process of animation
as possible, rather than delegating to assistants. The cartoon's
marginal status is also made manifest by the relative paucity of
critical writing on both the genre and its creators.[2] As John Robert
Tebbel has commented, Chuck Jones was one of the few animators who lived long enough 'to bask in a little overdue glory, after
having completed his greatest works in nearly complete obscurity'
(Tebbel, 1992: 64).

It is this marginality that might just have made it possible for
animation to escape the stultifying grasp of the studio, its execu-
tives, its power systems, its financial goals and its stars. It is this
marginality that gives permission for the *Pepe le Pew* project: a
sustained and consistent body of work exploring and celebrating
the malodorous, a project that could only have been undertaken
within the cartoon genre. It would be unthinkable to see or hear
the effects of Bogart or Bette Davis breaking wind, whereas when
Tex Avery farted he instructed an associate to 'catch that one and
paint it green' (Jones, 1999: 102).

The location of the animation department on the Warner Bros.
back lot fixes this cultural marginality in spatial terms. Renamed
by those working there as 'Termite Terrace', the animation department was mythically populated by geeky freaks. Avery was so
driven by his work he would resist the urge to urinate, resulting
in a regular sprint from his desk to reach a lavatory before he lost
bladder control. He once left it too long and ended up in hospital.
The animators' entomic address, evoking poverty and decay, is a
self-mythologisation, an appropriation by the animators of their
place at the margins, situating them as virtual outsiders within the
Hollywood studio system. Avery's bladder-driven antics express
the best in marginal behaviour: eccentric, oppositional, uncontainable within corporate culture, a bit of an embarrassment and,
above all, funny – like the silent, imagined farts never dropped
by Bogart. This marginality helps to construct for the cartoon a
minoritarian, counter-cultural status, which subsequently becomes
not only part of the cartoon's identity and cultural value, but
also, paradoxically, its commercial worth. The popular appeal of

animation, and hence its financial success, was in part due to the unruly image constructed for it by the animators themselves, cultivated in the public imagination through newspaper and magazine publicity. As Hank Sartin has pointed out, 'The popular press was happy to perpetuate these myths of the rebellious marginalized auteurs of the cartoon studio' (Sartin, 1998: 83).

Tex Avery's refreshingly literal line of flight is thought through sonically in the cartoon music of Carl Stalling, Musical Director for Warner Bros. animation from 1936 to 1958. It is predominantly through Stalling's termite music that I would like to consider the syntactic and morphological aspects of the cartoon genre, focusing particularly on the interaction of sound and image. In this sense I would like to turn my attention to the film text, not as a source of meaning, but rather as a material assemblage – a text woven from sound and image. There were, and are of course, notable and accomplished composers other than Stalling working in animated cartoons, whose work merits critical consideration. However, for the aesthetic and financial reasons explored later in this chapter, Stalling's own particular approach to composition threw the practices of quotation and montage, which I hold to be emblematic of the cartoon genre, into much sharper relief than the music of his best-known contemporary, MGM's Scott Bradley.

Ideas about the relationship between the sonic and the visual are thought through and manifest themselves differently in each historical period and film genre, but what is perhaps significant about the cartoon is its radical departure from the cinesonic model proposed by classical cinema, with its well-modulated, well-behaved and self-effacing soundtrack. And if film sound itself has traditionally occupied a marginal position in relation to the image, in terms of both production and criticism, then Stalling's Termite Art,[3] as subset of a subset, stands at the very outer limits of the world of mainstream cinema. However, does this marginality really allow the development or implementation of radical sonic practices, as some commentators have suggested?

> Separating his music from the images it was created to support, it becomes clear that Stalling was one of the most revolutionary visionaries in American music – especially in his conception of time. In following the visual logic of screen action rather than the traditional rules of musical form (development, theme, variations, etc.), Stalling created a radical compositional arc unprecedented in the history of music. (Zorn, 1990)

By what right, to what ends, and with what consequences do we follow John Zorn's suggestion of separating Stalling's music from the images it was composed to accompany? Stalling's use of montage, fragmentation and forms of dissonance might well place his compositional practice comfortably alongside the more overtly radical art practices associated with cubism, futurism, Soviet Montage, hip-hop, turntablism and video scratching, but how does the supposed radical potential of his music fare in the complex intersection of audiovisual relationships that define the cartoon genre?

Mickey-mousing

Sonic montage and the correspondence of sound and image are two tropes that are emblematic of Stalling's compositional practice. While the radical value of montage has been recognised in many art forms, the close correspondence of music and image in the audiovisual text has traditionally been denigrated and resisted, particularly in classical cinema. As an audiovisual practice, the sonic illustration of visual events referred to as 'mickey-mousing' is most often discussed in terms of 'redundancy', a notion that dogs proper discussion of sound–image relationships. This close matching of musical sound to the moving image has been consistently framed in negative terms. Scott Curtis observes, 'mickey-mousing seems to carry a pejorative meaning, both because of the lower status animated cartoons have traditionally held in film studies and because of the implication that exact illustration is a rather tedious and silly way to relate music and image' (Curtis, 1992: 201). Mickey-mousing is seen as poor practice; it is considered unsubtle, unnecessary, and creates humour when none is required. Max Steiner, whose status in the history of cinema is indicated by the fact that he is popularly referred to as the 'father of film music', arrived in Hollywood in 1929, and in a career that spanned four decades scored many major movies, including *King Kong* (1933), *Gone With the Wind* (1939), *Casablanca* (1942) and *The Searchers* (1956). Drawing heavily on the conventions of nineteenth-century European concert music, Steiner's lush orchestral scores did much to popularise the model of string-dominated melodic composition that came to dominate the soundtrack of classical Hollywood cinema. However, Steiner's otherwise unassailable reputation is blemished by his use of mickey-mousing. The following, from Irwin Bazelon's *Knowing the Score: Notes on Film Music* (1975), gives a clear indication of how this compositional practice has typically been viewed within the field of film music criticism:

> Steiner was one of the first practitioners of the device known in the trade as 'Mickeymousing' . . . Steiner had a special weakness for this practice, which often vulgarized the scenes he was scoring. Using highly illustrative music to echo the action and mood of the film, he translated into musical terms the very movements depicted on the screen – sometimes in precise synchronization. This redundancy – the viewer already sees the action unfolding before him – acts as a distraction, amplifying its own musical shortcomings. By constantly calling attention to itself, the Mickeymoused score becomes offensive and tiresome. (Bazelon, 1975: 24)

In addition to characterising mickey-mousing as 'vulgar' and 'redundant', and formulating Steiner's interest in it as a 'weakness', Bazelon also suggests that it is a primitive form of audiovisual expression, its practice representing a state of cultural and artistic under-development: 'It is easy to take a pejorative attitude toward the technique of Mickeymousing, but one must think of the practice in terms of its time. In those days nobody really understood anything about film music, and the filmmakers themselves were often as musically naive as their audience' (Bazelon, 1975: 25). In a similar vein, the composer Maurice Jaubert, writing on Steiner's use of mickey-mousing in John Ford's *The Informer* (1935), comments:

> Apart from its childishness, such a procedure displays a total lack of understanding of the very essence of music. Music is by nature continuous, organized rhythmically in time. If you compel it to follow slavishly events or gestures which are themselves discontinuous, not rhythmically ordered but the outcome simply of physiological or psychological reactions, you destroy in it the very quality by virtue of which it is music, reducing it to its primary condition of crude sound. (Jaubert, 1938: 108)

Here Jaubert objects to the fact that mickey-mousing responds to a set of determinants that are external to the established codes and structures of music itself, his critique articulating a belief that musical sounds should be organised according to a strictly musical logic.

While the critical reaction to the use of mickey-mousing in live-action drama might be understandable, given the dominance of other compositional modes used in film, what is surprising is that even within the small body of writing dedicated to cartoon music, mickey-mousing has also been framed in negative terms. Writing in 1949 on the role of the cartoon composer, Ingolf Dahl characterises the practice as musical illustration, advising, 'the degree to which illustration is lifted above the purely mechanical duplication of action depends . . . on the inventiveness of the composer' (Dahl, 1974: 187). Reflecting on the trends in contemporary scoring for animation, Dahl bemoans the fact that 'music is added to a predetermined course of hectic events and is in many cases required to do nothing more than duplicate the action by synchronous illustration, taking the role of sound effect together with the role of musical characterization' (Dahl, 1974: 184). Once again, the sense here is that mickey-mousing is somehow inferior to other compositional strategies, other ways of relating sound to image, and importantly, what seems to underpin Dahl's objection is the belief that music should *not* duplicate or illustrate the visual.

However, behind the value judgement commonly applied to this practice is the understanding that a sound can 'illustrate' an image, and that forms of audiovisual matching can be marked by degrees of closeness. Hence, music can follow the image *too* closely, and a composer like Steiner can be found guilty of mickey-mousing. But what exactly is it that determines this adhesion of sound to image, and what are the audiovisual parameters of mickey-mousing?

Musical morphology and the refrain

Perhaps unsurprisingly, the dominant modes of analysis brought to bear on sound–image relations in cinema tend to focus on film music's narrative functions. In their location of sound within significatory networks of meaning, these critical models lack the means by which to deal with material relations between sound and image. However, the notion of morphology, understood here in the sense of 'shape' as development over time, provides a useful conceptual resource with which we might better understand the phenomenon of mickey-mousing. By focusing on the morphological profiles of both sound and image, and the relationship between them, it becomes possible to conceptualise the material dimensions of the audiovisual text in ways that are not possible with significative modes of analysis.

First and foremost, what the notion of morphology brings to a study of sound–image relations is recognition of the temporal nature of the cinematic text. It is specifically the parallel development of sound and image within a temporal frame, rather than any other form of audiovisual correspondence, that produces the effect of mickey-mousing. If a film score were to be written in which a visual quality of texture was accompanied by some sonic equivalent, this would not be considered mickey-mousing, but probably good practice. Accordingly, it is unlikely that Vittorio Gelmetti's electronic score for *Il Deserto Rosso* (1964) would attract this label, despite the fact that the music seems to express feelings of intensity or diffusion that are also articulated simultaneously by the film's images – as, for example, in the scene in which the internal psychological state of the film's protagonist, Giuliana, finds expression in the amorphous coloured forms that appear on the walls of her bedroom, while at the same time the soundtrack's electronic tones convey a similar emotional mood. Rather, it is when *change* occurs within a temporal frame that mickey-mousing takes place. In this way, the term could be applied to Gelmetti's score if a *change* in the visual texture of the image was somehow mirrored by a change on the soundtrack. However, the term is almost exclusively identified with movement of and in the image, rather than other visual qualities. In response to visual movement the composer can vary tone, texture, timbre, amplitude, rhythm and other dimensions of sound to match the images on screen.

The notion of morphology offers a useful way of recognising, describing and tracking sonic and visual development within a temporal frame. In their work on musical morphology, Siegmund Levarie and Ernst Levy have attempted to understand musical phenomena in relation to fundamental structural principles, proposing that pairs of concepts such as growth and limitation, division and reconciliation, multiplicity and unity, can be applied to an analysis of music. Furthermore, they contend that musical events connect to physical and emotional experience through shared morphological profiles: 'A basic premise underlying all considerations is the correspondence of outer phenomena and inner experiences. This psycho-physical parallelism, implied or stated, may refer to the composer and his work, or to the work and the listener – it is always assumed to be present' (Levarie and Levy, 1983: ix). In this way they suggest that music has the ability to follow the 'motions and emotions' of the soul, because emotions, like music, present a morphological profile, and can thus be viewed as expressions of underlying principles of action–reaction, activity–response, increasing and decreasing levels of speed and power, and so on (Levarie and Levy, 1983: 4). According to Levarie and Levy, the shape or form of a phenomenon has resonance for the listener, since, through a form of psycho-physical parallelism, it is registered against 'inner experiences'. For example, the writers propose that cadence is a primary rhythmic event, central to their morphological formulation of music: 'cadence is the life form of music. It is its vital form' (Levarie and Levy, 1983: 93). In terms of morphology, they observe that the notion of cadence presupposes the existence of a departure point, an arrival point and an energetic process connecting the two. Thus, in its initial impulse, and subsequent tension and relaxation, cadence shares the morphological profile that characterises breathing form: 'Breathing proceeds as a life impulse from zero, accumulates energy during the tension of inhaling, and spends it during the relaxation of exhaling. Breathing is in effect the physiological symbol of the primordial form of an energetic process. Music is essentially energetic; it manifests itself through movement' (Levarie and Levy, 1983: 93). While not claiming that respiratory cadences provide the universal foundations of music, the writers propose that the energetic process that breathing form follows can also underlie musical development. For Levarie and Levy there exists, in the morphological figure of the building and relaxation of tension, a fundamental connection between rhythm, psychological experience and the physiological bodily processes of respiration and circulation. It is through its structural arrangement that music is therefore able to express or create different moods.

Levarie and Levy's work represents an ambitious attempt to map and analyse a large range of musical forms against a limited number of morphological principles, and while their analyses may be personal and provocative, their underlying structuralist approach is not unfamiliar. This structuralist tradition, and the assumptions it makes and relies upon, can be seen to underpin many other studies of music. For example, in an analysis of the ways in which musical soundtracks influence audience perception of filmed events, Marilyn Boltz (2001) characterises a number of pieces of music as expressing either a positive mood or a negative, suspenseful mood, which in turn she attributes to structural parameters. 'In general', she comments, 'negative music displayed a minor mode, atonality, and an irregular rhythm. Conversely, the positive music displayed a major mode, a consistent tonality scheme, and a very predictable rhythm' (2001: 434). If, in adopting a structural approach, the observations Boltz has to offer seem rather uncontentious, it is perhaps because these notions are so engrained within the craft of music. When a composer inscribes the word *misterioso* onto a score, they not only signal a feeling to be evoked, but also imply a technique to be employed – the two become indistinguishable. For the film composer, to be told that 'negative' music displays a minor mode, atonality and irregular rhythm, is not to be told very much. The inherent limitation of structural approaches to the study of music is the fact that the identification of a connection between structure and effect does not necessarily provide a satisfactory explanation of the processes at work; as is said in the disciplines of science and statistics, correlation does not imply causality. This form of analysis runs the risk of simply providing a parallel figuration that describes musical phenomena in other terms, rather than offering any meaningful critical insight. Thus, the explanation offered by Marvin Hatley, composer of the Laurel and Hardy theme tune, that 'The clash of the major second intervals is what makes it funny' (Shadduck, 1974: 179) is in some respects hardly an explanation at all, since it gets us no closer to understanding the way in which music creates an effect on the listener; Hatley's explanation simply raises the question, 'why is the clash of major second intervals funny?'

The potential limitations of morphology as a simple tool of parallel figuration are perhaps recognised by Levarie and Levy in their attempt to move beyond the identification of common structures by attributing them with significance and value. For these authors, the knowability of repeated structures stands against an abstract world of universal and absolute change: a world without order, a world of chaos that would be unknowable. It is, then, in its resistance to chaos that musical form takes on value. Thus, in their analysis of 'barbarianism' they write, 'From the unformed world of sound, such unadorned phenomena as noise, continuous pitch variation, and asystematic chance relations have been eliminated to reach the threshold of music' (Levarie and Levy, 1983: 73). For Levarie and Levy, music summons order from chaos. The order that results is seen as inherently positive, and thus much of their analysis of musical form equates morphology with life forces and energy.

In contrast to observable musical phenomena, it is perhaps harder to establish the nature of the 'inner experience' with which the morphological profile of a musical event supposedly resonates. While it is usually possible to observe parallels or connections between textual morphology and physiological or psychological states ('that music is driving me mad' and 'it's nice when it stops'), what Levarie and Levy offer as explanations of this connection are necessarily speculative. However, rather than considering specific points of contact with 'inner experience', or identifying the affective payload of a particular morphological figure, Levarie and Levy's formulation of morphology can be used to frame an analysis of audiovisual *materiality*. If it is possible to recognise morphological states in changes taking place over time, then changes in sound and image may share abstract similarities that serve to link both together; that is, the notion of morphology creates the possibility of making a material connection between two phenomena with the same morphological profile. What links sound to image in mickey-mousing is thus some degree of similarity between the morphological attributes of both sound and image: Wile E. Coyote sinks into the mud to the sound of a slide trombone.

While it might seem that the primary value of the notion of musical morphology is limited to its descriptive potential – producing the sort of parallel figuration criticised earlier – it can nevertheless serve as a starting point for critical analysis. By articulating morphology through the formulations of territorialisation proposed by Deleuze and Guattari, the notion can be productively applied to a consideration of the way in which sound–image relationships play through the motifs of control and containment that mark the cartoon. The notion of sonic morphology allows a critical engagement with the play between the radical potential of cartoon sound and the genre's broader audiovisual regime. While Levarie and Levy might suggest that music summons order from chaos, in their own work this emergent order remains an unexplored, fundamental positive: music equals civilisation, music equals life. However, in its Deleuzian formulation, morphology can be considered in spatio-political terms through the figure of the refrain – the equivalent, perhaps, of Levarie and Levy's cadence. Deleuze and Guattari conceptualise the refrain, like that of bird-song, as territorial; the refrain is a territorial assemblage. This concept of territorialisation proves useful in relation to a consideration of sound–image relationships, since it provides a way of thinking about the ways in which the film, as an audiovisual construct, claims its 'territory' from both sound and image. In the essay *1837: Of the Refrain*, Deleuze and Guattari (1988: 310–350) propose that territory is borrowed from milieus; and in considering an audiovisual construct like the film, we can adopt and transpose this Deleuzian formulation to think of sound and image as two separate milieus. Moment by moment, the film bites its territory from sound and image. Within the terms of the contract between sound and image required by the film, there are a number of possible relationships that can order cinesonic audiovisuality; but significantly, what the cartoon genre presents are moments when sound and image *echo to the same refrain* – moments of mickey-mousing.

The Deleuzian notion of the refrain brings to a consideration of morphology those issues of power and control that underpin the concept of territory. In contrast to the work of Levarie and Levy, this allows an exploration of what is *at stake* in the territorialising order imposed by morphological figures such as the refrain. Applied to a consideration of audiovisuality, the concepts of territorialisation and deterritorialisation provide a means to consider the ways in which the relationship between radical potential and containment plays through the cartoon; that is, how the notion of territorialisation engages with a micropolitics of audiovisuality. In order to explore the issues opened up by the critical potential of morphology, it is necessary to gain a fuller understanding of the elements that constitute the cartoon soundtrack, and the production practices that determine their articulation within an audiovisual context.

Sound practice

It is important to remember that the term mickey-mousing is derived from the practice of scoring for animated films, the assumption being that in cartoons music very closely matches what takes place on screen. However, this single term fails to acknowledge the variety of relationships that exist between sound and image in Stalling's Termite Art, or in Bradley's Cat-and-Mouse Music. It is possible to distinguish between two types or classes of musical sounds used by Stalling, which are to a certain extent emblematic of the cartoon genre: namely, quotation and musical sound effects.

Quotation

Of all aspects of cartoon music, the use of musical quotation is the best documented, particularly in terms of Stalling's own approach to composition.[4] The practice of scoring for cartoons, at least as it was done at Warner Bros. in the 1940s and 1950s, owes a great deal to the formal model of silent film accompaniment, and it is significant that Stalling began his career as a silent film accompanist and orchestra leader. Interviewed by Mike Barrier, Stalling commented on his own approach to scoring for films, 'I had played in theaters for about twenty years before sound came in. We improvised all the time, on the organ. I'd have to put music out for the orchestra, for features, but for comedies and newsreels we just improvised at the organ. So I really was used to composing for films before I started writing for cartoons. I just imagined myself playing for a cartoon in the theater, improvising, and it came easier' (Barrier, 1971: 26). In the era of so-called 'silent' cinema, an accompanist like Stalling would have had access to thematic musical catalogues that included pieces of music indexed by mood, situation, genre and so on.[5] A skilled accompanist, relying either on sheet music or on memory and experience, would be able to switch between various pieces, improvising to the image on screen. When Stalling was not supplied with a full score for a band or orchestra, which later became the trend for big-budget movies from the late 1910s onwards, his job as an orchestra leader was to act as a montagist, compiling short sections of various genres of music to create a score for his players, while as an accompanist he would have improvised a similar montage from fragments of music committed to memory. Whether or not the sequence of short musical pieces was well prepared and rehearsed, in the case of a single accompanist playing organ or piano the effect would be of the music chasing the image, taking its cue from the action, while at the same time interpreting and fixing the meaning of what was projected on the screen. In some sense, then, music improvised for silent film must logically echo the image, since its starting point is the accompanist's reading of the film's visuals. This practice lends itself to forms of audiovisual doubling, particularly in those instances where the refrain of the music transmutes into a synchronous effect; for example, when rhythm is used to accompany dancing on the screen. Thus, sonic montage and the correspondence of sound and image, which were later to characterise the cartoon, were an accepted part of cinema's audiovisual vocabulary prior to the introduction of synchronous sound recording.

In addition to writing original cues and using music in the public domain, at Warner Bros. Stalling was also able to draw upon the studio's extensive library of music when composing a soundtrack. The studio produced two series of cartoons during Stalling's tenure: *Looney Tunes*, which ran from 1930, and *Merrie Melodies*, which began the following year. Originally, *Merrie Melodies* was designed specifically to feature songs from the Warner library, and it was one of the responsibilities of the cartoon composer to include at least one complete chorus of a tune owned by the studio (Schneider, 1994: 39). This constraint was designed in part to help

Warners recoup the $8.5 million it had spent in 1929 buying music publishing companies, in anticipation of the success of sound film (Curtis, 1992: 193). What this meant was that Stalling's scores often quoted well-known pieces of popular music.

The relationship between cartoons and popular music had been important, even before the introduction of sound. A manual for film accompanists written by Edith Lang and George West in 1920 contains the following advice on animated cartoons and slap-stick comedy:

> This part of the show is admirably adapted to the introduction of all sorts of popular songs and dances. The player should keep in touch with the publications of popular music houses, since it will repay him to establish a reputation which will make the public say: 'Let's go to the Star Theatre – you always hear the latest tune there.' This will prove a never-failing drawing card for the younger generation of movie-fans, and it will react most decidedly to the advantage of the organist in his relation to box-office and his own earning power. It is well also to keep in touch with the monthly announcements of the latest phonograph records issued. As a rule, these numbers have proved assured successes, and people like to hear their favorite tunes, either those they already have at home, or new ones which they might want to add to their collection. The player's repertoire should always be kept alive by the infusion of new and up-to-date material. (Lang and West, 1970: 37)

The guidance given in the passage above suggests the potentially beneficial nature of the relationship between popular music and cartoons: cartoons plugged music, and music attracted audiences to the theatre. For Warner Bros., who were both music publishers and the producers of cartoons, the inclusion of music from their own library made sound economic sense. However, within the context of cartoon production, the jazz-influenced popular music of the 1930s and 1940s may have had significance beyond its commercial worth. During this era jazz music was, first and foremost, dance music, and it is the rhythm-driven physicality of dance that often *animates* the cartoon, especially in the films of the early sound era. Here it is not only people and animals that move to the rhythm of the jazz soundtrack, but also machines, buildings, plants and trees. Jazz's relationship with dance thus maps onto the centrality of mickey-mousing within the cartoon genre.

Jazz also serves to mark the development and differentiation of cartoon forms. The Disney aesthetic had already begun to reveal its cultural aspirations through the use of classical music in the

Silly Symphony films. This series, which began in 1929 and ran through the 1930s, had originally been developed in collaboration with Stalling before he moved to Warner Bros., and was conceived as a project in which music would be the primary term of the audiovisual relationship. Disney's choice of the word 'Symphony' stands in stark contrast to Warner's more overtly populist use of (Looney) 'Tunes' and (Merrie) 'Melodies', and represents a cultural difference that is echoed in other aspects of the two studios' approaches to animation. Thus, Disney's films aspire to the naturalism of the stage and the live-action film, while the Warner Bros. cartoons are more obviously heir to the cartoon strip and vaudeville. Disney works towards a form of illusionistic representation that includes the use of relatively naturalistic backgrounds, and, to add a further naturalistic dimension to the animated image, developed the multiplane camera, which enabled the separation of foreground images from various layers of background, creating a photographic depth of field that gave the illusion of depth in space. Disney's dissatisfaction with the two-dimensionality of the animated cartoon is further evidenced by his plans for *Fantasia* as a form of expanded cinema. He had considered producing the abstract *Toccata and Fugue* sequence in 3-D, and according to Culhane (1983: 10) had even discussed the possibility of diffusing the smell of flowers through the theatre to provide further sensory depth to the flower ballet sequence. The desire to resist the spatial limitations of the cartoon form found sonic expression in Disney's Fantasound system. Developed specially for *Fantasia*, this sound system employed three tracks of audio played over multiple speakers to create an early form of stereophonic surround-sound (Garity and Hawkins, 1941; Garity and Jones, 1942), thereby enveloping the audience within the audiovisual experience of the film, rather than situating them as spectators of a proscenium-style presentation.

If Disney's space becomes increasingly naturalistic, then it is occupied by a Mickey Mouse who becomes decreasingly plastic and malleable, and whose original rambunctious energy is replaced by a thoughtful sweetness. Contrast this with the flat, graphically pared-down world of the Warner Bros. animated cartoon, in which a character's malevolent energy finds expression in the destruction and deformation of their environment and their peers. Disney aspires to be judged according to the polite, old-world standards set by the European model of classical music, his most obvious bid for approval being *Fantasia*. On the other hand, in its sampling of popular music, and in the vital heterogeneity of its sonic montage, the Warner Bros. soundtrack seems to represent a slice of authentic Americana.

Various forms of interpolation, later to be celebrated in the euphoric terms of post-modern intertextuality, were common in studio productions of this era. Songs which had proved popular in one film would appear in others, regardless of the narrative context in which they might have originally been situated. So, for example, the hit song 'White Christmas', which was originally performed in the Paramount film *Holiday Inn* (1942), was reused in the 1954 film that adopted the song's title as its own. Similarly, studio stars like Bogart and the Marx Brothers made occasional 'guest appearances' in animated cartoons. Thus, Stalling's use of musical quotation was just one example of the intertextuality that was widely accepted within commercial film production during this period.

The use of musical quotation served several functions within the animated cartoon. Firstly, there is the use of specific named pieces of music that by convention are associated with particular events or situations; for example, Mendelssohn's *Wedding March*, or the all-purpose circus music of Fuččik's *Entry of the Gladiators* march. Then there are those pieces in a generic style that refer to specific activities or environments – fanfares, military marches, lullabies – and it is here that pastiche often moves into parody for comic effect. However, it is not just in its reference to, and its departure from, a known musical source that the quotation of music can create humour. Additionally, any composition might exploit what Boltz (2001) refers to as the 'structural elements of music' to generate a humorous effect. Thus, Jim Shadduck comments on part of Marvin Hatley's score for the Laurel and Hardy feature *Way Out West* (1937), 'In this sequence he used a lot of sickly, whiney oboe music to accompany the awkwardness' (Shadduck, 1974: 181), while on Hatley's famous Laurel and Hardy theme tune Shadduck proposes 'The top bugle-call-like theme represents Hardy, very domineering and the constant coo-coo part in the base represents little Stan Laurel, just a little off. They are dissonant together, always arguing' (Shadduck, 1974: 179).

In addition to the quotations that provide material for pastiche and parody, cartoons often sampled particular pieces of music because of the joke made by the relationship between their titles and the action on screen. For example, Stalling quotes the tune 'I'm Looking Over a Four Leaf Clover' as Roadrunner and Coyote

5.1 *Fast and Furry-ous*

run around a cloverleaf motorway intersection in *Fast and Furry-ous* (1949) (Figure 5.1). This particular approach to musical quotation has attracted the attention of a number of writers, including John Robert Tebbel (1992), Dick Blackburn (1990) and Daniel Goldmark (1997). Tebbel is critical of Stalling's compositional practice in this respect, suggesting that his habitual matching of song title to picture became trite, while the animator Chuck Jones, with whom Stalling worked for many years, commented that the composer would sometimes use songs that were no longer in the popular memory, thus making a joke that the audience would never get. In reference to Stalling's use of 'I'm Looking Over a Four Leaf Clover', Jones comments, 'It was kind of strange to me for him to do it, and it was okay, but I didn't think everybody knew that it was that music' (Goldmark, 1997). In contrast, however, other commentators have been more positive about this particular sampling technique. Stalling habitually quoted the virtually unknown song 'A Cup of Coffee, a Sandwich and You' as all-purpose food music, and both Goldmark (1997) and Friedwald (2002) argue that although an audience might not pick up on the specific references made by a song's title, if it is used often enough the audience will nevertheless make an unconscious connection between the few bars of a musical motif and the action on screen. While Goldmark characterises this as a gag in itself, Friedwald situates this form of quotation within the development of Stalling's compositional practice:

> As Stalling's tenure stretched from years into decades, he increasingly depended on the ability of the audience to decode his musical hieroglyphics and shorthand, and would fragment these familiar leitmotifs into ever tinier and tinier pieces of the musical mosaic. Just as Tex Avery made a systematic study of the ultimate minimum number of frames needed for an audience to comprehend a visual gag, Stalling could transmit a musical joke or idea with an ever-decreasing number of notes. (Friedwald, 2002: 139)

Friedwald's description of Stalling's technique suggests an aesthetic that is increasingly marked by two potentially radical musical strategies: firstly, the deconstruction and fragmentation of existing musical forms, and secondly, the use of montage as the means by which these fragments are articulated. To this list of potentially progressive musical practices we might also add the figure of quotation itself. The use of quotation as an intertexual strategy was not unknown in music before this time, as is demonstrated by Rachmaninov's *Rhapsody on a Theme of Paganini*, and the various reworkings of folk songs undertaken by generations of composers. However, a number of aspects of Stalling's particular formulation of musical quotation distinguish his use of this device from that of his forebears and peers. Stalling's use of quotation is largely indifferent to the source music: there is no totemic relationship with an original composition or its composer, nor is any attempt made to identify or align Stalling with a real or imagined community of artists. This contrasts with the classical sampling of folk song, or the reworking of well-known musical themes, whereby a composer seeks to celebrate, and perhaps romanticise, a social class, a real or imagined historical moment, a particular individual and so on. In this respect, Stalling's sampling also contrasts with that practised in contemporary hip-hop and turntablism. The cultural critic Diedrich Diederichsen[6] has suggested that artists working in these genres tend to be close to the material being quoted, to the extent that the act of sampling may be seen in some ways as an act of homage to the work of previous generations of musicians. Thus, the breakbeat is more than a convenient rhythmic device – it is a form of tribute, even if cannibalistic. As the DJ Matthew Herbert (aka Radio Boy) has commented, 'people only sample good stuff. They only sample Marvin Gaye, Curtis Mayfield and Miles Davis. People don't sample Andrew Lloyd Weber or Gilbert and Sullivan.

They'll sample brilliance from the past, and inherit some of that brilliance that lives on in those recordings'.[7] Stalling is only close to the material he samples in the sense that he must have been as a silent film accompanist, and as a working composer who turned out a score every ten days for twenty-two years at Warner Bros. For Stalling, source material is simply material at hand to be stretched, squashed and cut up, just as the people and animals that populate these cartoons are reduced to malleable, violently abused and abusable objects by the image track. Processed by the Stalling machine, the work of the great classical composers fares no better than anything else. Everything – popular music, Tin Pan Alley, folk, jazz and classical – is chopped up, deconstructed, reshaped and reconstructed in a montage of interspersed fragments. For John Zorn, this indifference to the traditional hierarchy of musical forms both identifies and recommends Stalling's compositional practice:

> On first hearing, Stalling's immense musical talents are immediately apparent, and certainly all these basic musical elements are there – but they are broken into shards: a constantly changing kaleidoscope of styles, forms, melodies, quotations, and of course the 'Mickey Mousing' . . . No musical style seemed beyond his reach – and his willingness to include them, any and all, whenever necessary (and never gratuitously, I might add) implies an openness – a non-hierarchical musical overview – typical of today's younger composers, but all too rare before the mid-1960s. All genres of music are equal – no one is inherently better than the other – and with Stalling, all are embraced, chewed up and spit out in a format closer to Burroughs's cut ups, or Godard's film editing of the 60's, than to anything happening in the 40's. (Zorn, 1990)

One of the things that Zorn celebrates here is a perceived democratic impulse in Stalling's work. Certainly the music exhibits an anarchic eclecticism that devalues the classical and violates its norms – and not only through the familiar cartoon tropes of pastiche and parody. In this respect, at least, the work undertaken by Stalling at Warner Bros. was certainly more radical than that produced for Disney. Despite personal indifference to classical music (Disney claimed that the idea for the Bach Toccata in D sequence in *Fantasia* came to him while dozing at a concert[8]), it was clear that it marked *Fantasia* as *the* serious Disney project – not a *cartoon*, but an animated film with artistic merit. As such, it inevitably provided the animators at Warner Bros. with an attractive target, which they were to ridicule subsequently in *What's Opera Doc?* (Chuck Jones, 1957).

Audible in Stalling's work is a logic of quotation in which every act of referencing is marked by a simultaneous act of deconstruction and destruction. Recognisable tunes can be heard, but the status of the original is reduced to a marker of difference, serving only to indicate the extent to which it has been cut up and distorted. Thus, Greg Ford observes, 'the songs themselves are not the thing but the brilliant manner in which they're squashed and stretched to suit cartoon purposes' (Ford, 1990). And if, as Zorn suggests, Stalling's reworking of source material represents the disempowerment of the hegemonic models and personalities of western art music, then it also represents the empowerment of the deconstructor. This logic of deconstruction signals a shift to a modernist objectivism in which everything not only has a material existence, but can also be reduced to a material *object*. What marks Stalling's use of quotation is the violence of its appropriation, which at its sharpest and most hard-edged comes close to a stop–start atomisation that finds no equal in the work of his peers. In contrast, the work of Scott Bradley, Stalling's contemporary at MGM, is dominated by a strong sense of melodic continuity, a difference in style that was, in part, determined by the economics of film production. Unlike Stalling, Bradley, who is best known for scoring the *Tom and Jerry* cartoons, did not have access to Warners' extensive library of popular music. Therefore, other than quoting tunes in the public domain (as did Stalling), Bradley had no option but to write original cues.[9] His scores do, however, reference various musical genres, and even specific pieces of music; for example, Bradley's score for Tex Avery's *T.V. of Tomorrow* (1953) repeatedly quotes Rossini's *William Tell Overture*. However, what distinguishes the two cartoon composers' styles most emphatically is the way in which their respective montages are structured.[10] Bradley's music has a sense of flow, his compositions working to create musical continuity through the unification of individual cues in a continuous track: 'My own method, if you could call it such, is in trying to maintain a continuous melodic line, and follow the action with new harmonization and orchestration of conventional patterns' (Bradley, 2002a: 117). Stalling's montage, however, is much more angular, its sense of fragmentation *foregrounded*; in Stalling's music, the listener is made aware of the suture, while with Bradley this is concealed.

Musical sound effects

In addition to quotation, another defining characteristic of the cartoon soundtrack is the use of musical sound effects, in which sounds are produced by the orchestra to accompany on-screen action; and it is here that we encounter the practice of mickey-mousing. A useful distinction can be made between two basic types of musical sound effect used in cartoons. The first category includes relatively realistic musical effects, such as the tapping of woodblocks to accompany the image of a character knocking on a door. The use of musical instruments in the creation of what are essentially non-musical effects is primarily a feature of early sound cartoons. In later work, effects of this type were replaced by spot effects, produced by sound-effects specialists – such as Treg Brown at Warner Bros. – rather than musicians. The early musical sound effects are of particular interest because of their status as sounds which have both a musical and a worldly dimension. This indeterminacy is illustrated by the use of music in the early sound cartoon *Felix the Cat in Astronomeows* (Otto Messmer, 1928). When the film industry began to move to sound in the late 1920s, the producer of the *Felix* cartoon series, Pat Sullivan, initially resisted conforming to the demands imposed by the new technology, hoping to wait it out until things settled down. But on seeing that a return to silence was increasingly unlikely, Sullivan had soundtracks retrospectively added to a number of silent cartoons (Canemaker, 1996: 129–130). One of these was the 1928 film *Felix the Cat in Astronomeows*, a cartoon that provides a clear illustration of the cinesonic practices that developed in cartoon production during the early years of sound. In one scene woodblocks are used to create the sound of the footsteps made by a robot walking on the surface of Mars (Figure 5.2). However, this walking sound also forms the rhythmic basis of the music that accompanies the action. There is thus a blurring of the distinction between sound effects and music. According to Scott Curtis (1992), this practice developed in early sound cartoon production because of the technical limitations of recording technology. Before 1933 there was effectively no way of mixing separately recorded sounds together without a drastic loss of quality. The playback system, which provided a basic form of mixing, entailed playing back recorded sounds from disc over loudspeakers in a studio, while at the same time other sounds – usually dialogue – were performed and recorded live (Altman, 1985: 46). While the resultant recording allowed various sound sources to be combined, the inevitable loss

5.2 *Felix the Cat in Astronomeows*

of quality meant the technique was not suitable for soundtracks with a musical element. The solution to this problem was to record all the elements of the cartoon soundtrack live. However, this created problems of competing volume levels, since, without mixing, only one microphone could be used to record everything, with the consequence that dialogue and effects might not be heard above the studio orchestra. This is certainly the case with *Felix the Cat in Astronomeows*, where the voices of the characters are sometimes barely audible above the underscoring.

The answer to this problem, at least as far as cartoons were concerned, lay in the arrangement of the music. Breaks were provided in the score, which was constructed of eight-bar phrases, allowing cartoonists to 'place significant action on the cadential accent at the end of every 8th measure' (Curtis, 1992: 198). It was within these breaks in the music that dialogue and effects were located. Thus, Curtis identifies an interesting paradox and an emblematic feature of the cartoon soundtrack: the arrangement of the music separates it from effects and dialogue, yet distinctions between sound elements are blurred as music is used as a sound effect, and all sound elements are orchestrated into a continuous musical track. Although the effects are located in the space provided in music, 'Produced by musical instruments, they became part of the music, entering at rhythmic breaks at a compatible pitch and volume' (Curtis, 1992: 198). In later years, although sounds could be mixed separately, the practice of integrating effects into a continuous musical score continued, even when many effects were no longer provided by the orchestra, but by sound effects specialists. This blurring of the distinction between music and effect is also a dissolution of the boundary between music and worldly sound, and between the abstract and the significative. In its acceptance of something approximating worldly sound, cartoon music marks a radical departure from the traditions of western art music, which has always resisted imitative sounds as unmusical.

However, the second category of musical sound effect used in cartoons in no way approximates worldly sounds. To illustrate this particular use of sound, consider the opening of a *Looney Tunes* or *Merrie Melodies* cartoon: the Warner Bros. logo expands as if rushing towards the viewer from the background, while simultaneously on the soundtrack we hear the familiar 'boinggg' of a chord played on the electric guitar. Here, sound and image are connected only by a common morphological profile, the sound having no naturalistic attachment to, or narrative relationship with, the action on screen. This particular use of sound is what we encounter in the audiovisual practice of mickey-mousing. The cartoon genre has developed a familiar vocabulary of musical sounds used in this way: swanee whistles invariably accompany movement up and down, cymbals mark collisions, pizzicato strings suggest tiptoeing, while notes played on the xylophone are synchronised with blinking. These are sounds that connect with the image only at a morphological level, and it is for this reason that they might best be described as morphological sound effects. These effects may be built into music, but can never fully be part of it, since their adherence to the image deterritorialises them as simple musical sounds.

The close relationship of sound and image

The term mickey-mousing refers not to a specific set of sounds, nor to any strictly musical dimension of the soundtrack, but rather to an audiovisual *relationship*; remove the picture and there is no mickey-mousing. In the cartoon, the precise synchronisation of sound and image that mickey-mousing entails is a direct outcome of the way in which compositional and film production practices mesh with one another. One illustration of this, referenced earlier, is the way in which both sound and image are designed according to a musical bar-structure. According to Dahl, it is this structural organisation that determines the visual rhythm of the cartoon: 'just as the dancer reserves his more spectacular tricks for the cadences at the end of musical phrases so the cartoonist, probably out of instinct, achieved some of his funniest effects by placing outstanding action (be it the bounce of a ball or the impact of a pie on a face) on the same cadential accents with which in popular music every eighth measure ends' (Dahl, 1974: 184). In respect to the work of the composer, Dahl views this structure as a potential curb on creative freedom, commenting that the limitation of working to a beat 'tends to impart a certain rhythmic squareness to his [the composer's] phrases and it takes much conscious effort on his part to overcome this' (Dahl, 1974: 188).

However, the close relationship between music and the visual in the cartoon runs deeper than the fact that sound and image are divided into roughly equal sections of corresponding duration. The cartoon production process predetermines, as a minimum, a *rhythmic* match between sound and image. On this rhythm hang the morphological changes of both the action of the film and the music on the soundtrack. Unlike live-action films, it was not always the case that the music for cartoons was recorded after the images. At Warner Bros., Stalling usually had the music recorded before the picture had been completed. As composer, he would meet with the film's director at the start of production, and, working from the script, a beat would be determined for each phase of action. This was measured not in musical time of beats per measure or beats per minute, but in frames per beat. Timings were worked out first on music sheets, and were only later transferred to the exposure sheets that provided timing instructions for the animators.[11] These sheets were tabulated according to the number of frame units on which the animation was based; for example ten or sixteen frames. This number represented the smallest *rhythmic* denominator of a scene, and thus its beat – the rhythm to which both music and action would conform. In this way the images were created to coordinate with bars of music that had yet to be written or recorded. Similarly, Stalling would be able to score the whole cartoon without ever seeing a single completed drawing. The foundational beat of each scene would then be reproduced during the recording session by the 'click track' – a metronomic loop of the appropriate number of film frames played over headphones, which enabled the conductor and musicians to achieve precise timing for each phase of the cartoon's action.[12]

Since both composer and director were working from the same exposure sheets, what this meant, at the level of production, was that there was a conflation of sound and image, of music and action, as if they were one and the same in *some respect*. Both the movement on screen and the music written to accompany it were planned in such a way that they would occupy the same duration (working to a bar structure) and would develop to the same rhythm. On this framework the composer would hang the morphological changes in tone, amplitude, texture and so on that seemed most appropriately to express the action first described in the script, and then later seen on screen. This is one explanation of why image and sound are so closely linked in these films; in the case of the Warner Bros. cartoons, both sound and image are conceived with, and drawn from, the same morphological profile.

However, synchronous sound is also a feature of most live-action filmmaking, particularly since so many films are dominated by lip-synched dialogue. What, then, are the factors that distinguish the audiovisuality of the animated cartoon – and in particular mickey-mousing – from other types of sync sound experience?

Sync sound and mickey-mousing

Unlike photographic forms of representation, which register the myriad visual details of profilmic space, animation creates a rarefied semiotic universe. At the same time, the cartoon lacks the subtle sonic rendering that characterises the naturalistic sound-tracks of most Hollywood narrative dramas. Although the Disney aesthetic attempted to resist the first of these two tendencies by striving to increase the naturalism of the animated image, more typical of the genre are the Warner Bros. cartoons, whose imagery is pared back, thinned out and lacking detail. The sonic world of the cartoon, like that of its image, is one of foreground and flatness, in which denial of depth allows no distraction from what is foregrounded, no opportunity for auditory wandering. The animated cartoon delivers continuously, up front; in an almost empty landscape, and in an almost empty frame, concentration is focused on every detail of what little is presented. The music echoes and supports the image's compression and focus, since it offers a sonic world without background; there is no ambient sync sound in the cartoon, just as there is no photographic micro-detailing of the image. Similarly, there is little foreground–background mixing outside of the dialogue/non-dialogue relationship. All non-dialogue sound is channelled into a single stream, orchestrated to include its various elements. Thus there is no folding of background and foreground in either sound or image. Rather, *it is the foreground that is folded, sound into image*, through the close synchronisation that characterises the audiovisuality of the cartoon.

The visual world of the cartoon appears as if under a microscope, in which everything is stretched, magnified and abstracted until it is reduced to simple graphic forms; and so it is with the soundtrack. Cartoon sound works with what could be considered micro textures, but which are hugely amplified. When Wile E. Coyote blinks in disbelief, the sprightly notes we hear played on the xylophone territorialise the whole soundtrack – sounds that in most musical modes would simply form part of a deeper sonic texture or linear continuum. This aesthetic of the foreground is cast against silence: there is no sound when the orchestra falls silent, no ambience of passing traffic, no rumble of air conditioning. The cartoon creates sound without sonic context, without environment or noise, and in this respect the sonic world of the cartoon parallels its pared down visual surface. If this is sound in close-up, then the cartoon has more in common with the pre-video pornographic film and the action movie than it does with other genres of film. While it might not seem productive to consider Stalling's music pornographic, it does display some of the same tendencies as the porn soundtrack and the action movie – that is, it works to foreground or isolate sounds in which strong morphological traits are themselves foregrounded: panting, grunting, moaning in the porn film, and punches, gunfire and squealing tyres in the action movie. It is precisely this simultaneous reduction and amplification that is registered in Dahl's pithy critique of the cartoon genre, and the creative opportunities it affords the composer: 'The scope of musical expression is . . . limited. For how long can a composer continue to restrict himself exclusively to the bright yellows and reds of the musical palette . . .?' (Dahl, 1974: 188).

What therefore links sound to image in mickey-mousing is not simply some degree of similarity between the morphological attributes of both sound and image, but a clear sonic and visual expression of that *relationship*. Mickey-mousing is not a by-product or an accident of sloppy scoring; along with violence and caricature, mickey-mousing is what the cartoon has to offer, one of its fundamental pleasures. In paring down both the sonic and visual fields, the cartoon works to privilege the relationship between sound and image, often above the minimal semantic content or narrative drive offered by either. In a sense, the repetitive, formulaic nature of the cartoon evidences the centrality of audiovisuality to its appeal. While we might enjoy the invention that the animator brings to each new Roadrunner gag, we know what the final outcome will be, since we are wholly familiar with the logic and laws of the Roadrunner–Coyote universe. In the same way, our familiarity with the sonic vocabulary of these cartoons gives a certain sense of predictability to the events that take place, and the way in which they are to develop. The already-knowness of the cartoon creates a form of audience involvement that downplays the role of enigma in narrative development, in favour of familiarity, repetition and predictability. The relative weakness of narrative attraction that results is contrasted with the affective impact of the cartoon's audiovisuality. This is strengthened, rather than reduced, by recognisability and repetition, experienced through the audience's predictive engagement in the audiovisual flow. In responding to the familiarity of the cartoon's sonic and visual cues, we prepare ourselves to submit to the affective pleasure of its audiovisuality, the most striking example of which is mickey-mousing.

Quotation revisited and a return to montage

The use made by the cartoon of montage and quotation might suggest that its soundtrack exhibits clear radical tendencies. Cartoon music displays many features that were, and would still be, considered unorthodox in many forms of western art music, and even within the broad genre of film music. In terms of a wider cultural and art-historical context, Stalling's use of montage, juxtaposition, fragmentation and collision make clear connections with modernist film practice, particularly that associated with Soviet Montage of the 1920s. Similarly, the parallels that might justifiably be drawn between Stalling's compositional use of fragmentation, and cubist and futurist art practices of the early twentieth century would seem to provide further evidence of the cartoon soundtrack's radical credentials. It has already been shown how Stalling's use of quotation challenges a number of musical orthodoxies and violates classical norms. However, in addition to the departure from normative modes of musical construction, quotation might also be considered in relation to a wider debate about the use of pre-existing material in the arts. From the vantage point of the twenty-first century, it seems clear that quotation fundamentally challenges the romantic notion of authorship that constructs the individual artist as god-like originator. But in the period and cultural context in which Stalling was working, quotation simply aligns the artist with the craft notion of *assemblage*, or 'montage' in its most general sense. The assignment of artisanal status within this particular cultural context emerges from the move to factory production, mass production, mass markets, mechanical reproduction and the growth of the culture industry that marks twentieth-century modernity. Paradoxically, rather than challenging the highly resilient model of authorship that associates true artistry with origination, the practice of quotation served to further strengthen this dominant model by providing the 'true' artist with a constitutive artisanal other. Within a cultural value system that placed a high priority on authorship, the use of pre-existing material excluded the quoting artist from those fields of creative production that were popularly understood to constitute high-status artistic activity. In reality, the notion of total and autonomous authorship is challenged by the fact that, for centuries, successful artists of all kinds have used assistants; and of course, the tradition of quotation surfaces in the visual arts whenever painters have tackled subjects undertaken by past masters.

Nevertheless, the differential status applied to various artistic practices, and to the cultural contexts in which they take place, undoubtedly meant that Stalling's work was seen as having little or no serious cultural merit at the time it was produced. The standing of composers working on cartoons in this period is evidenced by the fact that it was not until the late 1940s that their scores were given copyright protection. And if further proof of Stalling's craft status is needed, consider the critical profile granted to Stalling in comparison with that of his *peers* Schoenberg and Stravinsky. Stalling was interviewed only twice in his life, and then not until well after his retirement. But it is not necessarily differences in compositional practice that explain this critical imbalance. Stravinsky's 1945 *Ebony Concerto* sounds like (slow) cartoon music, with its montage construction, appropriation and quotation of jazz, and a use of dissonance that could quite easily signal comedic drunkenness or a broken merry-go-round if used within the context of a *Merrie Melodies* cartoon. Despite the potential similarity of their work, Stalling is viewed simply as an artisan working for the culture industry, while his contemporary is an artist of another order entirely. Of course, the context of production and reception has an important bearing on how this music is heard and appreciated – dissonance in Stravinsky is understood to be daring, while dissonance in Stalling's work is 'merely' funny.

When seen and heard in relation to the hegemonic model of the artist as autonomous originator, quotation becomes associated with forms of theft and parasitism. Thus, quotation attributes to the works making use of it a secondary, minor status. Quotation is seen as derivative: it does not produce, but reproduces. This perception is perfectly in tune with others that determine the minoritarian position of cartoons, of 'funny music', and even music itself within a visually dominated art of cinema. It is only by temporal displacement that the democratic impulse of Stalling's quotation, and its violation of classical norms, reveal themselves as potentially radical aspects of the composer's musical practice. Within the context provided by debates about post-modern forms of cultural appropriation, the removal of work from its original context becomes an act meaningful in itself, as with the sampling of U2's music by the audio collective Negativland, *or* John Oswald's plunderphonic reworking of Michael Jackson's *Bad*.[13] Hence, Diedrich Diederichsen has suggested that montage, used in conjunction with quotation, can be seen as the purposeful destruction of an old continuum.[14] For example, the act of cutting up and quoting a song by the band U2 can be thought of as an attack on the cultural dominance of U2-style über-rock and all that it connotes in terms of its stars, their status, the commercial music industry, the laws that support it and so on. The montage undertaken as part of sampling can, in this way, be heard as a decontextualisation of hegemonic sound objects.

Appropriating the title of a film made in 1965 by Jean-Marie Straub and Danielle Huillet, Diederichsen has suggested that another aspect of the radical value of montage lies in its status as the place of the *not reconciled*.[15] Transposed to the context of cinema, Diederichsen's formulation is evidenced by the example of Soviet Montage, in which editing reveals rather than conceals the cut joining, and separating, two shots. This marking of suture is a cinematic practice that makes evident the construction of film through editing, and is thus entirely at odds with classical film practice. Within the context of 1920s Soviet cinema, this approach to montage can be understood as a strategy of objectification, whereby the indexical and iconic power of the photographic image to signify the profilmic event or object is reduced in order to enhance the image's status as a complex sign. With Soviet

Montage, one plus one equals three, in the sense that the combination, collision or juxtaposition of shots generates a new element not present in the constituent material – normally an affective or intellectual construction. In this way, montage manifests a resistance to the power of the naturalistic image, and a desire for the signifier to no longer be dominated by the profilmic signified (the 'real' objects and events to which the photographic image seems to 'naturally' refer). This style of filmic construction stands in contrast to the practice of continuity editing, in which shots are arranged and recorded in such a way that they can be edited together as seamlessly as possible. Thus, conventions such as the match on action, adherence to the 180-degree rule, consistent screen direction and rough graphic matching between shots have developed to support narrative filmmaking, enabling a smooth flow of shots that will not distract the audience from its engagement with narrative or identification with characters. In the parlance of Brechtian debates, the continuity style of editing supports an illusionistic form of cinematic representation, while montage reveals itself, making the construction of the artwork visible.

In the animated cartoon there is indeed a sense in which sonic montage foregrounds musical construction. What is clearly audible in Stalling's music is its fragmentary nature, articulated through the rapid changes from quotation to morphological sound effect and back. Each element is audible as a brief sonic 'flash', the sections running together as a montage sequence, yet with each maintaining its identity, illuminated brilliantly as it passes. This sequence of audio events moves so rapidly that setting oneself the task of identifying the changes from sound effect to musical quotation to a morphological use of sound is an exhausting and almost impossible task. But of course, this sonic montage is not isolated from the changes taking place on the image track. The fractured nature of the soundtrack means the relationship between sound and image is not a fixed constant, but rather, is in *a constant state of flux*. This is a defining characteristic of the cartoon's audiovisuality, which impacts upon the supposed radical potential of the cartoon soundtrack.

Films on speed

If Stalling's use of sonic montage marks a point of contact with the formal vocabulary of modernism, then its rapidity connects with the spirit of modernity. Speed, of course, was one of modernism's emblematic enthusiasms, and in addition to its obvious celebration by futurism, it also becomes a key trope of modern jazz. In the mid-1940s, bebop introduced a form of playing that was so rapid it effectively removed jazz from the tradition of dance music. This turn of speed not only created excitement for the listener, but also served to foreground the virtuosity of the player. Bebop remained visceral and rhythmically infectious, but it also became intellectual and elite, empowering the black musicians who created and played it. A number like Dizzy Gillespie's 'Bebop' wasn't for humming or dancing to – it was designed for head-nodding, finger-popping admiration. In this way, when the cranking-up of tempo is combined with jazz's fondness for quotation, we encounter a form of music in which the player is demonstrably the master of the material he or she is reworking or appropriating. When bebop musicians play standards, they are judged not by fidelity to the original, but by their virtuosity in restructuring, referencing and distorting source material.[16] This mastery over material is central to the muscular appeal of early modern jazz, making manifest the transformative powers of the musician. Thus, if one makes the case for Stalling's work to be appreciated as democratic and anti-hegemonic, as John Zorn has done, then his twisting, stretching and compression of original tunes might also be seen in terms of the empowerment of the deconstructor, the empowerment of the montagist over hegemonic sound objects, particularly in relation to the sampling of classical music.

But there is also a sense in which speed qualitatively transforms a piece of music. In their introduction to *A Thousand Plateaus*, Deleuze and Guattari write, 'There are no points or positions in a rhizome, such as those found in a structure, tree, or root. There are only lines. When Glen Gould speeds up the performance of a piece, he is not just displaying virtuosity, he is transforming the musical points into lines, he is making the whole piece proliferate' (Deleuze and Guattari, 1988: 8). In the cartoon, speed retunes the radical potential of montage, transforming it from a potentially cognitive construction into a purely sensory experience. Quite simply, cartoons are films on speed, a line of flight with no destination. When Stalling puts source material through the sampling process, the resultant fragments are articulated with such rapidity that we experience the source music in new ways. To use Deleuze and Guattari's phrase, Stalling causes the sampled pieces to proliferate, in the sense that the music under his control develops affective and also significatory dimensions not present in the original material. Speed serves to intensify the affective dimensions of the cartoon, and in the same way that rhythm infects a listener, so the cartoon's rapidity abducts the audiospectator, taking them on its own line of flight.

Radical credentials

In its Soviet formulation, montage optimistically sought to enlighten, uncover and awaken the viewer on an intellectual level, thus bringing about a political awareness that might result in the eventual reconstruction of society. In its shaping of film material, and material film, montage thus plays an interventionist part in constructing a new world. While Stalling's montage also has transformative powers, these tend to work at a sensory rather than an intellectual level: Stalling's musical contribution to the cartoon's celebration of destruction evokes feelings of pleasure, rather than generating ideas.[17] For Eisenstein, destruction is not just a practical matter (clearing the decks for a new Soviet Union), but is also symbolic. For Bugs Bunny, destruction is sensory pleasure: toppling statues is a laugh, they do not necessarily have to be of a Tsar. Similarly, while the montage undertaken in sampling may be thought of as a means by which to decontextualise hegemonic sound objects, in the context of a *Merrie Melodies* cartoon, or even when framed retrospectively in the terms of post-modern appropriation, Stalling's quotation of the work of others seems to be subversion without political aim – which is to say, *just for fun*. How, then, should we understand and evaluate the radical potential of the cartoon's audiovisual poetics?

A number of critics have considered the distinguishing features of the cartoon soundtrack in terms of their divergence from traditional musical norms. We have already seen how John Zorn, probably Stalling's most active champion, has described the composer as a 'revolutionary visionary' who created a 'radical compositional arc unprecedented in the history of music' (Zorn, 1990). Kevin Whitehead simply describes Stalling as 'a great modernist composer' (Whitehead, 2002: 141), while Daniel Goldmark and Yuval Taylor comment, 'Cartoon music is among the most engaging and experimental forms of twentieth-century music, exploring the more outrageous extremes of instrumentation, rhythm and non-musical sound. It is a genre in which rapid tempo changes, unusual instrumental effects, experimental percussion, post-modern quotation, shock chords, and musical genre-shifting are de rigueur'

(Goldmark and Taylor, 2002: 5). Elisabeth Vincentelli assesses the value of Stalling's work in terms of its status as authentic Americana, commenting, 'Stalling worked within a particularly American tradition of abrupt interplay between high and low culture, and of orchestrated collisions between musical styles' (Vincentelli, 2002: 203). This particular feature of Stalling's work has enabled some writers to connect Stalling's compositional style with that of Charles Ives and, by this kind of association, attribute value and status to the cartoon composer's work. Thus, Ross Care describes Stalling's score for *Steamboat Willie* in the following celebratory terms:

> Key musical themes in *Steamboat Willie* were the title tune 'Steamboat Bill' (an old Irish folk tune) and 'Turkey in the Straw.' This same pastiche style was applied even more heavily to the *Plane Crazy* score (1928), which features a catalog of familiar public domain tunes – 'Ruben, Ruben,' 'Yankee Doodle,' 'Dixie,' 'Hail to the Chief' – fragments of which are dizzyingly stitched together by Carl Stalling in almost Ivesian fashion, and sometimes heard in two- and three-part contrapuntal development. (Care, 2002: 22)

This association of cartoon music with the musical avant-garde continues to be a means by which more recent work in animation has become valued. In an article on the work of Glen Daum – the composer responsible for scoring the TV series *Mighty Mouse: The New Adventures* (1987–88) and *Chip 'n' Dale's Rescue Rangers* (1989–92) – Neil Strauss makes a point of mentioning the fact that Daum studied with composer György Ligetti at Stanford University. Daum himself undoubtedly sees connections between his own work and that of 'serious' composers, commenting, 'You can be corny or contemporary; you can do anything . . . At one point, I had four different sections of the orchestra all playing different stuff at the same time. It was like Elliott Carter had scored the episode' (Strauss, 2002: 12).

The heterogeneity of cartoon sound seems guaranteed by a freedom not afforded to other genres of music. Writing in 1947 for *The Music Educator's Journal*, Scott Bradley states that, 'Established rules of orchestration are blandly ignored, since beauty in cartoons is rarely even skin deep, and we must employ "shock chords" which sometimes reach the outer limits of harmonic analysis' (Bradley, 2002b: 123). Here, the composer of the *Tom and Jerry* cartoons is clearly cognizant of the avant-garde, and of his relationship to it, commenting, 'Yes, from Schoenberg to Nelson Eddy all in one reel'

(Bradley, 2002b: 123). But, as suggested above, it is probably John Zorn who makes the most powerful case for both the artistic merit and radical value of cartoon music by associating Stalling's work with that of William Burroughs and Jean-Luc Godard. Referring to Burroughs's use of the cut-up, and Godard's jump cut, Zorn retrospectively allies an under-appreciated Stalling with two major radical figures; at the same time, by aligning Stalling's praxis with that of his own contemporaries in the 1980s and beyond, Zorn seeks to signal the avant-garde nature of Stalling's music.

Rupture

Although the writers referred to above seem to make a strong case for the cartoon soundtrack to be valued as inherently progressive, the limitation of the viewpoint adopted by these critics is that they tend to consider cartoon music in isolation – that is, extracted from the audiovisual complex of which it forms a part. Zorn's claim for the value of Stalling's work begins, 'Separating his music from the images it was created to support, it becomes clear that Stalling was one of the most revolutionary visionaries in American music' (Zorn, 1990); but, of course, in the context of the animated cartoon, Stalling's music is *not* separated from the images it was designed to accompany. Adopting a similar position, John Corbett writes, 'Some of the broadest implications of cartoon music have nothing at all to do with animated images, but are the result of what happens when the visual content is removed altogether and the listener is left to grapple with the sounds on their own terms' (Corbett, 2002: 279). This is not to say, however, that critics are unaware of the visual dimension of the cartoon, but rather that this has been bracketed in order to confirm the music's merit. Interviewed by Philip Brophy, Zorn notes, 'From a young age he was playing for silent movies. That helped create his weird sense of musical logic. His music was always connected with a visual counterpart, and that guided the music to non-musical development, more a filmic sense of development' (Brophy, 2002: 264). Although Zorn acknowledges the visual framework informing Stalling's music, his appreciation nevertheless relies upon the resituation of Stalling's work within a strictly musical context; it is here, rather than within the cartoon itself, that the music seems to take on a radical trajectory. By following a visual logic, Stalling's music challenges hegemonic forms of musical organisation. Placed in a musical context, these image-driven sounds conflict with existing frameworks of musical meaning: 'In following the visual logic of screen action rather than the traditional rules of musical form (development, theme, variations, etc.), Stalling created a radical compositional arc unprecedented in the history of music' (Zorn, 1990). It is therefore through displacement and recontextualisation that Stalling's Termite Art challenges the hegemonic sound-objects that constitute dominant forms of music; hence Zorn's claim that it is 'unprecedented *in the history of music*' [my emphasis], since Stalling's compositional approach is *not* unprecedented in the history of vaudeville or cartoon sound.

However, could these sounds have a radical value that goes beyond their resistance to existing models of musical organisation; that is, could cartoon music be considered, in a positive sense, an alternative to the hegemonic structural models of music? To engage with the radical potential of cartoon music in positive terms, consideration needs to be given to the ways in which its sounds create modes of experience, rather than simply negate established norms. Western art music has tended to reject those sounds it considers unmusical, and has been held up as the abstract art form par excellence. Douglas Kahn (1999) has argued that western art music has always been resistant to imitative sounds, and that even the futurist experiments with noise maintained music's isolation from a wider sonic environment: 'In keeping with the conventions of western art music at that time, Russolo rejected "imitation" and, in the end, simulated worldliness only through an expansion of timbre' (Kahn, 1999: 10). However, the intertextuality of Stalling's work represents an intrusion – albeit musicalised – of the outside into the sealed world of western art music. The self-contained, self-justifying compositions of post-classical western art music seem to engulf the listener, depriving them of a horizon beyond that of the composition's own making. Stalling's use of quotation, in signalling the material heterogeneity of musical forms and practices, precludes this form of total immersion in a single composition, and in the consistent, coherent sonic world it creates. Instead, Stalling objectifies music, rendering it 'audible' as music. His work is simultaneously able to sweep the listener along in its energetic montage while still objectifying the individual quotations it employs. Thus, through its heterogeneity this form of intertextuality, coupled with its articulation through montage, foregrounds the sonic materiality of both the whole and its constituent parts.

However, in a quiet and a noisy way, it is sound's *adherence* to the image, its lack of isolation that is one of the most radical aspects of Stalling's Termite Art. Mickey-mousing punctures the bubble in which western music has placed itself, forcing an acknowledgement of an 'outside', an other – in this case, constituted by the visual. Not only does mickey-mousing destroy the notion of isolated specificity that underwrites music – an abstraction from all else – it also introduces to music the possibility of other kinds of structuration, other ways of considering structure, other structural dimensions. What is under consideration here is *not* the Zornian model of a paradigm transplant that results in the extension of the existing range of musical structures, thereby further expanding music's mighty sonic empire; rather, mickey-mousing challenges the notion of how music might *be*. That is, instead of providing other ways of thinking *about* music, as a self-justifying substantive entity, mickey-mousing provides new ways of *thinking* music. Synaesthetic audiovisual experience, like that created by mickey-mousing, presents a sublation of sound and image, in which binary relations, hierarchies and identities are liquefied, where no one milieu is sacrificed to another, but rather where each milieu becomes permeable to the point of dissolution. For music, this marks an end to the notion of fixed boundaries, fixed identities and empires, to be replaced with a notion of audiovisual flux, of audiovisual becoming. The radical challenge that synaesthetic forms present to music is, consequently, not to be thought through in the wholly negative terms of destruction or eradication, but rather as a dissolution that is enacted without loss: a sublation. Such a liquefaction is liberating, a way out of the identity habit, a way of thinking beyond the parameters of identity and essence.

The refrain contained

Although Stalling's compositions might be considered radical within a musical context, within the cartoon their potentially turbulent elements are clearly contained. Cartoons are a central and inescapable part of popular culture, whose soundtracks seem to contribute to the genre's broad appeal and commercial success, rather than shaking the foundations of the culture industry, or disempowering hegemonic forms of western art music. Only when taken out of the context of the cartoon does Termite Art begin to build a radical space for itself. This is what has effectively been done by John Zorn, whose own musical practice – which draws on both the montage and humour of Stalling's cartoon work – situates him clearly within the contemporary avant-garde. This new context for Termite Art has been hard won by Zorn, whose 'maverick' status, and inhabitation of an indeterminate space between rock, jazz and art music, are indicative of the difficulty faced in inscribing this type of work within the dominant discourses constructed by music criticism.

But within the cartoon, what is it about the nature of sound–image relationships that seems to remove the music's potential for radical turbulence? To return to the idea of the refrain, we can conceptualise sound and image tracks as two separate milieus, in the terms proposed by Deleuze and Guattari. An audiovisual complex such as the film, which is neither a purely visual nor a purely sonic art form, territorialises these milieus: the film is precisely *audiovisual*, something other and different from either (or both) of its constituent terms. It is for this reason that we give this particular audiovisual complex its own name: *the film*. Moment by moment, the territory of the film is bitten out of the two milieus: 'A territory borrows from all the milieus; it bites into them, seizes them bodily (although it remains vulnerable to intrusions). It is built from aspects or portions of milieus' (Deleuze and Guattari, 1988: 314). In doing this, these two separate milieus may echo to the same territorial refrain; that is, both sound and image can be linked by a common morphology.

Of course, mickey-mousing is only one manifestation of the contract between sound and image that is required by the film. As has already been observed in relation to the cartoon, this contract is marked by flux, and relative positions of dominance within a visually oriented hierarchy. There are, however, moments when this contract breaks down, moments when the film fails to territorialise its sounds and images; for example, when Godard's camera wanders away from two characters conversing in a record store in *Vivre sa vie* (1962), to spy on Parisian street life through the shop window, while the characters continue talking off screen. Similarly, there is the sound of escaping steam in Antonioni's *Il Deserto Rosso* (1964), a sound that seems not to know its proper place in the soundscape of narrative cinema. This loosening of the audiovisual contract is also a feature of 'marginal' film forms and practices, including the 'badly' dubbed film and the pornographic film of the pre-video age. In these latter examples, selective matching, rather than total matching or total non-matching ('contrapuntal' sound) seems to challenge the legitimacy of the film's contract between sound and image. When not adhering to the terms of this contract, sounds may be able to reterriorialise the film on their own terms, carving out a chunk of time and space for themselves.

It is precisely this kind of moment that has been celebrated as radical by deconstructive film practice and criticism, which have long been at pains to disentangle the sonic from the visual within the audiovisual constructions of cinema. Here, deconstruction is championed as a form of enlightenment, an anti-illusionist strategy empowering the formerly passive viewer. In the mickey-mousing contract, however, such possibilities do not present themselves; but does this mean that within an audiovisual text mickey-mousing represents the deradicalisation of both sound and image? I would suggest not, for, as I hope to show, mickey-mousing also has a largely unrecognised, and perhaps even repressed, radical potential in respect to its deterritorialisation and reterritorialisation of sound and image. While mickey-mousing may disarm the radical potential of music within an audio-visual context, it has a more complex relationship with patterns and forces of containment within a work as a whole.

There is a widely held view within both filmmaking and criticism that the soundtrack should not simply echo or illustrate or reinforce the image. Consequently, the concept of redundancy is often called upon in discussions of film sound to denigrate certain forms of audiovisual correspondence. Similarly, a commonly accepted principle of 'good' filmmaking is that sound should maintain some form of independence from the image, rather than be determined by it. It was an objection to the coincidence of sound and image that motivated one of the first theorisations of film sound, the joint statement published in 1928 by the Soviet filmmakers Eisenstein, Pudovkin and Alexandrov. *The Sound Film: A Statement from the USSR* famously proposed a contrapuntal use of sound, in which the relationship between sound and image would be governed by strategies of montage rather than forms of naturalism. Thus, the use of montage would extend beyond the established 'horizontal' relations between images in a sequence, to encompass the 'vertical' relationship between sound and image. This move can be understood within the context of Soviet Montage, and specifically its Eisensteinian formulation, as a strategy to objectify sound: an attempt to reduce its power to refer to an original profilmic object-source, thereby enhancing the image's status as a complex sign. On the use of synchronous sound, to which these filmmakers were fundamentally opposed, the joint statement declared, 'To use sound in this way will destroy the culture of montage, for

every ADHESION of sound to a visual montage piece increases
its inertia as a montage piece, and increases the independence
of its meaning' (Eisenstein, 1977b: 258). The reference to inertia
expresses a modernist resistance to the naturalistic image, a desire
for the signifier to be no longer bound to the 'real'. In a modernist film practice of this type, sound and image could never be
allowed the transparency demanded by the classic realist text, but
rather should surrender their 'independence of meaning' – which
is to say, their naturalistic, representational capacity to refer to an
absent object – and submit to the authority of montage.

This theorised response to the model of sound proposed by
Hollywood's 'canned theatre' has been hugely influential. Entering
general critical vocabulary as the somewhat simplified notion of
counterpoint, the idea of vertical montage still occupies a kind
of cinematic moral high ground more than eighty years after it
was first proposed. In 2000 I attended a talk given by the sound
designer Claude Letessier to a large group of film sound profession-
als, academics and students at the School of Sound Symposium in
London. Letessier explained his contribution as sound designer to
Terence Malick's feature film *The Thin Red Line* (1998), and discussed other projects he had been working on at that time. Letessier
is a charismatic speaker with a solid professional track record,
and, with a strong sense of presence, was more than able to hold
the audience – that is, until he showed a clip from *The Last Days*
(1998), a project he had worked on two years previously. The film
is a documentary about five Hungarian survivors of the Holocaust,
and is composed largely of interviews, interspersed with both contemporary and archive footage of the concentration camps. As the
film's supervising sound designer, Letessier's job appeared to have
been fairly straightforward, since the interviews were powerful
and moving in themselves. However, he had taken the decision to
lay music under this interview footage – an unremarkable string
arrangement guaranteed to create an emotional response. Almost
instantly the moment the lights came back on, the audience turned
on him. He had broken one of the cardinal rules of sound design:
the music he had added, it was felt by the assembled crowd, was
redundant. It seemed to unnecessarily replicate what was already
present in the film, since the personal narratives related by the
interviewees, their voices and facial expressions, seemed to do
their own emotional work; the viewer did not need music to guide
their reactions. The strength of the audience's response was quite
extraordinary; Letessier temporarily lost control of the room and

the normal, orderly call-response of a question and answer session turned into an oceanic grumbling over which the sound designer was struggling to be heard. What this incident illustrates is the fact that a largely art-cinematic model of audiovisual counterpoint, originally formulated in the early years of sound cinema in opposition to an 'illustrative' use of sound, continues to inform critical understanding of sound–image relations. The Soviet notion of contrapuntal sound remains influential to this day, underpinning a belief within both filmmaking and criticism that sound should not simply echo or illustrate or reinforce the image.

Although Eisenstein's contribution to cinema as both a film-maker and a theorist has become almost exclusively associated with montage, he actually advised that 'There should be no arbitrary limits set on the variety of expressive means that can be drawn upon by the film-maker' (Eisenstein, 1977a: 61). This critical focus on montage ignores the fact that Eisenstein saw in the congruence of sound and image tremendous expressive potential. The congruence he argued for was that of mickey-mousing – a morphological congruence: 'we cannot deny the fact that the most striking and immediate impression will be gained, of course, from a convergence of the movement of the music with the movement of the visual contour' (Eisenstein, 1977a: 135). Given Eisenstein's interest in radical poetics, could it be possible that mickey-mousing offers a radical potential equal to that of montage? In his book *The Film Sense*, Eisenstein writes in detail the on synchronisation of the senses, referring, amongst other things, to synaesthesia – the condition in which a stimulus received by one sense gives rise to a perceptual response in another. The phenomenon has been of interest to a number of painters, composers and filmmakers, some of whom, like Wassily Kandinsky, had themselves encountered some form of synaesthetic experience. For many in the arts, synaesthesia provided inspiration for the development of creative practices that sought to transfer the essential qualities of one art form to another, or to fuse two art forms together as one. Thus, Kandinsky was to draw upon musical experience and musical modes of expression when developing his own form of painterly abstraction. However, the cultural historian Douglas Kahn has been somewhat critical of artistic interest in synaesthesia, while nevertheless acknowledging its potential as a productive means within the arts. At the heart of Kahn's criticism is the fact that synaesthesia is a wholly personal experience – the perceptions of one synesthete will not match those of another: 'their arbitrariness cannot be extended to the social sphere, let alone to form the rationalistic spiritual laws of the cosmos. Synesthesia more properly belongs to another class of considerations where private experience is mistaken as public, such as the schism involved in the voice one hears while speaking versus the voice others hear' (Kahn, 1999: 122). While Kahn's focus on the *condition* of synaesthesia rightly limits its impact to the sphere of personal experience, this view neglects the role that the *idea* of synaesthesia played in the development of abstract art in the nineteenth century. The championing of music as a formal model for abstract painting, and later as a temporal model for the abstract film, and the growth and popularity of the colour music movement, all point towards a shattering paradigmatic change in the visual arts. What synaesthetic experience presents is a haemorrhaging of inside into outside, one modality blending with another, as with Stalling introducing 'the world' into western art music through his use of quotation and mickey-mousing, bursting music's bubble, challenging its isolation. If paintings, like those by Kandinsky, could be structured like music, if they could work in the same way as music and create the same effects, then traditional territorial boundaries between art forms become subject to challenge. In the 1920s, when painterly concerns began to enter filmmaking through the work of Man Ray, Hans Richter, Viking Eggeling, Walter Ruttmann, Oskar Fischinger and other members of the European avant-garde, synaesthetic notions took on not just a structuring role, but also a radical trajectory. The 'visual music' experiments of animators Walter Ruttmann, Hans Richter and Oskar Fischinger had little future in Nazi Germany, where abstraction was simply seen as degenerate. Both Richter and Fischinger emigrated in the 1930s, their respective lines of flight once again signalling the relationship between violence, control and animation. Synaesthetic forms of audiovisuality, like those proposed by the films of Oskar Fischinger or John and James Whitney, surely confirm the radical possibilities of audiovisual correspondence, thus challenging the privileged status of montage as the model of choice for a radical audiovisual poetics.

Despite the actual complexity of Soviet formulations of montage editing, much of the value attributed to it retrospectively has rested on its deconstructive qualities: montage reveals rather than conceals filmic construction, while vertical montage separates sound and image, allowing both to exist as separate entities. However, what is neglected by the simplistic celebration of deconstruction as an intrinsically radical strategy is the truly audiovisual nature of film. Deconstruction proposes a binary model of the audiovisual construct: cinema as image and sound, or sound and image. This way of thinking about film sound and making film sound is problematic for two reasons. Firstly, it precludes engagement with the *transsensory* or *intersensory* experience of cinema (although in any case, deconstructive approaches to cinema tend to neglect the sensory, preferring instead to focus on textual construction and the meanings thereby created). Secondly, binary models deny access to modes of creative political thought proposed by art works that transcend certain forms of specificity and differentiation. Thus, what happens in mickey-mousing can never be understood within the conceptual framework upon which deconstruction is founded, and within which montage has been situated as a radical form. What the montagist celebrates is not suture as combination, so much as suture as the mark of separation – the place of the 'not reconciled'. The montagist follows a dominant modernist discourse that privileges individuation, separation and specificity, irrespective of whether this is articulated through the language of addition or collision. This can be seen in the joint statement published by Eisenstein, Pudovkin and Alexandrov, in which montage editing is conceptualised as the *essence* of cinematic expression, and thus the factor distinguishing cinema from other art forms: 'It is known that the basic (and only) means that has brought the cinema to such a powerfully affective strength is MONTAGE. The affirmation of montage, as the chief means of effect, has become the indisputable axiom on which the worldwide culture of cinema has been built' (Eisenstein, 1977b: 257).

What this idea of a separable and identifiable visual essence logically proposes is the notion that sound must in some sense be added to an already existing, fully functioning art of film. Sound therefore becomes the secondary term in a binary formulation of cinema. However, what the example of the cartoon demonstrates is a form of audiovisuality in which sound is not *added* to image, but rather is *folded* in with the image. To fully grasp the radical potential of mickey-mousing, what is therefore needed is a model that provides an alternative to the dominant binary formulations of cinema. Just such a model is provided by Deleuze and Guattari's concept of the refrain, which, when applied to cinema offers a creative means by which the understanding of sound–image relations might be productively reformulated.

Audiovisuality's refrain

In the essay *1837: Of the Refrain*, Deleuze and Guattari write, 'all kinds of milieus, each defined by a component, slide in relation to one another, over one another. Every milieu is vibratory, in other words, a block of space-time constituted by the periodic repetition of the component' (Deleuze and Guattari, 1988: 313). In relation to the conceptualisation of film as territory bitten from the milieus of sound and image, what the above suggests is that in some ways these milieus are distinguished from one another: each has its own internal 'periodic repetition', each has its own consistency, its own intensity, since image and sound are not the same phenomena. However, they are at the same time intimate, connected, and exist in relationship to one another: they 'slide in relation to one another'. Deleuze and Guattari continue:

> Every milieu is coded, a code being defined by periodic repetition; but each code is in a perpetual state of transcoding or transduction. Transcoding or transduction is the manner in which one milieu serves as the basis for another, or conversely is established atop another milieu, dissipates in it or is constituted in it. The notion of the milieu is not unitary: not only does the living thing continually pass from one milieu to another, but the milieus pass into one another; they are essentially communicating. (Deleuze and Guattari, 1988: 313)

The film as an audiovisual entity can be viewed in precisely these terms. Moment by moment, the relationship between sound and image changes – it is in a constant state of flux. Sometimes the image leads, sometimes the sound, while at other times we witness a mickey-mouse fusion of the two: 'one milieu serves as the basis for another, or conversely is established atop another milieu, dissipates in it or is constituted in it'. Thus, the slippery phenomenon we refer to as 'the film' is not the sum of sound and image, but is a living entity that passes from one milieu to another; as Deleuze and Guattari suggest, these milieus 'pass into one another, they are essentially communicating'.

What constitutes the film itself, as an audiovisual construct, is akin to what Deleuze and Guattari term 'rhythm': 'There is rhythm whenever there is a transcoded passage from one milieu to another, a communication of milieus, coordination between heterogeneous space-times' (Deleuze and Guattari, 1988: 313). The 'rhythm' of film – that which constitutes film as more than sound plus image, that which constitutes the *filmic* – is this communication or passage or flow between one milieu and another. This rhythmic flow between the milieus of sound and image constitutes film's audiovisuality. The film is not therefore to be understood as sound and image communicating (leave that perhaps to music and photography), but rather communication *between* sound and image. The quality of the filmic lies not in *either* sound or image, but in the movement between them: 'Action occurs in a milieu, whereas rhythm is located between two milieus, or between two intermilieus, on the fence, between night and day, at dusk, *twilight* or *Zweilicht*, Haecceity' (Deleuze and Guattari, 1988: 313–314). In cinema, each of the milieus of sound and image features its own 'action': each milieu has its own morphology, its own consistency, its own events. But what defines the filmic is the 'rhythm' that is established between sound and image. And since each milieu is 'in action' – in that both sound and image are constantly changing on a morphological level – so the 'rhythm' of the film is determined by the fact that sound–image relations are not fixed, but in a constant state of flux. Film is precisely audiovisual, both more than and other than the sum of its constituent elements: 'Whenever there is a transcoding, we can be sure that there is not a simple addition, but the constitution of a new plane, as of a surplus value. A melodic or rhythmic plane, surplus value of passage or bridging' (Deleuze and Guattari, 1988: 314). This formulation of audiovisuality embraces a range of possible relationships between sound and image, but most importantly, it allows for those moments when sound and image fuse and become indistinguishable. These are mickey-mouse moments, when for a brief period the identities of individual milieus are lost, moments when their individual periodic repetition can no longer be identified, when action within a particular milieu can no longer be perceived as such. Deleuze and Guattari draw upon the natural world to describe this close relationship between milieus: 'It has often been noted that the spider web implies that there are sequences of the fly's own code in the spider's code: it is as though the spider had a fly in its head, a fly "motif," a fly "refrain." The implication may be reciprocal, as with the wasp and the orchid, or the snapdragon and the bumblebee' (Deleuze and Guattari, 1988: 314).[18] When this reciprocity is absolute, we encounter a form of audiovisuality that animator Chuck Jones has described in the following euphoric terms:

> Here are two examples of what I believe to be the nearly perfect wedding of music and graphics which occurs when the visual and the

auditory impacts are simultaneous and almost equal. Both examples are from the picture *Fantasia*; both are bits. One consumed about four seconds in the *Toccata and Fugue* sequence. It pictured simply a ponderous, rocklike, coffinlike mass that waddled into a murky background accompanied by a series of deep bass notes. I should not say 'accompanied,' because this Thing was the music: to my mind there was no separation; the fusion of the auditory and the visual was perfect. (Jones, 1946: 365)

Articulated in these terms, the various relationships between sound and image employed in cinema need no longer be organised in a hierarchical fashion. Rather, by formulating cinema's audio-visuality according to the Deleuzian notions of territoriality and the refrain, mickey-mousing takes an equal place alongside other modes of audiovisual construction. Stripped of its pejorative associations, mickey-mousing becomes a valuable form of audiovisual expression, no less radical than montage, and certainly not inferior to other ways of relating sound and image.

'But where's the politics?'

Along with socially aware realist filmmaking practices associated with movements such as *cinéma vérité*, Free Cinema and Italian Neo-realism, montage has succeeded in territorialising the political, determining what political cinema might be. Accordingly, the radical aspect of cinematic practice is always thought to reside in the intellectual productivity of montage, or in the representational power of drama and documentary, but is rarely thought to have any sensory dimension. In 2002 I attended a sound studies conference[19] at which a performance was given by a video scratcher and a musician known at that time as Meta Forester and the Mighty Jungulator. Their performance took the form of a live audiovisual improvisation, using laptops to store, process and mix sounds and video footage. Like many performances of this kind, there was a close relationship between sound and image, either because both were being sampled together by the VJ, or because the music and images were evolving in relation to each other. As with many forms of live improvisation, each performer simultaneously took their lead from the other, creating a loop of two-way, instantaneous feedback. The performance was politely received by what must have been an atypical audience for two artists more used to performing in a club environment. It was followed by the usual question and discussion slot, during which one of the less-satisfied members of the audience commented to the performers, 'It's very nice, but where's the politics?'

In *A History of Montage*,[20] Diedrich Diederichsen concludes a discussion of the radical qualities of montage by referring to morphing, which he frames as a cheap show effect – a populist cinematic trick that nevertheless demonstrates political potential. However, Diederichsen constructs the value of morphing in terms of its ability to create a self-conscious moment of interruption within an otherwise continuous flow. In this respect, he suggests, morphing returns us to one of the creative origins of Soviet Montage, namely the circus's montage of attractions. This is a plausible argument, but it surely neglects the possibility that morphing itself might be radical, and perhaps political, in other ways – that is, rather than creating difference through interruption, morphing simply suggests the possibility of thinking outside of fixed identity. In this respect, morphing may present a somewhat utopian face, paralleling the view that saw synaesthesia as a liberatory overcoming of the senses. But nevertheless, identity does matter, and it is tempting to imagine the broader political applicability of the ideas prompted by morphing, and the ways in which creative conceptualisations based upon them might intersect with post-colonial debates and discourses, for example. Certainly issues of identity matter, for at the heart of identity lies the figure of negative differentiation, which, far from being a knotty linguistic and philosophical problem, is deeply political; it is what costs people their lives in ethnic conflict.

The audiovisuality of morphing and of mickey-mousing represent an important challenge to the dominant notions of what is understood to constitute the political in audiovisual terms. As mentioned previously, the political aspect of film is often seen to reside within, or in relation to, its representational dimensions. The centrality of the issue of representation to political discourse in cinema is demonstrated not only in debates about the responsiveness of the realist text to 'reality', but also in the rejection and deconstruction of these texts. Within the context of film practices that seek to resist the representational norms of realist cinema, the figures of contrapuntality and montage have certainly been privileged. These have now had an eighty-year run, and still continue to inform certain areas of filmmaking practice and their theorisation. Nicky Hamlyn's 2003 book *Film Art Phenomena* includes one chapter dedicated to a consideration of sound; entitled 'Sound, Sync, Performance', Hamlyn's commentary on the sonic strategies employed in the work of Jean-Luc Godard, Mike Dunford, William Raban and others is framed by the issue of synchronisation. In this respect, Hamlyn's contemporary commentary simply reiterates the well-rehearsed discourse on sound–image relationships first established in 1928 in *The Sound Film: A Statement from the USSR*. Hamlyn places his critical focus on work that is 'wary' of the binding of sound and image, and which therefore seems to resist or problematise illusionistic forms of cinema: 'Some [experimental filmmakers] have opted to avoid the use of sound as far as possible, while others have produced works in which the fit between sound and image – and, in a more technical sense, synchronisation – is examined, and in which these concerns become a key structuring element' (Hamlyn, 2003: 167). The context in which Hamlyn situates the adhesion of sound and image is thus limited to the discussion of cinema's mimetic capacities; the correspondence of sound and image is not discussed beyond its representational function. Similarly Diederichsen, in what is a highly creative but somewhat perverse argument, reworks morphing by inscribing it into the history of montage as 'part of the great discontinuous aesthetic of montage arts' (Diederichsen, 2005). Surely this critical take on morphing is a denial of its most significant feature: morphing transcends the *essential suture* of montage. However, what Diederichsen's problematic solution to the issue of morphing indicates is that there is no established discourse, no solid epistemological framework in which morphing can be situated in relation to radical creative practice. Perhaps morphing only seems banal – what Diederichsen refers to as a 'cheap show effect' – because it appears somewhat in advance of the conceptual vocabulary by which we might engage with its radical potential.

If we return to a careful re-reading of Eisenstein, we see that both the adhesive and the contrapuntal find a place in his thinking on cinema, despite the fact that it is the figure of montage that has come to dominate our understanding of his contribution to the poetics of film. The importance of this return to Eisenstein, and to a consideration of an audiovisuality of *adhesion*, is that it offers the possibility of a different notion of what constitutes the political. As I have attempted to demonstrate, contrapuntal and oppositional formulations, in all their various forms, have certain limitations, certain blind spots. This does not mean that the contrapuntal should simply be rejected or overturned, to be replaced by another model of relationality; rather, the key problem presented by the contrapuntal is its unchallenged dominance within the arena of what constitutes a radical poetics of film. In this context the figure of contrapuntal montage seems somewhat calcified – a fixed and unresponsive position from which to judge the audiovisual text. What an engagement with the audiovisuality of adhesion enables is an affirmative poetics that allows us to leave aside the rehearsal and reiteration of generational edicts based purely on the inscription of difference. This move from deconstruction to folding is difficult; it proposes modes of potential radicality that at present have no easy, ready-made framework in which to situate themselves as political. In this sense it is perhaps understandable why the disgruntled punter at the Metaforester and the Mighty Jungulator gig should have voiced his disappointment with their performance, or why Diederichsen should seek to situate morphing within a history of montage. The limitation of existing viewpoints on what constitutes political cinema is that they struggle to come to terms with the political dynamic that is immanent in poetics. The potentially radical dimension of an adhesive audiovisuality, and of other modes of sonic and visual articulation that work towards fusion, lies not in a series of political protocols 'flown in' from outside the audiovisual text, and applied unresponsively to an array of films, videos and performances, but is immanent in that audiovisuality itself. And if this is the case, then it follows that the political dimensions of audiovisuality might extend to matters of sensation and affect – issues to which I return in the next chapter.

Refrain

Montage and synaesthetic effect can be considered as two of the most radical aspects of Stalling's Termite Art, but in the cartoon the territorial appropriation of milieus disarms and dissolves the power of sonic montage. Within the audiovisual construct we call *the film*, the soundtrack's montage no longer maintains its identity as such. This is because, to paraphrase Eisenstein, every adhesion of image to a sonic montage piece increases its inertia as a montage piece, and increases its independence of meaning. Stalling's musical fragments, when auditioned independently of the images, do indeed present a form of sonic montage that thoroughly challenges classical notions of musical structure. However, these musical fragments, located within the audiovisual complex, are never heard without also being 'seen', and hence lose their sense of being located within a horizontal montage structure. At the same time, while total synaesthesia (total mickey-mousing) can be radically challenging, as it is in the work of the Whitney Brothers, this very montage ensures this never happens; instead, we witness only brief moments of mickey-mousing, followed by others in which the nature of the contract between sound and image differs. In this way, the potentially turbulent elements of Stalling's Termite Art remain under control, his challenge to the classical contained.

But does this mean that Stalling's sonic strategies can never fulfil their radical potential in an audiovisual context? History would indicate that this might be possible, if only briefly. The *model* of sound–image relationships offered by the cartoon genre represents a radical challenge to western film sound practices, and provides a way of thinking through filmic and other audiovisual texts. Part of the radical potential of Termite Art was realised briefly in the 1980s in some aspects of scratch video practice, in which the articulation of appropriated sounds and images briefly harnessed both montage and synaesthetic experience to political ends, before being reterritorialised by the music industry for marketing purposes. However, as I hope to demonstrate in the next chapter, the location of scratch within existing political frames of reference for avant-garde film and video was highly problematic, raising questions of how sensation and affect might be conceptually situated within radical forms of audiovisuality.

Notes

1 Released on *The Carl Stalling Project: Music from the Warner Bros. Cartoons 1936–1958* (1990) [Sound recording: CD].
2 One of the earliest and best-known critical commentaries on animated cartoons is that associated with the Frankfurt School, in the critiques of Disney offered by Theodor Adorno and Walter Benjamin. Adorno sees the work of Disney as essentially reactionary, and locates it squarely within his critiques of mass culture and the culture industry. While he is moderately approving of early cartoons marked by a strong narrative drive, he proposes the evolution of the cartoon as one towards a mere sequencing of violence and destruction: 'with the audience in pursuit, the protagonist becomes the worthless object of general violence. The quantity of organized amusement changes into the quality of organized cruelty' (Adorno and Horkheimer, 1997: 138). According to Adorno, the psycho-political impact of this on the viewer, and on society, is the promotion of a dehumanising, alienating barbarism and collective sadomasochism. The violence done to, and inflicted by, cartoon characters is seen by Adorno to impact on

the psyche of the viewer in a particularly negative and repressive manner: 'In so far as cartoons do any more than accustom the senses to a new tempo, they hammer into every brain the old lesson that continuous friction, the breaking down of all individual resistance, is the condition of life in this society. Donald Duck in the cartoons and the unfortunate in real life get their thrashing so that the audience can learn to take their own punishment. The enjoyment of the violence suffered by the movie character turns into violence against the spectator' (Adorno and Horkheimer, 1997: 138–139). Somewhat more positively, Benjamin proposes that the value of Disney's *Mickey Mouse* cartoons lies precisely in the fact that they *make visible* the naturalised, dehumanising effects of industrial modernity: 'here we see for the first time that it is possible to have one's own arm, even one's own body stolen' (Benjamin, 1999: 545). Thus, Benjamin suggests the reason for the popularity of these cartoons lies in the audience's identification with the condition of their protagonists: 'the explanation for the huge popularity of these films is not mechanization, their form: nor is it a misunderstanding. It is simply the fact that the public recognizes its own life in them' (Benjamin, 1999: 545). Furthermore, he also suggests that these cartoons may possess emancipatory potential, in proposing the possibility of surviving the most damaging aspects of urban-industrial modernity: 'In these films, mankind makes preparations to survive civilisation. Mickey Mouse proves that a creature can still survive even when it has thrown off all resemblance to a human being' (Benjamin, 1999: 545). Although the Frankfurt School analysis of Disney offers little direct commentary on sound, Adorno and Eisler do provide a few briefs comments on cartoon music in *Composing for the Films*. Here they recognise the creative potential of high-fidelity surround-sound in Disney's 'otherwise questionable' film *Fantasia* (Adorno and Eisler, 1994: 111), and bemoan the 'outdated' use of the whole-tone scale in films – while admitting that the disproportionate scale of this music can produce comic effects when 'mismatched' with certain images, as in animated cartoons (1994: 17). A brief comment made in relation to Eisenstein's observations on the correspondence of sound and image indicates that Adorno and Eisler share the general view that mickey-mousing is poor practice: 'If, in the name of higher unity, picture and music were to present this [shared] rhythm incessantly and simultaneously, the relations between the two media would be pedantically restricted, and the result would be unbearable monotony' (1994: 68). The work of Hansen (1993) and Leslie (2002) provides insightful critical commentary on the Frankfurt School's analysis of Disney, assessing the differences between the stances adopted by Adorno and Benjamin, and the ways in which the cartoon itself may have informed the broader critical project of the two writers. However, while Frankfurt criticism and the work that draws upon it might offer an interesting and potentially productive means by which to address some of the issues raised by my own study, the specificity of its commentary on cartoons does not engage with the issues of audio-visuality discussed here. Similarly, an engagement with the theoretical specificity of the Frankfurt School's concern with issues relating to the sociology of mass media, and the debates constructed around an opposition between 'high' and 'low' culture, falls outside the scope of my own study.

3 Manny Farber coined the term 'termite art' in the 1962 article *White Elephant Art Vs. Termite Art* (reprinted in Farber, 1998). Here, Farber describes films that self-consciously aspire to be 'great art' as white elephant art; thus, 'Antonioni's aspiration is to pin the viewer to the wall and slug him with wet towels of artiness and significance' (Farber, 1998: 143). In contrast, what Farber terms 'termite art' are those films and performances that appear modest and self-effacing, yet which prove to be, in his opinion, more powerful than 'white elephant art'. Accordingly, John Wayne is considered by Farber to be a great termite performer, while Lee Marvin is described as a 'flogging overactor' (1998: 136). Although connections could be made between Farber's use of the term and my own, I employ the phrase here simply to refer to the work of Carl Stalling, and to make the connection with Termite Terrace.

4 See Blackburn (1990), Ford (1990), Goldmark (1997), Tebbel (1992), Friedwald (2002) and Zorn (1990).

5 For example, *Sam Fox Moving Picture Music*, by J. S. Zamecnik, 1913. Volume I includes sheet music for twenty-six pieces in different styles and moods, including *Hurry Music for Duels*, *Hurry Music for Struggles*, *Hurry Music for Mob or Fire Scenes*, *Sailor Music*, *Death Scene*, etc.

6 Diederichsen's talk, 'A History of Montage', was given at Tate Modern, London on 8 November 2003 as part of the *Sample Culture Now!* public event. A different version of the talk can be found in Diederichsen's article 'Montage/Sampling/Morphing: On the Triad of Aesthetics/ technology/Politics', available at www.medienkunstnetz.de/themes/ image-sound_relations/montage_sampling_morphing/.

7 *Mixing It*, BBC Radio 3, 21 April 2002 [includes interview with Matthew Herbert].

8 See Care (2002: 23).

9 It is sometimes assumed that Stalling simply chose music written by others, and in this respect much has been made of his use of Raymond Scott's compositions. However, in an interview given to Mike Barrier, Stalling claimed that 80 to 90 per cent of his scores were original cues, written specifically for the cartoon in question (Barrier, 1971: 26).

10 Bradley's compositions can be heard on *Tex Avery Cartoons: Music from the Tex Avery Original Soundtracks Composed by Scott Bradley* (1993) [Sound recording: CD].

11 Also known as a 'dope sheet', this is a timing chart produced for the animators. It breaks down action and dialogue frame by frame, allowing the various layers of the image to be tracked, and includes instructions relating to camera movement and 'opticals' i.e. image dissolves, fades, etc.

12 Not every composer, however, would have had the opportunity to work with the director so early in production. According to Dahl (1974: 185), Scott Bradley would work directly from the exposure sheets produced for the animators, and from a rough cut of the 'pencil reel' of the film. The 'pencil reel' is a version of the visuals produced by the animators using only line drawings, its function being to check that action and timing work effectively – only then are individual drawings copied onto cels, and backgrounds and colour added.

13 In 1991 Negativland released a single entitled *U2*, which sampled the work of the Irish rock group of the same name. U2's label, Island Records, filed a suit against Negativland for violation of copyright regulations. Negativland argued that measures taken by Island Records showed a corporate giant crushing an independent label in response to the latter's challenge to the legal status quo. Chris Grigg of Negativland commented on the strategy of appropriation: 'It's extremely effective to actually apply our hands to this media barrage, cut it up, and turn it into something else that comments on it. That's one of the best ways to make art that we can see right now. But that's the central problem: the laws don't realize the legitimacy of this' (Berry, 1995).

14 See note 6, above.

15 See note 6, above.

16 In this respect it is worth pointing out that most original bebop tunes were, in any case, barely recognisable or unrecognisable reworkings of a limited number of standards, e.g., *How High the Moon, Blue Skies, I Got Rhythm.*

17 The close link between cartoon music and destruction is registered in the work of Survival Research Laboratories, who since 1978 have been mounting genuinely dangerous live events featuring self-destructing machines. The group was set up by founder Mark Pauline to reflect and appropriate the violence that he felt characterises the era we live in. Significantly, the soundtracks that are compiled to accompany the group's live events often feature cartoon music. Recordings of some of the shows can be heard on Pauline and Jupiter-Larsen (n.d.) [Sound recording: CD].

18 This formulation also allows for the contrapuntalism proposed in *The Sound Film: A Statement from the USSR*. In reference to the reciprocity of the relationship between the spider and the fly, the wasp and the orchid, and the snapdragon and the bumblebee, Deleuze and Guattari draw upon the work of biologist Jakob von Uexküll, the author of *The*

Theory of Meaning (1982 [1940]), who they claim 'has elaborated an admirable theory of transcodings. He sees the components as melodies in counterpoint, each of which serves as a motif for another . . .' (Deleuze and Guattari, 1988: 314). An English translation of von Uexküll's work appears in *Semiotica*, Vol. 42, No. 1 (1982).

19 *Sounding Out – an international symposium on the art and practice of sound.* 11–13 July 2002. Staffordshire University, Stoke-on-Trent.

20 See note 6, above.

6 Organised sound

◀◀ Back to the future ‖ 1935, 1937, 1940

The model of sound–image relations proposed by Eisenstein, Pudovkin and Alexandrov in *The Sound Film: A Statement from the USSR* (1928) was formulated as a reaction to the introduction of synchronous sound – a post-hoc theorisation offered in response to the international growth of the 'talkie'. In drawing on the established model of montage, the joint statement can be seen more as a prescriptive attempt to contain sound technology rather than a visionary celebration of its creative possibilities. However, while the Soviet approach to sound was fundamentally reactionary, for others the new technology presented a source of unforeseen creative potential. Although the use of sound in classical cinema was to confirm Soviet anxieties about the hegemonic power of theatrical and naturalistic modes of expression, the introduction of optical sound technology also opened up two new strands of sonic practice that were to have a profound influence on the soundscape of the twentieth century: the first of these was synthesis, the second was sound editing.

The primary creative opportunity that sound editing affords the filmmaker is the ability to organise sounds with a high degree of precision – to determine their relationships with one another, their placement within a temporal frame, and to shape and reshape source recordings. In this way, the technology of optical sound recording and reproduction presented the possibility of organising sound in ways other than those proposed by the mimetic or illustrative sound–image relations of classical cinema. However, in the 1930s and 1940s the creative potential of sound technology was not only being considered by those working within the film industry, but also by a number of composers who believed that these developments offered radical new possibilities for music. For the composers Jack Ellitt, John Cage and Edgard Varèse, film technology offered a form of control, and a degree of control over sound, hitherto unknown in music. Their thoughts on the creative potential of this new technology were recorded in three personal manifestos on sound, written between 1935 and 1940: Jack Ellitt's *On Sound* (1935), Cage's now famous *The Future of Music: Credo* (originally presented as a talk, and later published in *Silence: Lectures and Writings*) and Varèse's *Organized Sound for the Sound Film* (1940).

All three composers heard in the technology of film a means by which the range of sounds available to the composer could be extended. Thus, thinking through the opportunities afforded by developments in sound technology, Cage proposes the creation of a new form of music that would include the worldly sounds he termed 'noise': 'The sound of a truck at fifty miles per hour. Static between the stations. Rain' (Cage, 1999: 3). Similarly, Ellitt enthuses that, with access to recording equipment, 'all world sounds of interest now come within a sphere of creative control which may be termed Sound-Construction' (Ellitt, 1935: 182). Reflecting on the unexplored potential of the film soundtrack, Varèse comments, 'Any possible sound we can imagine can be produced with perfect control of its quality, intensity and pitch, opening up entirely new auditory perspectives' (Varèse, 1940: 205). In this respect, the three composers' individual responses to the creative potential of film sound technology was entirely in accord with the call raised earlier in the century, by the futurist Luigi Russolo, for the range of sounds available to the composer to be extended.[1] Like the futurists, Ellitt, Cage and Varèse heard in sound organised by editing an opportunity to break with existing musical paradigms, and the chance to explore sonic experiences that were somehow more in sympathy with the changing soundscape of the twentieth century. Accordingly, Ellitt proposes that 'Beauty in terms of sound-colours is not necessarily confined to orchestras, pianos, etc., and musical forms are only the chrysales [*sic*] from which more beautifully conceived forms will eventually burst forth in complete freedom and independence' (Ellitt, 1935: 185). In a similar vein, Varèse comments, 'We are now in possession of scientific means not merely of realistic reproduction of sounds but of *production of entirely new combinations of sound*, with the possibility of creating new emotions, awakening dulled sensibilities' (Varèse, 1940: 205). However, what also attracts these composers to film sound technology, and what distinguishes their approach from the futurist celebration of noises, is the opportunity to control, manipulate and organise recorded sounds. Thus, Ellitt proposes that sound recording technology be used to create a new sonic art form he terms 'sound-construction', while Cage suggests replacing the term 'music' with 'organization of sound', and Varèse offers the near-identical phrase 'organized sound'. These notions of organisation and construction, as proposed by Ellitt, Cage and Varèse, present a range of different creative possibilities for sound editing and mixing. In addition to allowing access to previously fugitive or indivisible worldly sounds, film technology provided the means by which recorded sound could be manipulated: 'We want to capture and control these sounds, to use them not as sound effects but as musical instruments. Every film studio has a library of "sound effects" recorded on film. With a film phonograph it is now possible to control the amplitude and frequency of any one of these sounds and to give it rhythms within or beyond the reach of the imagination' (Cage, 1999: 3). The degree of control offered by this technology allows Cage to imagine a new temporal domain for music, measured in fractions of a second. Before the development of optical film recording, it was not possible to isolate, combine or separate sounds of very short duration with any degree of control, and in this sense optical film opens the microsonic domain as a field of creative activity.[2] Of all three composers, Cage is the only one to identify the creative potential of microsound: 'The composer (organizer of sound) will be faced not only with the entire field of sound but also with the entire field of time. The "frame" or fraction of a second, following established film technique, will probably be the basic unit in the measurement of time. No rhythm will be beyond the composer's reach' (Cage, 1999: 5). In contrast, what Ellitt perceives in the new technologies of sound recording and reproduction is the opportunity for a personal and democratic exploration of sound – the potential for a new art of sound that might even find its way into the domestic sphere: 'When good recording apparatus is easily acquired, many people will record simple and everyday sounds which give them pleasure. The next step would be to mould these sound-snaps into formal continuity. Such sound-construction as this can have no more pretension or esoteric meaning than may be found in the energy expended on arranging some flowers in a vase' (Ellitt, 1935: 183).

While all three composers heard in film the potential to create radically new forms of sonic art, what they also shared in common was the fact that their dreams were never fully realised, at least in terms of film sound technology. Cage's attempts to gain access to the technical resources of Hollywood did not prove fruitful,[3] Varèse was not given the opportunity to compose for film, and Ellitt continued to work as a commercial film editor and director of documentaries. Rather, it was with quarter-inch tape that each realised their early enthusiasms for the radical creative possibilities of organised sound, in pieces that took the form of *musique concrete*.[4] But what was never realised by these composers, whose primary interest in film technology had been in its sonic potential, was the resituation of a radical art of organised sound within a cinesonic context. Of the three composers, it was Varèse who had most closely addressed the issue of how a radical sonic practice inspired by musical notions of organised sound might be employed within cinema; needless to say, it was many years before the kind of control and manipulation of film sound envisioned by the composer was realised in an audiovisual form.

▸▸ Fast-forward to the past ‖ 1984

In many ways, British scratch video of the 1980s can be seen as an audiovisual realisation of the ideas proposed by Varèse, Cage and Ellitt half a century earlier. If the call for an art of organised sound was realised sonically in the *musique concrete* experiments of the 1940s and 1950s, then it was video rather than film that finally provided the medium in which the composers' ideas took an audiovisual form. Based largely on the manipulation of sounds and images appropriated from film and television, in some ways scratch presented itself as a form of audiovisual *musique concrete*, the political dimensions of which seemed to realise the radical potential of organised sound. However, while in some ways scratch seems to continue a radical trajectory initiated by the development of film sound technology, the specificity of video naturally brings new considerations to the issue of what might constitute an art of organised sound. The cultural practices that arose from the introduction of consumer video in the early 1980s, and which were fundamental to scratch, signal a very different technological and cultural context to that in which Ellitt, Cage and Varèse were rethinking the use of film sound. Put another way, the issues and concerns of scratch indicate how musically informed models of sonic organisation may also be inflected by the specificities of audiovisual technology, and the way in which these technologies are deployed within specific cultural contexts. Thus, the organisation of sound becomes a more complex issue than is suggested by the simple authorial model of musical control proposed by Ellitt, Cage and Varèse in the 1930s and 1940s. Despite the fact that video is often treated as part of a seemingly coherent audiovisual continuity founded by film, video is in fact marked by differences and discontinuities that distinguish it from other audiovisual forms. Thus, the relationship between scratch and the radical modes of audiovisuality implied by the writings of Ellitt, Cage and Varèse raises two important issues: firstly, how are notions of control and organisation translated through the specificities of a particular medium situated within a particular historical and cultural context; and secondly, are the cinesonic practices of video best understood by way of continuity with other audiovisual forms, or in terms of difference and fracture?

While scratch represents a highly productive encounter between music and the audiovisual, that in some senses realises earlier radical visions of both an art of organised sound and an art of visual music, the musical dimensions of scratch proved problematic for those trying to situate its audiovisuality within existing political frames of reference. Central to its politically problematic status was the issue of how sensation and affect might be situated within radical modes of audiovisual practice. Scratch is intimately linked with music, which not only forms one of its key constituent elements, but also provides the primary formal model for its mode of articulation. Emerging from the London club scene of the 1980s, scratch video took its name, and in part drew its techniques and ethos, from New York hip-hop culture. In accord with the aims of the organised sound composers, scratch extends the sonic world of music to include worldly sounds, noises and sound effects. Furthermore, it enabled a democratic, personal exploration of an art of sound construction, similar to that proposed by Ellitt. In extending the control an artist-composer had over their sonic materials, scratch allowed what had already happened in *musique concrete*, and in hip-hop, to find audiovisual expression. Thus, if, in its organisation and manipulation of sound, scratch connects in spirit with *musique concrete*, its significant difference is that it is a truly audiovisual form, of the type suggested perhaps by Varèse. As the organised-sound composers had hoped, relatively cheap and readily available video technology finally provided the artist with the facility to place and manipulate sounds with a high degree of precision – even down to the level of the single frame. But perhaps most significantly, scratch enabled a form of listening not previously encountered in other forays into organised sound: that is, a transsensory, synaesthetic form of listening.

In 1984 Andrew Czezowski and Susan Carrington, owners of The Fridge nightclub in Brixton, set up a video lounge featuring the work of filmmakers and video artists such as Derek Jarman and John Maybury, and pieces by a small group of scratch video artists, including George Barber and Jeffery Hinton. Other clubs soon followed, including Heaven in London and The Zap Club in Brighton. At The Fridge work was shown on what, within a fine art context, would be thought of as an installation: a pile of TV monitors chained together, recalling the beginnings of video art in the sculptural works of Wolf Vostell and Nam June Paik. This form of visual presentation signals the fact that there was already a well-established sculptural mode of address for video art in the UK at this time. However, the fact that this work was exhibited not within a gallery, but within a club context, indicates that scratch was not completely aligned with the existing concerns and modalities of video art. While scratch seemed to invite the idea that it existed in continuity with established modes of video art practice, this relationship was perhaps marked to a greater extent by discontinuity and difference. This shift and disjuncture was to cause problems for the handful of critics who sought to engage critically with scratch, particularly as the majority of these writers were attempting to situate it within the dominant discourses relating to film and video practice during this period – discourses that were informed by the established tenets of political modernism.

Film as film, video as video

Scratch took place against a critical background that was dominated by political and aesthetic concerns inherited from the British avant-garde film culture of the previous decade; as Steve Hawley wrote at the time, 'There was a surprising degree of orthodoxy in British video in the seventies that did not apply on the continent or in the States. Here it was all structuralism and deconstruction' (Hawley, 1986: 9). During this period, British avant-garde film had been dominated by the critical and conceptual imperatives of modernism, most clearly articulated in structural film practice. In the work of Peter Gidal, this took the form of a wholesale rejection of narrative, and an attempt to demystify the illusion of film by foregrounding structure and materiality. Structural film demanded the involvement of a distanced yet active spectator who was to remain critically aware throughout a film's screening. Key to understanding this form of film practice was the ontological notion of 'film as film'.[5] Film was taken to be a substantive entity that could be differentiated from other art forms, and which would sustain a self-reflexive engagement with its own specificity. While those opposed to structural film practice argued that it was inward looking, lacking political engagement or contemporary relevance, the structural film was seen by some practitioners and critics as a political and cultural attack on representation in its various ideological, social, economic and sexual forms (Rees, 1999: 82). The severely reduced imagery of Gidal's films proposed a minimalist film as film: film as silver halide, the celluloid strip, the cone of light, the conditions of projection, space, perception and duration. In this way, structural filmmaking set the agenda for a politicised engagement with both the modernist concerns of specificity and materiality, and the problems of representation and narrative.

In 1975 Peter Wollen had argued in his influential article *The Two Avant-gardes* that, as a fundamental element of cinema, narrative had its place in avant-garde film practice.[6] While in the 1970s there had been a deep suspicion of narrative within avant-garde film culture, during the 1980s this attitude began to change. However, while there was a definite move by a number of film and video makers to engage with narrative form, their position on it remained critical – as is demonstrated by the work of John Smith. The concern with representation, which had been a central aspect of structural film practice, remained a key issue in the 1980s, its discussion further developed by the impact of feminism, a growing awareness of racism in British society and a desire to engage more directly with the social dimensions of the political. In some respects scratch video did seem to maintain the avant-garde's concern with the material and representational dimensions of the medium, but whereas avant-garde film and video addressed *itself* through materialist and self-reflexive practices, scratch turned its attention to the televisual image, prompted and supported by the widespread introduction of the domestic VCR in the early 1980s.

In addition to the critical and artistic concerns inherited from avant-garde film practice in the previous decade, radical film and video practice in the 1980s was also informed by an increasing awareness of the British party-political landscape. Socialism was in decline in Britain as the Conservative government began to dismantle the welfare state. Trade unions were under attack, and 1984 saw the beginning of a year-long miners' strike that ended in defeat for the National Union of Miners and marked the beginning of the downsizing of the British mining industry. Unemployment, at three million, was at its highest since the Depression of the 1930s. What can be seen in the avant-garde film and video of this period is a largely oppositional practice representing the concerns of an embattled Left; a final playing-out of a radical oppositional mode that had originally emerged from the events of May 1968.

The visual vocabulary of scratch is dominated by reworked images drawn originally from television and feature films, although artists such as Sandra Goldbacher and Kim Flitcroft also used live-action footage originated by themselves. In many ways, scratch was seen as a post-production aesthetic, relying heavily on certain editing techniques such as rapid cutting and the repeat edit. However, such a view would neglect the importance of the source material itself. Significantly, in scratching images from television, artists were using what was to hand – what surrounded them in their daily lives. This technological facility was made possible by the introduction of the domestic VCR. What this allowed was a time-shifting function that put broadcast images into alternative modes of circulation. Recorded on VHS, images of the miners' strike or a Conservative Party conference were no longer transitory, broadcast once and then gone forever (unless, of course, one had access to the archives of the broadcaster). The VCR allowed what was previously an uninterrupted flow of single iteration to be interrupted, stored and reiterated according to the designs of the scratcher. As Sean Cubitt put it, 'The domestic video cassette recorder (VCR) is itself a production device, as it can be used for seizing moments from TV's incessant flow, compiling, crash editing' (Cubitt, 1991: 4). For the first time ever, the sounds and images of broadcast television became permanently available to almost anyone who wanted to record them. This not only provided many scratch artists with the material content of their work, but also signalled a change in the relationship between the producers and consumers of television. In short, the VCR prompted and supported a culture of audiovisual appropriation that found its most immediate manifestation in scratch.

An oppositional use of the TV image is clearly apparent in the work of the Duvet Brothers,[7] whose agit-scratch videos dealt with unemployment, strikes, the dismantling of the welfare state, the Thatcher government and the arms race. Their 1984 tape *Blue Monday* (Figures 6.1–6.8) includes shots taken from documentaries and workers' films produced in the 1920s and 1930s, featuring images of the 1926 General Strike, fascist marches, mill workers, and the Chamberlain mannequin taken from Ivor Montagu's 1939 film *Peace and Plenty*. This material is montaged with contemporary images of Harrow schoolboys, the 1984 miners' strike, protest marches and scenes of urban desolation. The tape's use of montage editing works to critique the repressive and divisive aspects of life under Conservative rule. Shots of the Tory leadership are juxtaposed with images of Russian leaders taking the salute at a May Day parade in Red Square, while images of Soviet soldiers are cut together with those of members of the British police force attacking striking miners.

In the satirical *The President's World*, produced by Gorilla Tapes[8] in 1985, images from the films of Ronald Reagan are juxtaposed with contemporary news footage of Reagan engaged in presidential duties (Figures 6.9 and 6.10). Here, montage editing serves to make darkly comic connections between the two sets of images, suggesting perhaps that Reagan viewed his role as President of the United States in similar terms to the heroic characters he had played in his movie career.

When scratch was required to provide its own soundtrack, it sometimes adopted techniques from hip-hop, but rarely its specific sound. Much more common was the use of contemporary post-punk rock and pop, produced by British groups such as New Order and Joy Division. In its close association with popular music, scratch was not only informed by, but also influenced the pop video – one of the defining cultural forms of the 1980s. Thus, the scratch aesthetic went on to be incorporated into many of the techno videos of the late 1980s. While there were certainly many scratch videos that simply illustrated or interpreted a pre-existing music track, or even worked 'contrapuntally' against it, there were also others that worked in more varied cinesonic modes,

6.1–6.8 *Blue Monday*

6.9–6.10 *The President's World*

employing sync sound alone, or using it in conjunction with music. What the combination of different sound sources produces in scratch is a complex flux of sound–image relationships, rather like that of the cartoon. But unlike in the cartoon, synaesthetic effects dominate the audiovisual texture of scratch, rather than simply representing one constituent element. Thus, scratch lies in an interzone between a number of milieus: it is like pop video, but isn't pop video; its imagery and style of construction is sometimes reminiscent of Soviet montage and agit-prop, but at the same time its musical dimensions and its place within club culture mark it apart from these traditions; and in its use of synaesthetic effects, it seems to align itself with earlier experiments in visual music – but in scratch, representational, rather than abstract, images and sounds are central to its mode of address.

This indeterminacy is mirrored in scratch's problematic critical status. In relation to contemporary discourse relating to avant-garde film and video practice at this time, the arrival of scratch represented a challenge to both the existing understanding of the political nature of sound–image relationships, and to the dominance of the visual. The critical difficulties faced by avant-garde film and video in its attempt to territorialise scratch mark the point at which established conceptual models reveal their own deficiencies and biases, in terms of the way in which they conceptualise the cinesonic, and the cinesonic experience. What we see and hear in the case of scratch is the point at which dominant modernist formulations of sound–image relations are challenged by other radical conceptual models of the cinesonic.

Sound and scratch

One needs to look quite hard in the critical material of the time to find mention of the sonic strategies employed by scratch. The common use of the ready-made music soundtrack, to which appropriated TV and film footage was edited, or which was simply selected to accompany a dominant visual track, proved to be a problem for a number of critics of the period. Reviewing a tape by Kim Flitcroft and Sandra Goldbacher in 1986, the critic Philip Hayward describes the work as 'a disappointingly routine visualisation of Joy Division's vintage "Love Will Tear Us Apart"' (Hayward, 1986: 10). Similarly, in a review of work by Mike Jones and Graham Ellard, Ben Keen refers to 'the obligatory sugar coating of the up-tempo soundtrack' (Keen, 1986: 10), while elsewhere Nick

Houghton bemoans what he sees as the contemporary 'reliance on the supposedly populist appeal of music-tracked tapes' (Houghton, 1986: 9).

However brief this commentary, it nevertheless expresses a number of widely held beliefs about what is considered to be the appropriate place of music on the film or video soundtrack. There is perhaps a sense in which Hayward's negative response to Flitcroft and Goldbacher's tape reflects a widespread feeling that *visualisation* of music is somehow an unworthy filmmaking practice, and certainly less acceptable than the strategy of using music to *accompany* an image track. This latter cinesonic model has a long, although largely unattended, history in avant-garde film, and conforms to a dominant hierarchical formulation of sound–image relations, in which image is seen as the primary term, and sound as adjunct. The negative attitude towards visualisation reveals itself with great clarity in the discourse surrounding the work of animator Oskar Fischinger. In the 1930s Fischinger produced a series of films in which abstract graphics were tightly synchronised with well-known pieces of light classical or popular music. Writers championing Fischinger's work have long been at pains to describe this relationship between sound and image as something other than a visualisation of the music track. Thus, Richard Whitehall figures Fischinger's work in terms of 'audio-visual harmony' (Whitehall, 1988: 60), while William Moritz argues that music was only used in these films in order to help the audience engage with potentially challenging abstract imagery: 'Fischinger never intended to illustrate music, but rather hoped that the viewer, reminded that music is really abstract "noise" with a 1000-year artistic tradition behind it, would more easily be able to relate to his graphics' (1979: 61). Fischinger himself commented obliquely on the issue when describing the process by which he had added music to his first experimental abstract film, stating, 'On the wings of music faster progress was possible' (Fischinger, 1947: 38). But the fact remains that the movements, transformations and design of Fischinger's abstract lines, dots and wedges are not simply suggested but are actually determined by the rhythm, development and repetition of the music. Fischinger would begin work on these films by marking a phonograph record into sections, like slices of a pie, and would then painstakingly transcribe the sonic events held by each groove in each section of the disc.[9] This provided a visual 'score' for the film, according to which drawings could then be produced and animated.

But why resist the model of visualisation; why should Fischinger's defenders, or the critics of scratch, figure it as a problem? By constructing the relationship between Fischinger's imagery and music in terms not of dependence, but rather of support, his champions set out resist the idea that visualisation is merely an interpretation or augmentation of another art form. What this in turn points to is the modernist notion that each art form should distinguish itself from others, drawing upon and exploring its own 'essential' and defining qualities, rather than borrowing from elsewhere. Thus, musical *accompaniment* is an accepted cinesonic strategy in avant-garde and experimental filmmaking because it does not seem to threaten the integrity of the image track. The views expressed by Fischinger's supporters, and the critics of scratch, adhere to the belief that the essence of film resides in its visual dimensions; accordingly, the visualisation of music is framed in negative terms, since this practice necessarily positions sound as the primary term of the audiovisual relationship. Thus, we are returned to the celebration of silent cinema as the true art of film, and the conceptualisation of sound film as simply 'canned theatre' – or in this instance, canned music.

In terms of the prioritisation of the visual over the sonic, the avant-garde proves no different from classical Hollywood cinema. Although, as previously stated, music had an important influence on the development avant-garde film, this was limited to providing a model of how an abstract visual experience might be organised in time. As Wollen notes in *The Two Avant-gardes* (1975), in many ways early avant-garde film simply extends established painterly concerns – particularly those regarding abstraction – into a temporal dimension. The work of the pioneers of avant-garde film, like that of Man Ray, Hans Richter, Viking Eggeling, Moholy-Nagy and Fischinger, proposed kinetic solutions to pictorial problems. In the book *Painting, Photography, Film*, Moholy-Nagy wrote, 'The traditional painting has become a historical relic and is finished with. Eyes and ears have been opened and are filled at every moment with a wealth of optical and phonetic wonders' (Moholy-Nagy, 1969: 45). The book proposes a progressive evolution of the visual arts, from the easel painting to film, beginning with a chapter entitled 'From Painting with Pigment to Light Displays', and ending with 'Simultaneous or Poly-cinema'. Thus, for Moholy-Nagy, cinema provides the visual arts with kinetic and temporal dimensions that were absent in photography and painting; film is conceptualised as an extension of existing forms, and the inheritor of their concerns. In this way, Moholy-Nagy tacitly supports the dominant view of cinema as an *essentially* visual art form. Hence, when identifying the medium's defining properties, Moholy-Nagy's focus is entirely visual: 'everyone today has some idea of what is meant by the proposition – revolutionary in its effect in the early days – of the FILMIC, that is, of the film which proceeds from the potentialities of the camera and the dynamics of motion' (Moholy-Nagy, 1969: 122). The visual bias of avant-garde film practice is more overtly expressed in the work and writing of Stan Brakhage, many of whose films were purposely produced without a recorded soundtrack. Brakhage took the view that the filmic image has an inherent sonic dimension which, when articulated through editing, provides film with its own internal rhythmic and musical qualities: 'The sound sense which visual images always evoke and which can become integral with the esthetic experience of film under creative control, often makes actual sound superfluous. On this premise alone, one could disqualify almost every sound film from consideration as a work of art. There is no definition of a work of art which will admit superfluity' (Brakhage, 1960: 67). Brakhage's approach to filmmaking is in part underpinned by a belief in the importance of medium specificity. Thus he took the decision to film members of his family rather than actors, and to record events in daily life rather than staged narratives, in order to reduce or eliminate the influence of other arts on filmmaking – in this case drama (Ganguly, 2002: 141). While his comments on the silent sound sense are not dismissive of sound per se, they nevertheless clearly express the view that film does not require a soundtrack to function as an art form. By figuring sound as dispensable, Brakhage tacitly locates the essence of film in the image. This optically oriented view of cinema is deeply inscribed in what Wollen has referred to as the 'first' avant-garde. It was this visually dominated tradition of avant-garde film and video practice that provided the context in which scratch video, a profoundly and disturbingly audiovisual form, was situated by critics of the time.

In relation to scratch, the deafness associated with Wollen's 'first' avant-garde translates into a critical distrust of music. When Keen refers to 'the obligatory sugar coating of the up-tempo soundtrack' (Keen, 1986: 10) his comments imply that the popular music employed by scratch renders something that is essentially difficult more palatable. Keen's choice of metaphor gives the sense that this form of musical moderation is inappropriate, in that this 'sugar coating' might be deceptive, mystificatory, perhaps even manipulative. A similar position is adopted by Houghton, who describes 'a reliance on the supposedly populist appeal of music-tracked tapes' (Houghton, 1986: 9). Here the sense is that music makes the work of the video artist popular and digestible in a way that is unacceptable to this particular critic. A profound mistrust of popular music is thus expressed by both critics, whose comments suggest that its sounds are not properly aligned with the bitter realities and tough messages that scratch might be trying to address in its *images*. Situated against the overt political imagery of scratch, much of which was taken from news broadcasts of the time, popular music is figured as somehow out of sync with the harsh political and social realities faced by the Left. This view is expressed in very direct terms by the video artist and critic Catherine Elwes, who writes, 'Some artists are now trying to make direct social comments with scratch. The Duvet Brothers for instance, cut together urban wastelands and well-fed Conservative politicians. The pace is snappy and the images are well-oiled by the inevitable disco soundtrack. We are left wondering whether to debate the evils of unemployment or get up and dance' (Elwes, 1985: 22). What Elwes's comments indicate is a perceived tension between politically committed imagery, engaging with the issues of the time at an intellectual level, and a cinesonic *experience* engendered by the use of dance music. Significantly, Elwes's criticism extends beyond the specific nature of the soundtrack to address the perceptual and experiential dimensions of scratch, signalled in her reference to the 'well-oiled' nature of sound–image relations. In common with Keen and Houghton, Elwes figures the musical dimension of scratch as somehow standing in opposition to what is properly 'political'.

In addition to anxieties centring on the perceived indifference of the ready-made soundtrack to scratch's politicised imagery, some critics were also concerned about the nature of the context in which scratch was exhibited. Experienced within a club environment, it was unlikely that the visuals of scratch would command the full attention of its audience. Scratch's origins in the London club scene, and specifically its place within dance culture, thus proved problematic for writers on the subject:

> A bank of TV monitors, a bar, dancefloor, live bands. Nice. But while the sounds might be wild by contrast the vision will probably be dull, decontextualised and operating at a level of attractively vacuous video wallpaper. Shown without the sub-text of sound, primarily because this might disrupt the DJ's programme of vinyl goodies, and

located within a situation where the viewers [*sic*] concentration is likely to be minimal, video-art here taken [*sic*] on the appearance of empty gesture, image without meaning, an impacted form where the tendency toward spectacle serves only to amplify the worst in dominant television and film. (Funking the Frame/Framing the Funk, 1986: 9)

What appears to lie behind this particular writer's antagonism towards scratch is a feeling that, in a club situation, the visual is not allowed to occupy its rightful place as the primary term of the audiovisual contract, and is instead usurped by the dance music of the club environment.

Informed by the visually oriented discourses supporting avant-garde film and experimental video practice during this period, criticism of the musical dimensions of scratch reveals a lack of understanding of the political potential of sound, and of synaes-thetic audiovisuality; hence, critics were only able to view the work in terms of insufficiency. Rather than revealing some fundamental flaw in the logic of scratch, the critical response indicates, perhaps, that there was no conceptual vocabulary in place to engage with the affective dimensions of scratch's audiovisuality. Thus, the comments of these critics simply revisit a set of established and well-rehearsed notions about what constitutes a radical poetics of film or video in primarily visual terms.

This continued prioritisation of the image returns us to Moholy-Nagy's assertion that the radical potential of film emerges from its specificity, which in turn is founded on the medium's visual qualities: 'everyone today has some idea of what is meant by the proposition – revolutionary in its effect in the early days – of the FILMIC, that is, of the film which proceeds from the potentialities of the camera and the dynamics of motion' (Moholy-Nagy, 1969: 122). But perhaps it is possible revisit Moholy-Nagy's ideas to suggest that by the 1980s the ongoing prioritisation of the visual, and the concern with specificity manifested in critical writing on scratch, was no longer revolutionary, and perhaps even conservative. What can be perceived quite clearly in scratch criticism is an established notion of the political that is figured in purely visual terms; but what also lurks behind these comments is an uneasiness about pleasure and its relationship with the audiovisual experience. The tension between established forms of political representation and modes of audiovisual experience is manifested within the works themselves, which suggest a kind of crisis of the visual. What we see in a tape like the Duvet Brother's *Blue Monday* is a use of juxtaposition that returns us to the intellectual montage of Soviet cinema. When the image of Margaret Thatcher is juxtaposed with that of Soviet military leaders reviewing a May Day parade, a third meaning is created, implying that the Conservative government is dictatorial and repressive. Elsewhere in the same tape we see a shot of a surgeon, taken from a black and white documentary, made perhaps in the 1940s (Figure 6.11). After several seconds this image is frozen, and the word 'private' superimposed over it (Figure 6.12). This composite visual is then mixed with a shot of a graveyard (Figure 6.13), producing a combination of images which spells out the formula HOSPITALS + PRIVATISATION = DEATH. Here the images are organised to operate at a *significative* level, as in the Eisensteinian formulation of intellectual montage.

But there are other forces at work here, challenging the dominance of significatory and linguistic modes of address. Although the soundtrack of the tape (Joy Division's *Blue Monday*) features lyrics, the song is clearly not only operating at the level of linguistic signification; importantly, music also works through affect. This is also true of the image track, where the affective dimensions of the 'political' imagery are enhanced through the use of cutting. Thus, in a sequence that uses news footage of police battling with striking miners, shots are jump cut to the accents of the music. This use of editing is clearly problematic for critics like Elwes, who writes, 'We are left wondering whether to debate the evils of unemployment or get up and dance'. What this cutting creates is a synaesthetic intensification of affect that cannot be understood or valued within critical discourses dominated by the conceptual traditions of semiology and structuralism, and concerned primarily with meaning. Deconstructive modes of criticism, founded on structuralist principles, have no way to engage with certain modes of synthesis. Consequently, at this particular moment in history, there was no space in which to consider the radical possibilities of synaesthetic experience. The critical discourse brought to bear on scratch was geared towards separating rather than blending sound and image.

The way in which images are combined using video technology also adds to the challenge that scratch presented to the dominance of the significative political image. Here, images lose their essence as they are folded and mixed one into another through the use of chroma key and luma key superimposition – a technique that renders them mutually perforated, and which of course, in its sonic form, is central to music production (i.e., mixing). The tension

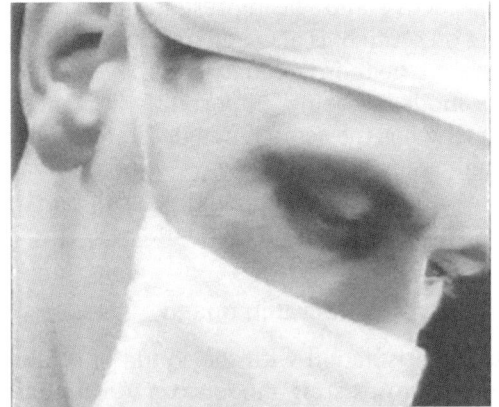

6.11–6.13 *Blue Monday*

between the affective and the representational, signalled by the critical writing on scratch, is also apparent in the tapes themselves. What we see and hear in scratch is a movement of the visual towards other modes of being. Importantly, it is music that stands as the marker of what the scratch image aspires to become, just as the image might represent other ways of being for music, in the case of mickey-mousing. At the juncture of these two becomings lies the audiovisual experience of scratch.

Scratch image

While critical dissatisfaction with the sound of scratch shows that it did not conform to existing models of radical audiovisual practice, paradoxically, it is criticism of the scratch image that serves to indicate the political potential of the form's cinesonic dimensions. Turning briefly to the way in which the appropriated image was understood within avant-garde film and video practice at this time, the discontinuities that mark scratch and its soundtrack from the work with which it was initially assumed to be comparable become clear. In the early days of video art Nam June Paik had declared, 'Television has been attacking us all our lives . . . now we can attack it back' (Youngblood, 1970: 302), and at first sight, scratch seems to realise Paik's dream of a democratic, oppositional televisual form. However, despite appearances, this model of radical appropriation does not account adequately for the factors that motivate scratch. What differentiates scratch from the model of deconstructive appropriation proposed by Paik is the nature of the relationship between the appropriator and the appropriated, and the way in which pleasure figures within this relationship. If the scratchers attacked the images transmitted by television, this did not necessarily mean that television itself was their target. Unlike the form of appropriation proposed by Paik, scratching was not always motivated by an oppositional desire to deconstruct or destroy; this becomes most apparent in scratch's use of images appropriated from feature films. VHS rental made films available on demand, providing scratch with a plentiful source of audiovisual material. However, when film images were appropriated by scratch, it was certainly not always the case that they were used to deconstruct Hollywood film, or to attack the political values Hollywood movies seemed to represent. Despite its concern with the medium, scratch did not in fact offer the same type of self-reflexivity perceived in, or demonstrated by, video art. Nevertheless, claims were still made for its formalist potential. Thus, Catherine Elwes wrote at the time, 'There is no doubt that the fragmentation of seamless television footage robs the image of its narrative anchor and exposes it as a fictitious construct' (Elwes, 1985: 22). However, while critics saw radical potential in the visuals of scratch – judged, of course, according to established notions of what constituted 'progressive' video practice – the dominant view was that this potential was not being realised. Rather than being seen as radical, scratch's appropriation of images was sometimes perceived as being highly problematic. The case against scratch centred on issues of representation, and in particular on problems relating to the issue of the male gaze.

Central to scratch's problematic relationship with the theoretical and critical frameworks supporting film and video practice at this time was the issue of the personal nature of sampling, and how this might relate to politicised notions of representation. In Jeffrey Hinton's tape *Bucks Fizz*, the inclusion of a revealing shot of a dancer locates the problem of scratch within the image itself. Here the appropriated footage retains its sexual charge despite transplantation and recontextualisation. In this respect, Hinton's work would have been seen as simply reproducing, rather than deconstructing, the sexist images of the mainstream media. In a period where film criticism drew heavily on the theoretical resources provided by semiology, the image became subject to close analysis, discussed in political terms through debates about representation. What troubled the avant-garde community about scratch's appropriation of the TV image was that it did not automatically radicalise that image. An article written by Catherine Elwes in 1985, entitled *Through Deconstruction to Reconstruction*, articulates this problem in the following terms:

> There has been a sustained attempt to establish the political credentials of Scratch, but the question remains, does scratch deconstruct television by reconstructing it? There is no doubt that the fragmentation of seamless television footage robs the image of its narrative anchor and exposes it as a fictitious construct. But the deconstructions are also reproductions, they reproduce highly seductive television imagery made all the more captivating by the ingenious new configurations scratchers are inventing. Scratch is being trapped by its own prey. (Elwes, 1985: 22)

Here the question of what constitutes a properly political form of scratch revolves around the issue of deconstruction. Elwes

6.14 *Yes Frank, No Smoke*

'Sumptuous as Barber's reworkings of Nestor Almendros' images may be, does their recontextualisation substantially alter the 'core attraction' element of the exploitation of Brooke Shield's (often naked) body in the source film "Blue Lagoon."'?' (Hayward, 1986: 10)

6.15 *Night of a 1000 Eyes*

'The glamour-scratch tapes of Kim Flitcroft and Sandra Goldbacher are pure celebration. Their video vamps do little to undermine the sexism of their media originals.' (Elwes, 1985: 22)

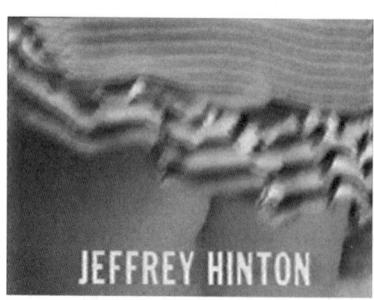

6.16 *Bucks Fizz*

'The entire existence of a problematic of representation seems unknown to these artists, who operate as if the last 20 years of film history had never occurred or had been so successfully repressed as to have disappeared from the cultural horizon. The political relationships, the ideology encapsulated in television, and in the imagery of television seems unseen.' (Dunford, 1986: 6) concedes that scratch may possess radical potential, but that this can only be realised under certain conditions: 'only when s/he unrelentingly attacks and undermines the dominant readings of the footage s/he is using, when her vision remains clear and unclustered by arty aspirations, when s/he eradicates any weakness s/he might have for the glamour of those flickering fantasies on the screen' (Elwes, 1985: 22). Thus, the issue of pleasure is situated as a problem in relation to a radical politics of deconstruction.

For Mike Dunford, one of scratch's most unforgiving critics, the practice of using television's images is fraught with problems. He writes, 'Tremendous confusion exists about what it is that television actually does. Many video artists see it as either a source of neutral imagery to be copied, or reused, or as an example to be emulated for its production values, its narrative models' (Dunford, 1986: 6). Here Dunford suggests a kind of naïveté on the part of scratchers who, he proposes, seem ignorant of the debates about representation that had occupied a central place in the work of theoretically (and politically) aware film and video makers. What Elwes, Dunford and their fellow critics have a problem reconciling is the fact that the appropriation practised in scratch is not necessarily in tune with the kind of oppositional deconstruction proposed by the work of the previous decade. However, Dunford is incorrect in suggesting that the scratchers saw TV and film as source of 'neutral imagery to be copied, or reused'. Rather, these tapes often reveal the scratcher's attraction to their source material, rendering it anything but neutral. As Kodwo Eshun has written in relation to scratching with vinyl, 'The sample, a window into psychoaffective time, exposes and externalizes the instamatic mechanism that is your innermost taste' (Eshun, 1998: 58). Thus, it is hip-hop's model of organised sound that serves to highlight the logic of appropriation proposed by scratch video. The imagery of scratch, as an externalisation of the scratcher's innermost taste, thus signals a move from oppositional deconstruction to a form of cannibalism motivated, in part, by pleasure, and which needs to be understood in terms other than those proposed by the critical writing of the time.

Can you dig it?

In its focus on the issue of the ready-made pop soundtrack, the small body of writing that offers critical comment on the sound of scratch neglects the range of cinesonic strategies the form employed. Rather than editing mute visuals to pre-recorded music, many scratch video makers created work that would use both appropriated footage and its accompanying synchronous soundtrack. In this case, the sounds from the source material were often incorporated into, and synchronised with, pre-existing or specially composed music, as in George Barber's *Yes Frank, No Smoke* (1986). Here, Barber samples and scratches a number of American feature films of the period, including *The Deep* (1977) and *The Blue Lagoon* (1980). What is significant in terms of the cinesonic approach developed by Barber is that the original material is being raided as much for its sounds as for its images. Thus, single words, or even parts of words, are scratched, just as in hip-hop, except that here the sampled sounds remain attached to their accompanying visuals. Barber may repeat these samples over and over again, reverse them, or manipulate them by the addition of effects. These reworked samples are then bedded into a composed music track that runs throughout the piece. In one section of the tape Barber works on a sampling of a Hollywood movie starring Roy Scheider, scratching the phrases 'no smoke' and 'yes Frank' into a stuttering, rhythmic, hip-hopish 'n/n/n/-/n/n/n/-/n/n/no smoke' and 'y/y/y/-/y/y/y-/y/y/yes Frank/-/yes Frank'. In addition, quite banal pieces of action might be scratched to create synaesthetic effects, as when Barber builds a rhythmic structure from repeated shots of an actor putting down a telephone handset.

While Barber's manipulation of appropriated dialogue seems to move towards the kind of control and manipulation of sound proposed by Cage, Ellitt and Varèse fifty years earlier, the composers' ideas are perhaps more fully realised in sonic terms by those video scratchers who worked without a continuous music track, simply using the sound of the appropriated footage as a form of *musique concrete*. In the Duvet Brothers' 1984 tape *War Machine*, looped sounds of heavy artillery create the basis of a powerful, unrelenting sonic accompaniment to sometimes shocking images of war. The soundtrack also features loops and scratches of significant words and phrases: thus we hear 'threat' and 'safety net' taken from a contemporary speech by Ronald Reagan, the phrase 'war machine' lifted from a TV advertisement for a military magazine of the same name, and an ominous 'you ain't seen nothin' yet'.

A much more technically straightforward, yet equally effective, piece of audiovisual *musique concrete* comprises the Duvet Brothers' 1984 tape *Take It*. Lasting only 30 seconds, the tape has been produced by scratching a short section from the 1971

blaxploitation movie *Shaft*. As with *War Machine*, no music has
been added, and its makers work only with the synchronous sound
accompanying the image. The tape opens with the actor Richard
Roundtree emerging from the shadows to deliver the line, 'Hey,
I don't know about you guys, but me, I've had it up to here,' and
closes with the actor delivering an aggressive 'Take it!' The Duvet
Brothers isolate and repeat short sections of the scene, which
begins with the ominous sound of the detective's approaching
footsteps. Following this, Shaft's exclamation 'Hey!' is repeated
five times through looping. During the course of articulating this
single sound, Rowntree's head moves slightly, from the top right of
the screen towards the bottom left. This is a small movement that
would not attract any attention in the original sequence. However,
the jump cut that results from scratching this section creates a
strong kinetic effect, as the actor's head flicks from one side of
the screen to the other, in synchronisation with the sonic accent
created by repetition of the vocal exclamation. The same effect
is produced when the actor's partial line 'I've had it . . .' is looped
a number of times. In this case, Roundtree is seen drawing an
imaginary line across his chest – a gesture that illustrates the line
'I've had it up to here,' and which is finally delivered in its entirety
after several partial samplings. The tape closes with Roundtree
gesticulating aggressively towards the camera, his fist and teeth
clenched as the words 'Take it!' are repeatedly looped, once again
producing a strong kinetic effect that synchronises precisely with
the repetitions of the soundtrack.

What this particular tape demonstrates is the way in which
cutting can generate synaesthetic effects. Scratch often employed
the repeat edit – a short clip of video looped over and over with
great rapidity; when video and sound are cut synchronously in this
way, the correspondence of sound and image strikes the viewer
more clearly than when longer samples are used. The effect of
repeating short samples of video with sync sound is to bond sound
and image ever more strongly. A clip of video may feature sounds
that do not have a particularly strong morphological relationship
with the image, and if played only once, the clip will probably
not demonstrate any significant synaesthetic potential. However,
when that clip is repeated, the connections between sound and
image begin to crystallise, as by synchresis an element of the image
begins to align itself with part of the soundtrack, and vice versa.
The shorter the clip, the fewer visual and sonic events it includes,
thus giving the extract a more concrete morphological profile than

clips of longer duration. Indeed, this kind of editing can release a micro-event, like the slight movement of a head, that would otherwise not offer itself up to synchresis. The more times we have the opportunity to view and hear the clip, the more opportunity we have to explore this micro-morphological domain, and nuances of movement and sound that can be missed at first viewing begin to reveal themselves in repetition. Thus a synaesthetic bond between sound and image is actively shaped by the repeat edit.

By working and reworking source material in this way, scratch created a range of audiovisual experiences that had little to do with the forms of deconstructive appropriation that had been championed by its critics. While scratch did rework film and video footage in order to engage in social and political critique, adopting an oppositional political stance that could be understood within existing political discourse, its capacity to negate and attack was much less significant than its capacity to create and generate. While not necessarily recognised by critics of the time, the productive nature of scratch was certainly understood by its practitioners. Thus, Rik Lander's critical reflection on *Take It*, which had been made by his partner Peter Boyd Maclean, offers a model for a positive poetics of re-articulation, rather than simply viewing scratch as an essentially negative act of deconstruction: 'The feeling is great when something this simple and powerful comes together. It's like what Barbara Hepworth says about a piece of rock – that there's a form inside the material that you have to reveal with your hacking and tapping. With scratch there's a sense of chipping away and layering and moulding an existing form into something new' (Lander, 2005). Further, what Lander suggests in his choice of sculpture as a positive model for scratch is the idea that scratching releases a potential that already lies within the material itself. What proved problematic for the critics of the time was that the deconstruction of source material undertaken in scratch was rarely the same kind of semiotic deconstruction they were familiar with. Rather, the deconstruction practised in scratch works in a positive way to liberate the kinaesthetic and synaesthetic potential of its source material.

What is notable about the critical commentary on scratch is that it tends to neglect, or merely hint at, the affective payload delivered by the kinetic-sonic shocks that are central to the form. The rapidity of the scratch edit, and the possibility of endless repetition, are made sense of by Elwes in terms of an *excess* that aligns scratch with television in a problematic way:

Today, a general disenchantment with structuralist prohibitions has led to a euphoric return to television aesthetics. Yesterday's taboos are today's imperatives. Where the deconstructed image of the 70s was as unlike television as possible, today's deconstructions are more like television than television itself – 'General Hospital on Acid' as John Sanborn put it. Scratch, the most fashionable form of television deconstruction is proposing excess as the new video aesthetic. Excess is a refusal to engage in rational exchanges with a system which it regards as irrational, autocratic and unassailable through normal political channels. (Elwes, 1985: 21–22)

Elwes picks up on the idea that scratch may not be concerned primarily with rationality – that is to say, it may not operate purely at a cognitive level. However, she views the 'irrationality' of excess as simply a rational response to the irrationality of another system. Ironically, she touches on the key issue relating to the radical potential of scratch when she opposes 'excess' and 'normal political channels', suggesting that the audiovisual poetics of scratch, figured here in terms of excess, do not relate to the established notions of what is understood to constitute the political. Her formulation offers the failure of excess as an oppositional strategy, a refusal to engage when 'normal political channels' are no longer operative. What this shows is an understanding of the radical that is entirely limited to established political norms; there is no comprehension that modalities like 'excess' may have immanent political potential. Her logic thus belies a faith in the order of the rational, proposing that irrationality should be challenged by any means if 'normal' political discourse is to no avail.[10] What Elwes cannot comprehend is that the 'excess' of scratch may have value beyond its deployment as a Dadaistic oppositional technique. Scratch sidesteps the logocentrism that proposes, supports and requires forms of individuation and notions of essence – the same logocentrism upon which a range of modernist approaches to the visual are founded. The excess of scratch replaces the single, isolated, meaningful and representational image or sound with a multiplicity that simply engulfs the audiospectator in a stream of kinetic-sonic affective shocks. While, above, I have described in detail some of the basic structural elements of the Duvet Brother's tape *Take It*, this has been done with the aid of a VHS tape and the video player's pause button; that is, my own deconstruction of the tape is somewhat removed from the actual experience of watching it and listening to it. When experiencing the tape without the benefit of freeze-frame, the viewer is swept up in its flow, unable to track or identify the techniques being used, unable to reflect upon the complexity of its synaesthetic dimensions; rather, the viewer simply registers the *flow* of kinetic-sonic shocks as sound and image become increasingly fused.

The rapidity of the scratch edit, and the possibility of endless repetition, links the video edit controller with another technological phenomenon of this period, namely the drum machine. In regard to the speed and rhythm generated by this particular piece of music technology, Kodwo Eshun writes, 'This "humanly impossible" time, this automization of rhythm which is rhythmatics, opens up the posthuman multiplication of rhythm: the rhythm synthesizer's spastic pulses seize the body, rewiring the sensorium in a kinaesthetic of shockcuts and stutters, a voluptuous epilepsy' (Eshun, 1998: 79). Eshun makes the point that the body is 'seized' by the drum machine's rhymatics; it is overtaken, possessed. The sensory and embodied nature of this experience not only parallels that created by the rapidity and 'excess' of scratch video, but also sheds light on the effects and affects created by scratching. Eshun proposes that the scratching of vinyl can be understood as the creation of new textures in sound. In turn, these textures can be thought of as a 'switching on' of the material potential of the scratch (Eshun, 1998: 176). Thus, scratching with vinyl may be seen as a means by which the powerful morphological dimensions of sound are isolated and articulated. The textures produced by manipulation, and the articulation of individual isolated sounds by sampling, set up an experience that is felt or 'understood' at a bodily rather than an intellectual level. For Eshun, musical samples, scratches and the breakbeat all pay off in kinetic or dermal ways. Making a clear link between morphology, bodily experience, film sound and music, he comments:

> To me, it makes complete sense to see action movies in the same stratum as skratchadelia. There are the same velocities, the same vectors, the same sounds: the sound of a car as it skids round a corner is the same sound the wheels of steel make as they ride around. You're captured, abducted by the same sounds in each. It's this fantastic sound of velocity, as 2 surfaces in friction literally converge and then shoot apart at fantastic speeds. (Eshun, 1998: 180)

Here vectors, velocities and convergence all point to the material and morphological features of sound, by which music captures and abducts the listener.

Standing in stark contrast to the logocentric, deconstructive critical models applied to video practice in the 1980s, Eshun's analysis of musical scratching provides an alternative frame of reference for scratch video's re-articulation of appropriated images and sounds. When scratch video switches on the material potential of a moving image or a recorded sound, it switches on not *only* the potential to create meaning, but also its affective potential. Releasing the latent kinaesthetic and synaesthetic power of its source material, scratch video follows the imperatives of music, disengaging with linguistic models of meaning in favour of an intensification of affect.

If Eshun's observations on sensory and embodied experience provide a way of understanding the audiovisual dimensions of scratch video, then they also indicate why its true home was in the club environment rather than the gallery or cinema. The club experience itself can be thought of as a form of sensory blending, a fusion of sound and image and bodily movement. And in some ways it is this form of transsensoriality to which scratch video aspires in its synaesthetic articulation of sound and image; scratch is a mode of articulation that places emphasis on blending and folding rather than isolation and specificity.[11] Little wonder, then, that scratch got the reception it did in the 1980s, a period in which British avant-garde film and video practice was dominated by a visually oriented critical culture founded on modernist notions of specificity.

'People only sample good stuff': the pleasures of cannibalism

Critical resistance to the discussion of pleasure meant that many of the key elements of scratch were either ignored by writers of the time, or dismissed because of their assumed lack of political relevance. In this way, the synaesthetic possibilities of scratch were completely overlooked by those hoping to make sense of the phenomenon. Similarly, in neglecting the issue of pleasure, critics proved unable to understand the complexity of factors motivating creative acts of appropriation. In simply formulating appropriation according to an approved model of cultural opposition, writers on scratch were only able to find it wanting as a form of radical video practice.

To fully appreciate the radical potential of scratch, it is necessary to situate it within a more complex and nuanced model of cultural appropriation. In the book *Timeshift*, Sean Cubitt makes reference to scratch's use of rapid repetition in the following way: 'Grab-frames, the repetition of a frame or a group of frames to give the impression of a repeated gesture, is one of the most common of mid-1980s video techniques and one which seems to drive on-screen characters to the level of puppets in a particularly disturbing way' (Cubitt, 1991: 95). Cubitt proposes that when this technique is applied to hegemonic images of power and masculinity, taking as his example the Roy Scheider performance sampled in Barber's *Yes Frank, No Smoke*, the re-articulation that results can be read as an attack on the original material, and thus an attack on the values this material is seen to represent. In a similar fashion, Diedrich Diederichsen has formulated montage as a partial act of destruction, stating, 'everywhere a cut interrupts a continuum and is joined together with another one, a context, an image is also always lost' (Diederichsen, 2005). The disruption of continuity proposed by Diederichsen's model of montage, and observed by Cubitt in scratch's use of the 'grab-frame', can be interpreted as an attack on a hegemonic cultural object. Accordingly, Cubitt views scratch's form of deconstruction very much in oppositional terms, as an assault on the original source material, and all that it might stand for and represent. This means, of course, that he sees deconstruction as an essentially representational strategy; the act of deconstructing, and the deconstructed artefact, stand for something other than themselves, declaring an oppositional stance to what is *represented* by the source material. This critical viewpoint inevitably fails to offer a positive consideration of the material act of deconstruction, or the materiality of the deconstructed.

However, the example of musical scratching suggests that scratch video may not always be driven by wholly oppositional imperatives. As the musician and DJ Matthew Herbert put it so succinctly, 'people only sample the good stuff'.[12] Going beyond the oppositional gesture, the creative complexity of appropriation might be further adumbrated by considering some of characteristics of fine art collage and montage proposed by Gregory L. Ulmer (1985). Ulmer suggests that collage can be understood as the transfer of materials from one context to another, while montage involves the dissemination of appropriated material through a new setting. In this sense, the compositional pair montage/collage offers immediate parallels to scratch video practice. The operation of both compositional forms, according to Ulmer, is marked by four characteristics: *découpage* (severing); preformed or extant messages or materials; assemblage (montage); and discontinuity or heterogeneity. The logic of appropriation proposed by scratch negotiates a desire that relates both to the act of *découpage* and to the extant materials being severed. When the scratcher picks out a single moment from the continuum of images and sounds being sampled, they appropriate atmosphere and style as well as a particular audiovisual event. In this way the background sounds of film, optical crackle, the hiss of video tape and the specific sonic qualities rendered by a particular type of microphone are all bought into in the scratch, just as much as the on-screen action, or the visual qualities rendered by the actor, the setting, props, lighting, film stock and so on. Thus, a scratch tape such as Barber's *Yes Frank, No Smoke* does not simply *refer* to the Hollywood movies it quotes, but at some level it also takes on their qualities, plugging into the whole artistic and cultural complex that inhabits and surrounds a clip. Multiple associations of historical period, lifestyle, attitude and atmosphere permeate the images and sounds culled from source material. In this way, a fragment taken from a film can embody and articulate many of the characteristics of the original source.

However, this act of sampling should not be understood as an articulation of the aspirational desires of a 'wannabe' Hollywood director. The act of *découpage* represents a form of cannibalism that is both respectful and predatory. The Brazilian poet Haraldo de Campos has suggested that anthropophagy (in this case used as a metaphor for translation) might be viewed not as an act of furious aggression, but rather as an irreverently amorous devouring. If some forms of cannibalism are informed by an animistic belief in the inseparability of matter and spirit, then the killing and consumption of an enemy may be seen as a form of tribute, the victor eating the defeated in order to take on their strength. Working through de Campos' formulation in terms of literary translation, Else Ribeiro Pires Viera describes 'a translation project which murders the father . . . yet reveres him by creating a continued existence for him in a different corporeality' (Viera, 1999: 97). Both de Campos and Viera's formulations of 'cannibalistic' translation help to describe a key aspect of the appropriation undertaken in scratch video. If scratch is to be conceptualised as an oppositional form, then it is so because it exhibits a positive desire to appropriate the power of its victim. Scratch's use of film and television footage needs therefore to be viewed according to a complex and positive model of appropriation, rather than as a simple form of negation or destruction.

The problematic complexity of the relationship between source and re-articulation is signalled, perhaps, by Derrida's phrase 'participation without belonging' (Derrida, 1992: 227). Applied to the scratch video, this formulation proposes that scratched footage forms part of a new text, while simultaneously referring to its original source. The 'participation' of the sample within a scratch tape takes place, initially, at the material level. While the ruptures and contrasts of fine art collage may serve an anti-illusionist, deconstructive function, in scratch these ruptures, although still visible and audible, are subsumed by the organisational logic of the piece – whether this is rhythmic structuring, or scratch's updated form of Eisenstinian Intellectual Montage. In addition to this material participation, the clip also plugs into the scratch tape's representational regime. The referential element of the clip is guaranteed by its otherness, its belonging elsewhere. In this way, the clip leads to a double 'reading' – of its place in the edit, and of its relationship with an original source. Even though we may not be able to identify the source of a clip when watching a scratch tape, the status of recorded sound and image as representation without reference guarantees the possibility of this double reading. In fact, it is the weakness of a clip's attachment to its source that allows its reanimation within the scratch video, enabling a smooth passage into a new context, and allowing the potential for it to take on a range of other meanings. In this way, while we may not recognise a particular clip as an extract from *Shaft*, we know the kind of film it stands for, and all the cultural baggage it carries. Severed from its original context, the clip's re-articulation not only becomes possible, but also fluid and unresisted. However, as Derrida's phrase might suggest, collage never entirely suppresses the alterity of the elements it makes use of. This proved highly problematic for many critics, who felt that scratch ran the risk of reproducing, rather than challenging, hegemonic forms of representation:

> What we are seeing here is the old problem of how to demonstrate sexism, say, without reproducing a sexist image. The 70s solution was to eliminate the image altogether. Todays exposition through excess unwittingly traps the artist in a circular argument with television itself. S/he oscillates between totally denying television imagery and wholeheartedly embracing it. S/he never steps outside it. (Elwes, 1985: 22)

The material sampled in scratch clearly had significance to those making the tapes, and this in itself became an issue for video scratchers working within the context of the critical and intellectual climate of the 1980s. Dianne Waldman has written of fine art collage that it 'seemed to document the social and political life of the artist – the brand of cigarette he or she smoked, the newspaper he or she read, the articles the artist chose to single out to represent himself or herself to the world' (Waldman, 1992: 11). What we observe in scratch are the images and sounds that surrounded the artists in their daily lives; but in sampling what was to hand, the video scratchers not only worked with materials they wished to deconstruct, but also with materials to which they were attracted. It is possible, in this respect, to make a distinction between scratch's use of television and film footage. Television footage tends to be employed by scratchers in a significatory, critical manner, in the sense that the images of Thatcher and Reagan culled from news programmes could be employed in a very straightforward and traditional 'political' fashion – for example, in the creation of meaning through juxtaposition. However, where film footage is used, there is more of a sense that scratch becomes a window onto the artist's innermost tastes, even when its images seem to be presented, almost half-apologetically, through the filter of irony. Thus, scratch rendered the personal investment made in the selection of the appropriated material both audible and visible. This expression of personal desire met with resistance and incomprehension within the politicised art climate of the 1980s: as far as Catherine Elwes was concerned, scratch could only have radical potential if the scratcher 'eradicates any weakness s/he might have for the glamour of those flickering fantasies on the screen' (Elwes, 1985: 22).

Refrain: opening the circle

Both the cultural position of scratch in the 1980s and the intervention made by the scratchers may be usefully articulated through reference to Deleuze and Guattari's concept of the refrain. In the opening to their essay on this topic, the authors describe three aspects of the way in which the refrain territorialises. First, 'A child in the dark, gripped with fear, comforts himself by singing under his breath' (Deleuze and Guattari, 1988: 311) – in this way a calm, stable centre is created in the heart of chaos; second, 'The forces of chaos are kept outside as much as possible, and the interior space protects the germinal forces of a task to fulfil or a deed to do' (1988: 311) – here, territory is demarcated around a point of order; third, 'one opens the circle a crack, opens it all the way, lets someone in, calls someone, or else goes out oneself, launches forth' (1988: 311). However, the authors explain that the three aspects of the refrain do not represent a linear, chronological or historical model for the development of territorialisation, stating, 'These are not three successive moments in an evolution. They are three aspects of a single thing, the Refrain' (Deleuze and Guattari, 1988: 312).

The dominant modernist history of avant-garde film and video, articulated according to the dynamics of differentiation and specificity, might be understood in terms of the first two aspects of Deleuze and Guattari's refrain. That is, we observe in the history of modernism a tendency towards differentiation of the arts, and a quest for specificity. In relation to avant-garde film practice, these are the imperatives to which Moholy-Nagy responds when he writes, 'everyone today has some idea of what is meant by the proposition – revolutionary in its effect in the early days – of the FILMIC, that is, of the film which proceeds from the potentialities of the camera and the dynamics of motion' (Moholy-Nagy, 1969: 122). The attempt to establish an art form's specificity, and to work with its 'essential' qualities, is a territorialising move that may be understood both as the establishment of a centre, and as the declaration of territory surrounding that centre. This particular act of territorialisation thus has two key elements: the declaration of an essence (a point of focus worthy of, and demanding its own territory and territorial boundaries), and the differentiation of that essence from others. Deleuze and Guattari's description of this second dimension of the refrain provides a faithful account of the modernist search for specificity: 'The forces of chaos are kept outside as much as possible, and the interior space protects the germinal forces of a task to fulfil or a deed to do. This involves an activity of selection, elimination and extraction' (Deleuze and Guattari, 1988: 311). This search for essence reaches its apotheosis in the minimalist concerns of structural film in the late 1960s and early 1970s, and the pursuit of 'film as film'.

This form of minimalism is, in the end, reassuring; that is, while minimalism seems on the one hand to be a radically challenging stripping away or erasure, what remains is hugely comforting; after all, what could be more grounded and reassuring than one of Carl Andre's floor sculptures? Minimalist works like those by Andre, or films like Snow's *Wavelength*, seem to present us with something that is completely known, and completely knowable in all its dimensions. Minimalist sculpture, like structural film, is rock solid, stable, predictable, measured and consistent. This, then, was the conceptual mindset that informed notions of what constituted radical video practice during 1970s and early 1980s. The arrival of scratch, however, marked a 'new' artistic and epistemological space, sidestepping the creative embargo set up by structural film. As critical commentary on scratch demonstrated, its presence in the territory staked by and for avant-garde film and video proved problematic. It is in this disjuncture between scratch video and the established critical norms informing film and video practice during this period that we observe the third of Deleuze and Guattari's aspects of the refrain: 'one opens the circle a crack, opens it all the way, lets someone in, calls someone, or else goes out oneself, launches forth' (1988: 311). This last aspect of the refrain can be seen both as the attempt made by the established film and video avant-garde of the early 1980s to (unsuccessfully) territorialise scratch, and more positively, as the line of escape that opens the territory of avant-garde film and video to an 'elsewhere'. For radical forms of film and video practice, the line of flight made by scratch marks a move from art concerned with specificity and territorial demarcation, to an encounter with something radically different. What we observe in scratch are modes of synthesis that can never be known within the traditions of deconstruction articulated by the dominant avant-garde film and video practice of the early 1980s. As noted in Chapters 3 and 4, synaesthetic audiovisual experience presents a sublation of sound and image, in which binary relations, hierarchies and identities are liquefied, where no one milieu is sacrificed to another, but in which each milieu becomes permeable to the point of dissolution. This is registered by the audioviewer not just at an intellectual or cognitive level, but also by a sensorium and a body that is seized by the affective shocks of scratch. In this sense, the sensory and affective pleasures associated with scratch mark a radical break with the kind of logocentrism that came to dominate avant-garde film and video production in this period.

As Deleuze and Guattari state, the three aspects of the refrain do not represent an evolution – the synaesthetic and affective possibilities of montage were, after all, recognised by Eisenstein fifty years before scratch. But the neglect that this aspect of Eisenstein's work has suffered simply highlights the dominance of certain critical modes over others. In this sense, the case of scratch represents a clear transvaluative moment; as Al Rees has commented in regard to scratch's departure from the norms set down for avant-garde

film and video practice by structural film, 'This was a sure sign
that something new was in the air' (Rees, 1999: 96). What we see
in this moment is the emergence of an affective or sensory turn,
arising before the vocabulary was in place to deal with it. For the
critics of the time, scratch simply did not make sense; they were
unable to situate the affective and sensational dimensions of the
form's audiovisuality within existing critical and theoretical frameworks. All the critics of scratch could see were insufficiencies, and
it has taken more than two decades for this moment to be affirmed
as a radical departure from the critical and creative agenda set
in motion by the linguistic turn of structuralism. What video
scratching inherits from its vinyl forebears is the 'physical' act of
scraping away at source material to release a potential that cannot
be understood in purely *significative* terms. In this sense, scratch
revealed itself to be an irritant to the established discourses of
political audiovisuality. If it is useful to describe scratch as a post-
modern form, then it is because its *postness* signals a break with
the modernist notions that have dominated thinking about radical
film and video practice for so many years.

The role played by mutual interaction, interdependence and
dissolution in the aesthetics of scratch returns us to the question
of what constitutes the 'properly' political in a radical poetics
of audiovisuality. Processes and forms that aren't dialectic have
always seemed to have an oblique political potential at best, or
none at all. An illustration of this is the problematic place occupied
by the synaesthetic in accounts of political modernism. Despite the
fact that the affective potential of the synaesthetic was recognised
by Eisenstein, it has been sidelined by the figure of montage, since
this seems in many ways to represent and manifest the radical
rupture presented by modernism. But this sidelining is, in part,
the neglect that results from the fact that nobody knows what to
do with the synaesthetic at a theoretical level, and certainly not
within a political context. Thus, Doug Kahn raises the figure of its
medical manifestation to dismiss the synaesthetic as an entirely
personal phenomenon. Similarly, studies of those filmmakers who
have explored synaesthetic forms, like those on the work of John
and James Whitney, Oskar Fischinger and Norman McLaren, con-
centrate on technology, technique or on matters of authorship.
Outside of these frames of reference, the only other consistent
discourse offered for the synaesthetic is the cosmic and the psyche-
delic, like that proposed by Gene Youngblood in *Expanded Cinema*
– a book that opens with the line, 'Gene Youngblood became a

passenger of Spaceship Earth on May 30, 1942' (Youngblood, 1970). Four decades after the publication of Youngblood's book, his take on film and video may seem mildly eccentric, and certainly personal; but viewed in another way, the launching of the synaesthetic into space is a declaration of its unknowability within existing epistemological regimes. It is this unknowability that is its political dimension, opening a window onto alternate political modes in which the ways we engage with sound, the ways we hear sound, the ways we feel and live with sound, and the ways in which we make sound, are as important as the ways in which sound signifies.

Notes

1 In the 1913 manifesto *The Art of Noises*, Luigi Russolo wrote, 'The ear of the Eighteenth Century man would not have been able to withstand the inharmonious intensity of certain chords produced by our orchestra (with three times as many performers as that of the orchestra of his time). But our ear takes pleasure in it, since it is already educated to modern life, so prodigal in different noises. Nevertheless, our ear is not satisfied and calls for even greater acoustical emotions' (Russolo, 1986: 24). Referring to concert halls as 'hospitals for anemic sounds' (1986: 25), Russolo called for music to embrace what had previously been considered noise. While not featured in Russolo's own compositions – which used specially built *intonorumori* to produce noises – his manifesto nevertheless prompts consideration of the musical value of worldly sounds.

2 While discs allowed the incorporation of worldly sounds into music – as in the work of Pierre Schaeffer in the late 1940s – it was not possible to isolate, combine or separate sounds of very short duration before the introduction of optical sound film or magnetic recording tape. Schaeffer's montage in first-generation *musique concrete* works, such as the *Etude aux chemins de fer* (1948), was produced by playing sections from discs in succession, rather like a modern turntablist. Schaeffer developed a technique of locking the stylus in a record groove to create what we would now refer to as 'loops' of sound; these could not be shorter than one rotation of the disc. With a 78 rpm disc, this technique determines a minimum loop duration of approximately 0.75 seconds.

3 Cage did not fare better with the radio industry. The composer's desire to control and manipulate sounds, outlined in *The Future of Music: Credo* (1937), translated five years later into a 250-page score for CBS Radio's production of Kenneth Patchen's *The City Wears a Slouch Hat*. On being told by a member of staff at CBS that there was no

limit to what could be done on radio, Cage laboured on a mammoth orchestration of sound effects, notating each sound in terms of timbre, loudness and pitch. On his return to the studio a week before the programme was to air, Cage's score was rejected as being too complex to be realised within budget and on schedule. Cage then worked solidly for four days on a much more modest score for percussion. The resulting work can be heard on Cage and Patchen (2000) [Audio recording: CD]. See Pritchett (1995), Kostelanetz (2003: 164–165) and Kahn (1999: 137) for accounts of his work on this programme.

4 Cage's first work on tape was the 1953 composition *Williams Mix*, for which over 2,000 pieces of sound tape, created from 350 separate recordings, were cut and edited according to Cage's graphic score (Austin, 2005). Varèse composed two pieces for tape: *Déserts* (1954) was written for orchestra and tape, and features electronic interludes that employ modified recordings of factory sounds and percussion instruments; *Poème électronique* was commissioned for the Philips pavilion – designed by Le Corbusier and Xenakis for the 1958 World Fair – and includes machine noises, bells, piano, percussion and electronic tones. Although Jack Ellitt became a pioneer of *musique concrete*, there are no commercial recordings of his work currently available. However, extracts from his compositions feature on the soundtrack of Keith Griffith's 1987 documentary *Doodlin' – Impressions of Len Lye*. According to Roger Horrocks – one of the few people to have interviewed Ellitt – in later years Ellitt composed only for his own satisfaction, 'no longer interested in the effort required to find sponsors or audiences' (Horrocks, 2001: 168).

5 This was the title of a major exhibition held at London's Hayward Gallery in 1979. 'Film as Film: Formal Experiment in Film 1910–1975' (3 May–17 June) featured the work of many of the key avant-garde filmmakers of the period. The exhibition attempted to trace a connection between contemporary avant-garde films and earlier modernist works, situating current film practice in terms of its continuity with the traditions of avant-garde filmmaking. The exhibition's title constructed the history of avant-garde film from 1910 to 1975 around the concern with formal issues, central to which was the notion of medium specificity.

6 Published in the journal *Studio International*, Wollen's article identified two strands of avant-garde film practice that differed in terms of aesthetic assumptions, institutional framework and historical and cultural origins. Wollen proposed that the first of these avant-gardes – the so called 'co-op' avant-garde – had its roots in the work of artists such as Hans Richter, Man Ray, Moholy-Nagy and Rene Clair, whose interests had been essentially visual, and whose film practice grew out of the concerns of painting. The other strand of avant-garde film practice, represented by the work of Godard, Straub and Huillet, was more

closely associated with the traditions of Soviet cinema, and embraced narrative and language. Wollen's article called for a re-unification of the two traditions. He writes, 'The way into narrative cinema is surely not forbidden to the avant-garde film-maker, any more than the way into verbal language. Cinema . . . is a multiple system – the search for the specifically cinematic can be deceptively purist and reductive. For most people, after all, cinema is unthinkable without words and stories. To recognize this fact is by no means to accept a conventional Hollywood-oriented . . . attitude to the cinema and the place of stories and words within it' (Wollen, 1975: 175).

7 The collective name of video artists Rik Lander and Peter Boyd Maclean.

8 The collective name of video artists Jon Dovey, Gavin Hodge and Tim Morrison.

9 The process is described by Fischinger's widow Elfriede in Keith Griffiths' 1992 documentary *Oskar Fischinger: Visual Music*.

10 Elwes has re-evaluated scratch in *Video Art: A Guided Tour* (2005), in which she frames scratch's televisuality in terms of a refreshing opposition to the theoretically driven work of the previous decade: 'Scratch's populist approach to image making was also a healthy antidote to the conceptual acrobatics of a 1970s avant-garde, steeped in theory' (Elwes, 2005: 115). However, Elwes's approach to what constitutes a properly political poetics of video remains unchanged, and the focus of her analysis continues to centre on the problematic relationship between the affective and political dimensions of scratch, figured in mutually exclusive, binary formulations: 'internal contradictions arose when the glamorous aesthetics of the pop video were too thickly overlaid onto political sentiments. Many artists accompanied their video découpages with pulsating disco beats that, like [Paul Hardcastle's] '*19*', left the viewer wondering whether she should write to her local M.P. or throw a party' (Elwes, 2005: 112). Regarding the use of 'scratched' footage of the Vietnam war in the video for Hardcastle's 1985 hit single *19*, she writes: 'Faced with repeating images of explosions and mutilated bodies, it was hard to know whether to weep or get up and dance to the music' (Elwes, 2005: 109).

11 While not understood at the time, scratch's engagement with folding signals an important cultural and epistemological shift that was affirmed more readily in other arts; for example, the concept of folding presented radical possibilities for architecture in the 1990s. See Lynn (1993).

12 *Mixing It*, BBC Radio 3, 21 April 2002 [includes interview with Matthew Herbert].

References

Abel, R. and R. Altman (eds) (2001) *The Sounds of Early Cinema.* Bloomington, Indiana University Press.

Adorno, T. (1997) *Negative Dialectics.* Collected Works, Volume 6. [Internet]. Frankfurt am Main, Suhrkamp Verlag. Translated from the German by D. Redmond. Available from: Centre for Research in Modern European Philosophy <www.efn.org/%7Edredmond/ndtrans.html> [Accessed 31 December 2004].

Adorno, T. (2002) *Essays on Music.* Selected, with introduction, commentary and notes by R. Leppert. Translated from the German by S. H. Gillespie. Berkeley, University of California Press.

Adorno, T. and H. Eisler (1994) *Composing for the Films.* London, Continuum.

Adorno, T. and M. Horkheimer (1997) *Dialectic of Enlightenment.* Translated from the German by J. Cumming. London, Verso.

Alten, S. R. (2005) *Audio in Media.* 7th edn. Belmont, CA, Thompson Wadsworth.

Altman, R. (1980) Introduction. *Yale French Studies,* No. 60, Cinema/Sound, pp. 3–15.

Altman, R. (1985) Evolution of Sound Technology. In: E. Weis and J. Belton (eds) *Film Sound: Theory and Practice.* New York, Columbia University Press, pp. 44–53.

Altman, R. (ed.) (1992) *Sound Theory Sound Practice.* AFI Film Readers. New York, Routledge.

Altman, R. (2004) *Silent Film Sound.* New York, Columbia University Press.

Apollonio, U. (ed.) (1973) *Futurist Manifestos.* London, Thames and Hudson.

Arts Council of Great Britain (1979) *Film as Film: Formal Experiment in Film 1910–1975.* London.

Attali, J. (1985) *Noise: The Political Economy of Music.* Theory and History of Literature, Volume 16. Translated from the French by B. Massumi. Minneapolis, University of Minnesota Press.

Augoyard, J. and H. Torgue (2005) *Sonic Experience: A Guide to Everyday*

Sounds. Translated from the French by A. McCartney and D. Paquette. Montreal, McGill-Queen's University Press.

Austin, L. (2005) *Larry Austin – Program Notes.* [Internet]. Denton, University of North Texas College of Music, The Center for Experimental Music and Intermedia. Available from: <http://cemi.music.unt.edu/larry_austin/LApnotes.htm> [Accessed 5 August 2009].

Baron, S. (1986) The Daisy Pulled. *Wire Magazine,* Issue 33, November, pp. 38–39.

Barrier, M. (1971) An Interview with Carl Stalling. *Funnyworld,* 13, Spring, pp. 21–27.

Barron, B. (1997) Making Music for Forbidden Planet: Bebe Barron interviewed by Mark Burman. In: J. Boorman, J. Donohue and W. Donohue (eds) *Projections 7.* London, Faber and Faber, pp. 252–263.

Barthes, R. (1977) *Image–Music–Text.* Translated from the French by S. Heath. London, Fontana Paperbacks.

Bazelon, I. (1975) *Knowing the Score: Notes on Film Music.* New York, Van Nostrand Reinhold.

Beck, J. and T. Grajeda (eds) (2008) *Lowering the Boom: Critical Studies in Film Sound.* Urbana and Chicago, University of Illinois Press.

Belton, J. (1985) Technology and Aesthetics of Film Sound. In: E. Weis and J. Belton (eds) *Film Sound: Theory and Practice.* New York, Columbia University Press, pp. 63–72.

Benjamin, W. (1999) *Selected Writings: Volume 2, 1927–1934.* Edited by W. Jennings, H. Eiland and G. Smith. Translated from the German by R. Livingstone. Cambridge, MA, Belknap Press/Harvard University Press.

Bergson, H. (1991) *Matter and Memory.* Translated from the French by N. M. Paul and W. S. Palmer. New York, Zone Books.

Bernds, E. (1999) *Mr Bernds Goes to Hollywood: My Early Life and Career in Sound Recording at Columbia with Frank Capra and Others.* Filmmakers Series, No.65. Lanham, MD, The Scarecrow Press Inc.

Berry, C. (1995) The Letter U and the Numeral 2. *Wired Magazine* [Internet], January 1995 (3.01). Available from: <www.wired.com/wired/archive/3.01/negativland_pr.html> [Accessed 4 August 2009].

Blackburn, D. (1990) Untitled essay. In: unpaginated booklet accompanying C. Stalling (1990) *The Carl Stalling Project – music from Warner Bros Cartoons 1936–1958.* Warner Bros. CD 9 26027-2 [Sound recording: CD].

Bogue, R. (2003) *Deleuze on Cinema.* London, Routledge.

Boltz, M. G. (2001) Musical Soundtracks as a Schematic Influence on the Cognitive Processing of Filmed Events. *Music Perception,* Vol. 18, No. 4, Summer, pp. 427–454.

Bordwell, D., J. Staiger and K. Thompson (1985) *The Classical Hollywood Cinema: Film Style and Mode of Production to 1960.* London, Routledge.

Bradley, S. (2002a) Music in Cartoons. In: D. Goldmark and Y. Taylor (eds) *The Cartoon Music Book.* Chicago, A Cappella Books, pp. 115–120.

Bradley, S. (2002b) Personality on the Soundtrack: A Glimpse Behind the Scenes and Sequences in Filmland. In: D. Goldmark and Y. Taylor (eds) *The Cartoon Music Book*. Chicago, A Cappella Books, pp. 121–124.

Brakhage, S. (1960) The Silent Sound Sense. *Film Culture*, No. 21, pp. 65–67.

Brecht, B. (1962) *Mother Courage and Her Children: A Chronicle of the Thirty Years War*. Translated from the German by E. Bentley. London, Methuen.

Brecht, B. (1964) *Brecht on Theatre: The Development of an Aesthetic*. Translated from the German by J. Willett. London, Methuen.

Brophy, P. (2002) An Interview with John Zorn. In: D. Goldmark and Y. Taylor (eds) *The Cartoon Music Book*. Chicago, A Cappella Books, pp. 263–267.

Brophy, P. (2004) *100 Modern Soundtracks*. BFI Screen Guides. London, British Film Institute.

Brougher, K. et al. (2005) *Visual Music: Synaesthesia in Art and Music Since 1900*. London, Thames and Hudson.

Buchanan, I. and P. MacCormack (eds) (2008) *Deleuze and the Schizoanalysis of Cinema*. London, Continuum.

Bull, M. and L. Back (eds) (2003) *The Auditory Culture Reader*. Sensory Formations Series. Oxford, Berg.

Cage, J. (1985) *A Year from Monday: New Lectures and Writings*. London, Marion Boyars.

Cage, J. (1999) *Silence: Lectures and Writings*. London, Marion Boyars.

Canemaker, J. (1996) *Felix: The Twisted Tale of the World's Most Famous Cat*. New York, Da Capo Press.

Care, R. (2002) Make Walt's Music: Music for Disney Animation, 1928–1967. In: D. Goldmark and Y. Taylor (eds) *The Cartoon Music Book*. Chicago, A Cappella, pp. 21–36.

Carroll, N. (2006) Film, Emotion and Genre. In: N. Carroll and J. Choi (eds) *Philosophy of Film and Motion Pictures: An Anthology*. Oxford, Blackwell.

Chion, M. (1994) *Audio-vision: Sound on Screen*. Translated from the French by C. Gorbman. New York, Columbia University Press.

Chion, M. (1999) *The Voice in Cinema*. Translated from the French by C. Gorbman. New York, Columbia University Press.

Chion, M. (2003) The Silence of the Loudspeakers, or Why with Dolby Sound it is the Film that Listens to Us. In: L. Sider, D. Freeman and J. Sider (eds) *Soundscape: The School of Sound Lectures 1998–2001*. London, Wallflower, pp. 150–154.

Chion, M. (2009) *Film, A Sound Art*. Translated from the French by C. Gorbman. New York, Columbia University Press.

Christie, I. (1981) How to Do Things with History. In: R. Stoneman and H. Thompson (eds) *The New Social Function of Cinema: Catalogue: British Film Institute Productions '79/80*. London, British Film Institute, pp. 34–39.

Corbett, J. (2002) A Very Visual Kind of Music: The Cartoon Soundtrack Beyond the Screen. In: D. Goldmark and Y. Taylor (eds) *The Cartoon Music Book*. New York, A Cappella, pp. 279–287.

Cornwell, R. (1972) Some Formalist Tendencies in the Current American Avant-garde Film. *Studio International*, Vol. 184, No. 948, October, pp. 110–114.

Cowan, L. (ed.) (1931) *Recording Sound for Motion Pictures*. New York, McGraw-Hill.

Cowie, E. (1981) At the Fountainhead (of German Strength). *Framework*, 15–17, pp. 73–74.

Cox, C. and D. Warner (eds) (2004) *Audio Culture: Readings in Modern Music*. London, Continuum.

Crafton, D. (1999) *The Talkies: American Cinema's Transition to Sound, 1926–1931*. Berkeley, University of California Press.

Cubitt, S. (1991) *Timeshift: On Video Culture*. London, Routledge.

Culhane, J. (1983) *Walt Disney's Fantasia*. New York, H. N. Abrams.

Curtis, S. (1992) The Sound of the Early Warner Bros. Cartoons. In: R. Altman (ed.) *Sound Theory Sound Practice*. New York, Routledge, pp. 191–203.

Dahl, I. (1974) Notes on Cartoon Music. In: J. L. Limbacher (ed.) *Film Music: From Violins to Video*. Metuchen, NJ, The Scarecrow Press, Inc. pp. 183–189. [Originally published in *Film Music Notes*, 8:5, May–June 1949, pp. 3–13.]

Davis, E. (2002) Recording Angels: The Esoteric Origins of the Phonograph. In: R. Young (ed.) *Undercurrents: The Hidden Wiring of Modern Music*. London, Continuum, pp. 15–24.

Day, T. (2000) *A Century of Recorded Music: Listening to Musical History*. New Haven, CT, Yale University Press.

Del Rio, E. (2008) *Deleuze and the Cinemas of Performance: Powers of Affection*. Edinburgh, Edinburgh University Press.

Deleuze, G. (1989) *Cinema 2: The Time-Image*. Translated from the French by H. Tomlinson and R. Galeta. London, Athlone Press.

Deleuze, G. and F. Guattari (1988) *A Thousand Plateaus: Capitalism and Schizophrenia*. Translated from the French by B. Massumi. London, Athlone Press.

Deleuze, G. and F. Guattari (1994) *What Is Philosophy?* Translated from the French by G. Burchill and H. Tomlinson. London, Verso.

Derrida, J. (1992) The Law of Genre. Translated from the French by A. Ronell. In: D. Attridge (ed.) *Jacques Derrida: Acts of Literature*. London, Routledge, pp. 221–252.

Diederichsen, D. (2005) *Montage/Sampling/Morphing: On the Triad of Aesthetics/Technology/Politics*. [Internet]. Karlsruhe, Media Art Net/ Center for Art and Media Karlsruhe. Available from: <www.medienkunstnetz.de/themes/image-sound_relations/montage_sampling_ morphing/1/> [Accessed 23 September 2005].

Doane, M.A. (1985) Ideology and the Practice of Sound Editing and Mixing. In: E. Weis and J. Belton (eds) *Film Sound: Theory and Practice*. New York, Columbia University Press, pp. 54–62.

Drummond, P. (1979) Notions of Avant-garde Cinema. In: Arts Council of Great Britain, *Film as Film: Formal Experiment in Film 1910–1975*. London, pp. 9–16.

Dunford, M. (1986) Subverting Television? *Independent Video*, Issue 55, June, pp. 6–8.

Dyer, R., J. Fisher, and P. Wollen (2004) *Electronic Shadows: The Art of Tina Keane*. London, Black Dog.

Eisenstein, S. (1977a) *The Film Sense*. Translated from the Russian by J. Leyda. London, Faber and Faber.

Eisenstein, S. (1977b) *Film Form: Essays in Film Theory*. Translated from the Russian by J. Leyda. San Diego, Harvest/Harcourt Brace Jovanovich.

Eisenstein, S. M., W. I. Pudowkin and G. V. Alexandrov (1928) The Sound Film: A Statement from the USSR. *Close Up*, No. 3/4, October, pp. 10–13. [Reprinted in Eisenstein (1977b)].

Ellis, J. (1981) At the Fountainhead (of TV History). *Screen*, Vol. 21, No 4, pp. 45–55.

Ellis, J. (1992) *Visible Fictions: Cinema, Television, Video*. London, Routledge.

Ellitt, J. (1935) On Sound. *Life and Letters Today*, December, pp. 182–184.

Eluard, P. and B. Péret (1995) Proverbs for Today. In: M. Gooding (ed.) *A Book of Surrealist Games*. Compiled by A. Brotchie. Boston and London, Shambhala.

Elwes, C. (1985) Through Deconstruction to Reconstruction. *Independent Video*, Issue 48, November, pp. 21–23.

Elwes, C. (2001) Trespassing beyond the Frame. *Filmwaves*, Issue 15, Autumn, pp. 12–17.

Elwes, C. (2005) *Video Art, A Guided Tour*. London, I. B. Tauris.

Erlmann, V. (ed.) (2004) *Hearing Cultures: Essays on Sound, Listening and Modernity*. Oxford, Berg.

Eshun, K. (1998) *More Brilliant than the Sun: Adventures in Sonic Fiction*. London, Quartet Books.

Farber, M. (1998) *Negative Space: Manny Farber on the Movies*. New York, Da Capo Press.

Figgis, M. (2003) Silence: The Absence of Sound. In: L. Sider, D. Freeman and J. Sider (eds) *Soundscape: The School of Sound Lectures 1998–2001*. London, Wallflower, pp. 1–14.

Fischinger, O. (1947) My Statements Are in My Work. In: F. Stauffacher (ed.) *Art in Cinema*. San Francisco, San Francisco Museum of Art, pp. 38–40.

Flaxman, G. (2000) *The Brain is the Screen: Deleuze and the Philosophy of Cinema*. Minneapolis, University of Minnesota Press.

Ford, G. (1990) Untitled essay. In: unpaginated booklet accompanying

C. Stalling (1990) *The Carl Stalling Project – music from Warner Bros Cartoons 1936–1958*. Warner Bros. CD 9 26027–2 [Sound recording: CD].

Fraisse, P. (1982) Rhythm and Tempo. In: D. Deutsch (ed.) *The Psychology of Music*. New York, Academic Press, pp. 149–180.

Freud, S. (1958) *On Creativity and the Unconscious*. Translated from the German by A. Strachey. New York, Harper and Row.

Friedwald, W. (2002) Sublime Perversity: The Music of Carl Stalling. In: D. Goldmark and Y. Taylor (eds) *The Cartoon Music Book*. Chicago, A Cappella Books, pp. 137–140.

Funking the Frame/Framing the Funk (1986) *Independent Video*, Issue 50, January, pp. 8– 9.

Ganguly, S. (2002) Stan Brakhage: The 60th Birthday Interview. In: W. W. Dixon and G. A. Foster (eds) *Experimental Cinema: The Film Reader*. London, Routledge, pp. 139–162.

Garity, W. E. and J. N. A. Hawkins (1941) Fantasound. *Journal of the Society of Motion Picture Engineers*, Vol. 37, August, pp. 127–146.

Garity, W. E. and W. Jones (1942) Experiences in Road-Showing Walt Disney's Fantasia. *Journal of the Society of Motion Picture Engineers*, Vol. 39, July, pp. 6–15.

Gidal, P. (1975) Theory and Definition of Structural/Materialist Film. *Studio International*, Vol. 190, No. 978, November/December, pp. 189–196.

Gidal, P. (ed.) (1978) *Structural Film Anthology*. London, British Film Institute.

Gidal, P. (1989) *Materialist Film*. London, Routledge.

Goldmark, D. (1997) Carl Stalling and Humor in Cartoons. *Animation World Magazine* [Internet], April, Issue 2:1. Available from: <www. awn.com/mag/issue2.1/articles/goldmark2.1.html> [Accessed 4 August 2009].

Goldmark, D. and Y. Taylor (eds) (2002) *The Cartoon Music Book*. Chicago, A Cappella Books.

Gorbman, C. (1987) *Unheard Melodies: Narrative Film Music*. Bloomington and Indianapolis, Indiana University Press.

Gormley, P. (2005) *The New-Brutality Film: Race and Affect in Contemporary Hollywood Cinema*. Bristol, Intellect.

Greenberg, C. (2002) Modernist Painting. In: C. Harrison and P. Wood (eds) *Art in Theory: 1900–2000 An Anthology of Changing Ideas*. Oxford, Blackwell, pp. 773–779.

Hall, S. and S. Maharaj (2001) *Modernity and Difference*. London, Institute of International Visual Arts.

Hamlyn, N. (2003) *Film Art Phenomena*. London, British Film Institute.

Handzo, S. (1985) A Narrative Glossary of Film Sound Technology. In: E. Weis and J. Belton (eds) *Film Sound: Theory and Practice*. New York, Columbia University Press, pp. 383–426.

Hansen, M. (1993) Of Mice and Ducks: Benjamin and Adorno on Disney. *South Atlantic Quarterly*, Vol. 92, No. 1, pp. 27–62.

Hartog, S. (1978) Ten Questions to Michael Snow. In: P. Gidal (ed.) *Structural Film Anthology*. London, British Film Institute, pp. 36–37.

Hawkins, G. (2002) Documentary Affect: Filming Rubbish. *Australian Humanities Review* [Internet], September–December, Issue 27. Available from: <www.australianhumanitiesreview.org/archive/Issue-September-2002/hawkins.html> [Accessed 4 August 2009].

Hawley, S. (1986) Hard Times For Video Art. *Independent Video*, Issue 53, April, p. 9.

Hayward, P. (1986) Second Wave Scratch. *Independent Video*, Issue 52, March, p. 10.

Hein, B. (1979) The Structural Film. In: Arts Council of Great Britain, *Film as Film: Formal Experiment in Film 1910–1975*. London, pp. 93–105.

Horrocks, R. (1999) Jack Ellitt: The Early Years. *Cantrills Filmnotes*. Nos 93–100, December 1999–January 2000, pp. 20–26.

Horrocks, R. (2001) *Len Lye: A Biography*. Auckland, Auckland University Press.

Houghton, N. (1986) Infermental: Institute Contemporary Arts December 1985. *Independent Video*, Issue 51, February, p. 9.

Jaubert, M. (1938) Music on the Screen. In: C. Davy (ed.) *Footnotes to The Film*. London, Lovat Dickson and Readers' Union.

Jayamanne, L. (2001) 'Forty Acres and a Mule Filmworks' – DO THE RIGHT THING – 'A Spike Lee Joint': Blocking and Unblocking the Block. In: P. Pisters (ed.) *Micropolitics of Media Culture: Reading the Rhizomes of Deleuze and Guattari*. Amsterdam, Amsterdam University Press, pp. 235–249.

Jones, C. (1946) Music and the Animated Cartoon. *Hollywood Quarterly*, Vol. 1, No. 4, pp. 364–370.

Jones, C. (1999) *Chuck Amuck: The Life and Times of an Animated Cartoonist*. New York, Farrar, Straus and Giroux.

Kahn, D. (1999) *Noise Water Meat: A History of Sound in the Arts*. Cambridge, MA, MIT Press.

Kalinak, K. (1992) *Settling the Score: Music and the Hollywood Film*. Madison, WI, University of Wisconsin Press.

Keane, T. (2009) *Deviant Beauty*. [Internet]. London, Luxonline. Available from: <www.luxonline.org.uk/artists/tina_keane/deviant_beauty.html> [Accessed 5 August 2009].

Keen, B. (1986) Reviews. *Independent Video*, Issue 50, March, p. 10.

Kennedy, B. M. (2002) *Deleuze and Cinema: The Aesthetics of Sensation*. Edinburgh, Edinburgh University Press.

King, N. (1984) The Sound of Silents. *Screen*, Vol. 25, No. 3 May–June, pp. 2–15.

Kittler, F.A. (1999) *Gramophone, Film, Typewriter*. Writing Science Series. Translated from the German by G. Winthrop-Young and M. Wutz. Stanford, Stanford University Press.

Kostelanetz, R. (2003) *Conversing with Cage*. 2nd edn. London, Routledge.

Kozloff, S. (1988) *Invisible Storytellers: Voice-over Narration in American Fiction Film*. Berkeley, University of California Press.

Kozloff, S. (2000) *Overhearing Film Dialogue*. Berkeley, University of California Press.

LaBelle, B. and C. Migone (eds) (2001) *Writing Aloud: The Sonics of Language*. Los Angeles, Errant Bodies Press.

LaBelle, B. and S. Roden (1999) *Site of Sound: Of Architecture and the Ear*. Los Angeles, Errant Bodies Press/Smart Art Press.

Lander, R. (2005) *oni baba/take it II*. [Internet]. London, Duvetbrothers.com. Available from: <www.duvetbrothers.com/media/oni.html> [Accessed 9 October 2005].

Lang, E. and G. West (1970 [1920]) *Musical Accompaniment of Moving Pictures: A Practical Manual for Pianists and Organists*. New York, Arno Press and the New York Times. [Reprint of the original 1920 edition, published by The Boston Music Company.]

Lastra, J. (2000) *Sound Technology and the American Cinema: Perception, Representation, Modernity*. New York, Columbia University Press.

Le Grice, M. (1977) *Abstract Film and Beyond*. London, Studio Vista.

Leslie, E. (2002) *Hollywood Flatlands: Animation, Critical Theory and the Avant-garde*. London, Verso.

Levarie, S. and E. Levy (1983) *Musical Morphology: A Discourse and a Dictionary*. Kent, OH, Kent State University Press.

Levin, T. Y. (2003) Tones from Out of Nowhere: Rudolph Pfenninger and the Archaeology of Synthetic Sound. *Grey Room* [Internet], Vol. 12, Summer, pp. 32–79. Available from: <www.centerforvisualmusic.org/LevinPfen.pdf> [Accessed 26 January 2006].

Lynn, G (ed.) (1993) *Architectural Design 102: Folding in Architecture*. Chichester, John Wiley and Sons.

Mackenzie, D. (1931) Sound Recording by the Light-valve System. In: L. Cowan (ed.) *Recording Sound for Motion Pictures*. New York, McGraw-Hill, pp. 84–95.

McLaren, N. (1953) Notes on Animated Sound. *Quarterly of Film Radio and Television*, Vol. 7, No. 3. pp. 223–229.

McMahon, O. D. (2009) An Analysis of the Soundtrack in the Work of Malcolm Le Grice. [Internet]. London, British Artists' Film and Video Study Collection, St Martin's College of Art and Design. Available from: <www.studycollection.co.uk/soundtracts.html> [Accessed 24 August 2009].

Manvell, R. and J. Huntley (1975) *The Technique of Film Music*. Revised and enlarged edition. London, Focal Press.

Marks, L. U. (1998) Video Haptics and Erotics. *Screen*, Vol. 39, No. 4, Winter, pp. 331–348.

Marks, L. U. (2000) *The Skin of the Film: Intercultural Cinema, Embodiment, and the Senses*. Durham, NC, Duke University Press.

Massumi, B. (2002) *Parables for the Virtual: Movement, Affect, Sensation*.

Post-Contemporary Interventions. Durham, NC, Duke University Press.

Mazière, M. (1983) John Smith's Films: Reading the Visible. *Undercut*, No. 10/11, Winter/Spring, pp. 40–44.

Mertens, W. (1988) *American Minimal Music: La Monte Young, Terry Riley, Steve Reich, Philip Glass*. London, Kahn and Averill.

Moholy-Nagy, L. (1969) *Painting, Photography, Film*. London, Lund Humphries.

Moritz, W. (1979) Non-objective Film: The Second Generation. In: Arts Council of Great Britain, *Film as Film: Formal Experiment in Film 1910–1975*. London, pp. 59–71.

Moritz, W. (2006) *You Can't Get Then From Now*. [Internet]. Los Angeles, The William Moritz Archive, The iotaCenter. Available from: <www.iotacenter.org/program/publication/moritz> [Accessed 6 January 2006]. [Originally published in *Southern California Art Magazine*. Los Angeles Institute of Contemporary Art, No. 29, Summer 1981, pp. 26–40 and 70–72.]

Mulvey, L. (1975) Visual Pleasure and Narrative Cinema. *Screen*, Vol. 16, No. 3, Autumn, pp. 6–18.

Neale, S. (1985) *Cinema and Technology: Image, Sound, Colour*. London, British Film Institute.

Nickerson, C. (1998) Montreal Metro: Tenors vs. Toughs Subway Stations Blast Opera to Chase Off Loiterers. *Boston Globe*, 31 December, p. A1.

Oram, D. (1972) *An Individual Note of Music, Sound and Electronics*. London, Galliard Paperbacks.

Pasolini, P. P. (1980) Observations on the Long Take. *October*, Vol. 13, Summer, pp. 3–6.

Peirce, C. S. (1991) *Peirce on Signs: Writings on Semiotic by Charles Sanders Peirce*. Edited by J. Hoopes. Chapel Hill, NC, University of North Carolina Press.

Pisters, P. (ed.) (2001) *Micropolitics of Media Culture: Reading the Rhizomes of Deleuze and Guattari*. Amsterdam, Amsterdam University Press.

Pisters, P. (2003) *The Matrix of Visual Culture: Working with Deleuze in Film Theory*. Stanford, Stanford University Press.

Powell, A. (2005) *Deleuze and Horror Film*. Edinburgh, Edinburgh University Press.

Pritchett, J. (1995) *The Story of John Cage's The City Wears a Slouch Hat*. [Internet]. Princeton, Music Department, Princeton University. Available from: <www.rosewhitemusic.com/cage/texts/slouch.html> [Accessed 4 August 2009].

Rees, A. L. (1999) *A History of Experimental Film and Video: From the Canonical Avant-garde to Contemporary British Practice*. London, British Film Institute.

Rees, A. L. (2002) Associations: John Smith and the Artists' Film in the

UK. In: *John Smith: Film and Video Works 1972–2002*. Bristol, Picture This Moving Image/Watershed Media Centre, pp. 14–31.

Richter, H. (1965) *Dada: Art and Anti-art*. London, Thames and Hudson.

Roads, C. (2001) *Microsound*. Cambridge, MA, MIT Press.

Rodowick, D. N. (1994) *The Crisis of Political Modernism: Criticism and Ideology in Contemporary Film Theory*. Berkeley, University of California Press.

Rodowick, D. N. (1997) *Gilles Deleuze's Time Machine*. Durham, NC, Duke University Press.

Russolo, L. (1986) *The Art of Noises*. Monographs in Musicology No. 6. Translated from the Italian by B. Brown. New York, Pendragon Press.

Rutherford, A. (2003) Cinema and Embodied Affect. *Senses of Cinema* [Internet], March–April, No. 25. Available from: <www.sensesofcinema.com/contents/03/25/embodied_affect.html> [Accessed 2 August 2006].

Sartin, H. (1998) From Vaudeville to Hollywood, From Silence to Sound: Warner Bros. Cartoons of the Early Sound Era. In: K. S. Sandler (ed.) *Reading the Rabbit: Explorations in Warner Bros. Animation*. London, Rutgers University Press, pp. 67–85.

Sartre, J. (1969) *Being and Nothingness: An Essay on Phenomenological Ontology*. Translated from the French by H. E. Barnes. London, Methuen.

Saussure, F. (1964) *Course in General Linguistics*. Translated from the French by W. Baskin. London, Peter Owen.

Scarth, R. N. (1999) *Echoes from the Sky: A Story of Acoustic Defence*. Hythe, Kent, Hythe Civic Society.

Schaeffer, P. (2004) Acousmatics. Translated from the French by D. W. Smith. In: C. Cox and D. Warner (eds) *Audio Culture: Readings in Modern Music*. London, Continuum, pp. 76–81.

Schafer, R. M. (1977) *The Tuning of the World*. New York, Alfred A. Knopf.

Schafer, R. M. (1994) *The Soundscape: Our Sonic Environment and the Tuning of the World*. Rochester ,VT, Destiny Books.

Schneider, S. (1994) *That's All Folks: The Art of Warner Bros. Animation*. London, Aurum Press.

Screen (1984) Vol. 25, No. 3. May–June, 'On the Soundtrack' special issue.

Selwood, S. (1981) 'The Development from Abstract Art to Abstract Animated Films'. M. Phil. thesis, University of Essex.

Sergi, G. (2004) *The Dolby Era: Film Sound in Contemporary Hollywood*. Manchester, Manchester University Press.

Serres, M. (1995) *Genesis*. Translated from the French by G. James and J. Nielson. Ann Arbor, MI, University of Michigan Press.

Shadduck, J. (1974) The Ku-Ku Song Man! In: J. L. Limbacher (ed.) *Film Music: From Violins to Video*. Metuchen, NJ, The Scarecrow Press, pp. 176–181.

Shannon, C. E. (1948) A Mathematical Theory of Communication. *The*

Bell System Technical Journal [Internet], Vol. 27, July–October, pp. 379–423, 623–656. Available from: Bell Laboratories Computing and Mathematical Sciences Research <cm.bell-labs.com/cm/ms/what/shannonday/shannon1948.pdf> [Accessed 19 January 2005].

Sharits, P. (1972) Words per Page. *Afterimage*, No. 4, Autumn, pp. 26–43.

Silverman, K. (1988) *The Acoustic Mirror: The Female Voice in Psychoanalysis and Cinema*. Bloomington and Indianapolis, Indiana University Press.

Sitney, P. A. (1969) On 'Structural Film'. *Film Culture*, No. 47, Summer, pp. 1–10.

Sitney, P. A. (ed.) (1971) *Film Culture: An Anthology*. London, Secker and Warburg.

Sobchack, V. (1992) *The Address of the Eye: A Phenomenology of Film Experience*. Princeton, Princeton University Press.

Sobchack, V. (2004) *Carnal Thoughts: Embodiment and Moving Image Culture*. Berkeley, University of California Press.

Sterne, J. (2003) *The Audible Past: Cultural Origins of Sound Reproduction*. Durham, NC, Duke University Press.

Stockhausen, K. (1959) . . . .How Time Passes. . . . . *Die Reihe* (English edition), Vol. 3, pp. 10–40.

Strauss, N. (2002) Tunes for Toons: A Cartoon Music Primer. In: D. Goldmark and Y. Taylor (eds) *The Cartoon Music Book*. New York, A Cappella, pp. 5–13.

Taylor, T. D. (2001) *Strange Sounds: Music, Technology and Culture*. New York, Routledge.

Tebbel, J. R. (1992) Looney Tunester. *Film Comment*, September/October, pp. 64–66.

Thompson, E. (2002) *The Soundscape of Modernity: Architectural Acoustics and the Culture of Listening in America*. Cambridge, MA, MIT Press.

Tönende Handschrift (1932) *Völkischer Beobachter*, 25 October.

Toop, D. (1999) *Exotica: Fabricated Soundscapes in a Real World*. London, Serpent's Tail.

Toop, D. (2004) *Haunted Weather: Music, Silence and Memory*. London, Serpent's Tail.

Uexküll, J. von (1982 [1940]) The Theory of Meaning. *Semiotica*, Vol. 42, No. 1, pp. 25–87. Translated from the German by B. Stone and H. Weiner.

Ulmer, G. L. (1985) The Object of Post-Criticism. In: H. Foster (ed.) *Postmodern Culture*. London, Pluto Press, pp. 83–110.

Varèse, E. (1940) Organized Sound for the Sound Film. *The Commonweal*, Vol. 33, No. 8, 13 December, pp. 204–205.

Viera, E. R. P. (1999) Liberating Calibans: Readings of Anthropofagia and Haraldo de Campos' Poetics of Transcreation. In S. Bassnett and H. Trivedi (eds) *Post-colonial Translation: Theory and Practice*. London, Routledge, pp. 95–113.

Vincentelli, E. (2002) Merrie Melodies: Cartoon Music's Contemporary Resurgence. In: D. Goldmark and Y. Taylor (eds) *The Cartoon Music Book*. New York, A Cappella, pp. 203–206.

Waldman, D. (1992) *Collage, Assemblage and the Found Object*. London, Phaidon.

Weis, E. and J. Belton (eds) (1985) *Film Sound: Theory and Practice*. New York, Columbia University Press.

Weiss, A. S. (ed.) (2001) *Experimental Sound and Radio*. A TDR Book. Cambridge, MA, MIT Press.

Weiss, A. S. (2002) *Breathless: Sound Recording, Disembodiment and the Transformation of Lyrical Nostalgia*. Middletown, CT, Wesleyan University Press.

Whitehall, R. (1988) Bildmusik – Art of Oskar Fischinger. In: R. Russett and C. Starr (eds) *Experimental Animation: Origins of a New Art*. 2nd edn. New York, Da Capo Press, pp. 59–61.

Whitehead, K. (2002) Carl Stalling, Improviser and Bill Lava, Acme Minimalist. In: D. Goldmark and Y. Taylor (eds) *The Cartoon Music Book*. New York, A Cappella, pp. 141–150.

Whitney, J. (1980) *Digital Harmony: On the Complementarity of Music and Visual Art*. Peterborough, NH, Byte Books/McGraw-Hill.

Whitney, J. and J. Whitney (1947a) Film notes. In: F. Stauffacher (ed.) *Art in Cinema*. San Francisco, San Francisco Museum of Art, pp. 60–61.

Whitney, J. and J. Whitney (1947b) Audio-Visual Music. In: F. Stauffacher (ed.) *Art in Cinema*. San Francisco, San Francisco Museum of Art, pp. 31–34.

Wollen, P. (1972) Counter Cinema: Vent D'Est. *Afterimage*, No. 4, Autumn, pp. 6–17.

Wollen, P. (1975) The Two Avant-gardes. *Studio International*, Vol. 190, No. 978, November–December, pp. 171–175.

Wollen, P. (1976) Ontology and Materialism in Film. *Screen*, Vol. 17, No. 1, Spring, pp. 17–23.

Yale French Studies (1980) No. 60, 'Cinema/Sound' special issue.

Young, L. and M. Zazeela (1969) *Selected Writings*. [Internet]. Munich, Heiner Friedrich. Available from: ubu.com <www.ubu.com/historical/young/young.html> [Accessed 29 November 2004].

Youngblood, G. (1970) *Expanded Cinema*. London, Studio Vista.

Zamecnik, J. S. (1913) *Sam Fox Moving Picture Music*. Vol. I. [Internet]. Cleveland, OH, Sam Fox Publishing Co. Available from: Cinemaweb <www.cinemaweb.com/silentfilm/bookshelf/> [Accessed 4 August 2009].

Zorn, John (1990) Carl Stalling: An Appreciation. In: unpaginated booklet accompanying Stalling, C. (1990) *The Carl Stalling Project – music from Warner Bros Cartoons 1936–1958*. Warner Bros. CD 9 26027–2 [Sound recording: CD].

Selected filmography and videography

Abbreviations: Prod. = production; Dist. = distribution.

Alphaville (1965) Directed by Jean-Luc Godard. London, Connoisseur Video [Video: VHS].

Anthology: George Barber (1997) London, London Electronic Arts [Video: VHS].

Anthology: John Smith Vols 1 & 2 (1997) London, London Electronic Arts [Video: VHS].

Associations (1975) Directed by John Smith. Prod. London, John Smith/ Royal College of Art. Dist. Lux [Film: 16mm] Available on the compilation *Anthology: John Smith. Volume 1.* (1997) London, London Electronic Arts [Video: VHS].

At the Fountainhead (of German Strength) (1980) Directed by Anthea Kennedy & Nick Burton. Prod. and Dist. London, British Film Institute [Film: 16mm].

Birdman (1975) Directed by Anthea Kennedy & Nick Burton. Prod. London, World Service/Royal College of Art. Dist. Anthea Kennedy [Film: 16mm].

Birds, The (1963) Directed by Alfred Hitchcock. Hollywood, Universal Pictures. [Video: DVD].

Black Tower, The (1985–87) Directed by John Smith. Prod. London, Arts Council of Great Britain. Dist. Lux [Film: 16mm]. Available on the compilation *Anthology: John Smith. Volume 1.*(1997) London, London Electronic Arts [Video: VHS].

Blue Lagoon, The (1980) Directed by Randal Kleiser. Culver City, Columbia Pictures Corporation [Film: 35mm].

Blue Monday (1984) Directed by The Duvet Brothers. Prod. London, The Duvet Brothers. Dist. Lux [Video]. Available on the compilation *The Greatest Hits of Scratch Volume One* (1985) Directed by George Barber. London, Scratch Video [Video: VHS].

Bucks Fizz (1984) Directed by Jeffrey Hinton [Video]. Available on the compilation *The Greatest Hits of Scratch Video Volume One* (1985) Directed by George Barber. London, Scratch Video [Video: VHS].

Casablanca (1942) Directed by Michael Curtiz. Burbank, Warner Bros. [Film: 35mm].

Catalog (1961) Directed by John Whitney. Prod. Motion Graphics Inc. Dist. BFI [as part of the *Whitney Brothers Programme*] [Film: 16mm].

Central (2001) Directed by Scott Rankin. Prod. Hong Kong, Videotage [video]. Dist. Scott Rankin [Video: DVD].

Chelsea Girls, The (1966) Directed by Paul Morrisey & Andy Warhol. New York, The Film-makers' Cooperative [Film: 16mm].

Crack-up (1946) Directed by Irving Reis. Atlanta, Turner Home Entertainment [Video: VHS].

Deep, The (1977) Directed by Peter Yates. Los Angeles, Casablanca Filmworks/EMI Films [Film: 35mm].

Deviant Beauty (1996) Directed by Tina Keane. Prod. London, London Production Fund [video]. Dist. Lux [Video: VHS].

Diagonal Symphony (1925) Directed by Viking Eggeling [Film: 35mm]. Available on the compilation *Experimental Cinema of the 1920s and '30s*. (Films from the Raymond Rohauer Collection). New York, Kino Video [Video: DVD].

Doodlin': Impressions of Len Lye (1987) Directed by Keith Griffiths. London, Illuminations for Channel 4/ESTV New Zealand [Video: VHS].

Fantasia (1940) Produced by Walt Disney. Burbank, Walt Disney Pictures [Film: 35mm].

Fast and Furry-ous (1949) Directed by Chuck Jones. Available on the compilation *Looney Tunes Golden Collection*. Burbank, Warner Home Video [Video: DVD].

Felix the Cat in Astronomeows (1928) Directed by Otto Messmer. New York, Pat Sullivan Films [Film: 35mm] Available on the compilation *Felix the Cat in Bold King Cole*. Diamond Films [Video: VHS].

Five Film Exercises (1943–44) Produced by John and James Whitney. Prod. Hollywood, John and James Whitney [Film: 16mm] Dist. Lux [Film: 16mm].

Forbidden Planet (1956) Directed by Fred M. Wilcox. Taipei, Great Music [Video: DVD].

Gone With the Wind (1939) Directed by Victor Flemming. Los Angeles, Selznick International Pictures [Film: 35mm].

The Greatest Hits of Scratch Video Volume One (1985) Directed by George Barber. *Volume Two* (1986) Produced by George Barber, The Duvet Brothers, Tim Morrison. London, Scratch Video [Video: VHS].

Holiday Inn (1942) Directed by Mark Sandrich. Hollywood, Paramount Pictures Inc. [Film: 35mm].

Il Deserto Rosso (1964) Directed by Michelangelo Antonioni. London, Connoisseur Video [Video: VHS].

Informer, The (1935) Directed by John Ford. Hollywood, RKO Radio Pictures Inc. [Film: 35mm].

King Kong (1933) Directed by Merian C. Cooper & Ernest B. Schoedsack. Hollywood, RKO Radio Pictures Inc. [Film: 35mm].

Lapis (1963–66) Produced by James Whitney, Hollywood, [Film: 16mm]. Dist. London, Lux [Film: 16mm].

Last Days, The (1998) Directed by James Moll. Los Angeles, Survivors of the Shoah Visual History Foundation/Ken Lipper-June Beallor [Film: 35mm].

L'avventura (1960) Directed by Michelangelo Antonioni. London, Connoisseur Video [Video: VHS].

L'eclisse (1962) Directed by Michelangelo Antonioni. New York, Criterion Collection [Video: DVD].

M. Hulot's Holiday (1953) Directed by Jacques Tati. London, Connoiseur Video [Video: VHS].

My Favourite Wife (1940) Directed by Garson Kanin. Watford, Herts., Cinema Club [Video: VHS].

Neighbours (1952) Directed by Norman McLaren. Available on the compilation *Norman McLaren: Selected Films*. London, Connoisseur Video [Video: VHS].

Night of a 1000 Eyes (1984) Directed by Kim Flitcroft and Sandra Goldbacher. Dist. Lux [Video]. Available on the compilation *The Greatest Hits of Scratch Volume One* (1985) Directed by George Barber. London. London: Scratch Video [Video: VHS].

Om (1986) Directed by John Smith. Prod. London, John Smith. Dist. Lux [Film: 16mm]. Available on the compilation *Anthology: John Smith. Volume 1.* (1997) London, London Electronic Arts [Video: VHS].

On the Waterfront (1954) Directed by Elia Kazan. Culver City, Columbia Pictures Corporation/ Horizon Pictures [Film: 35mm].

Oskar Fischinger: Visual Music (1992) Directed by Keith Griffiths. London, Koninck International [Video: VHS].

Passing, The (1991) Directed by Bill Viola. Amsterdam, Éditions à voir [Video: DVD].

Path (2003) Directed by Scott Rankin. Prod. Normal, IL., Scott Rankin. Dist. Video Data Bank [Video: DVD].

Peace and Plenty (1939) Directed by Ivor Montagu. Prod. London, Kino. Featured in the compilation *Workers films of the 1930s* (1981) Directed by Victoria Wegg-Prosser. London, BFI [Film: 16mm].

Piccadilly (2004) Directed by Scott Rankin. Prod. & Dist. Normal, IL., Scott Rankin. [Video: DVD].

President's World, The (1985) Directed by Gorilla Tapes. Dist. Lux [Video]. Available on the compilation *The Greatest Hits of Scratch Video Volume Two* (1986) Produced by George Barber, The Duvet Brothers, Tim Morrison. London, Scratch Video [Video: VHS].

Psycho (1960) Directed by Alfred Hitchcock. Hollywood, Paramount Pictures [Film: 35mm].

Pull My Daisy (1959) Directed by Robert Frank and Alfred Leslie. New York, G-String Enterprises [Film: 35mm].

Pure, The (1993) Directed by Scott Rankin. Prod. Chicago, Center for New Television. Dist. Video Data Bank [Video: DVD].

Reichstag Fire Part I, The (1976) Directed by Anthea Kennedy and Nick Burton. Prod. London, World Service/Royal College of Art. Dist. Anthea Kennedy [Film: 16mm].

Searchers, The (1956) Directed by John Ford. Burbank, Warner Bros. [Film: 35mm].

Shaft (1971) Directed by Gordon Parks. Los Angeles, MGM/Shaft Productions [Film: 35mm].

Spellbound (1945) Directed by Alfred Hitchcock. London, Pearson Television International [Video: DVD].

Swing, The (1978) Directed by Tina Keane. Prod. London, Tina Keane. Dist. Lux [Video: VHS].

Synchromy (1971) Directed by Norman McLaren. Montreal, National Film Board of Canada [Film: 35mm] available on the compilation *Norman McLaren: Selected Films* (2000) London, Connoisseur Video [Video: VHS].

Take It (1984) Directed by The Duvet Brothers. Prod. London, The Duvet Brothers [Video]. Available on the compilation *The Greatest Hits of Scratch Video Volume One* (1985) Directed by George Barber. London, Scratch Video [Video: VHS].

Thin Red Line, The (1998) Directed by Terence Malick. Los Angeles, Twentieth Century Fox Home Entertainment [Film: DVD].

This and That (Part Two) (1990) Directed by Scott Rankin. Prod. Chicago, Centre for New Television/ National Endowment for the Arts/New York, Art Matters Inc. Dist. Scott Rankin [Video: VHS].

T.V. of Tomorrow (1953) Directed by Tex Avery. Los Angeles, MGM [Film: 35mm].

Vivre sa vie (1962) Directed by Jean-Luc Godard. Hereford, Nouveaux Pictures [Video: DVD].

War Machine (1984) Directed by The Duvet Brothers. Prod. London, The Duvet Brothers. Dist. Lux [Video]. Available on the compilation *The Greatest Hits of Scratch Video Volume One* (1985) Directed by George Barber. London, Scratch Video [Video: VHS].

Wavelength (1967) Directed by Michael Snow. New York, Michael Snow [Film: 16mm]. Dist. London, BFI [Film: 16mm].

Way Out West (1937) Directed by James W. Horne. Culver City, Hal Roach Studios/Stan Laurel Productions [Film: 35mm].

What's Opera Doc? (1957) Directed by Chuck Jones. Burbank, Warner Bros. [Film: 35mm].

White Christmas (1954) Michael Curtiz. Hollywood, Paramount Pictures [Film: 35mm].

White Zombie (1932) Directed by Victor Halperin. Elstree, Herts, Elstree Hill Entertainment [Video: DVD].

Yantra (1950–58) Directed by James Whitney. Prod. Uroboros Films. Dist. London, Lux [Film: 16mm].

Yes Frank, No Smoke (1985) Directed by George Barber. Dist. Lux [Video]. Available on the compilation *Anthology: George Barber* (1997) London, London Electronic Arts [Video: VHS].

Selected audio recordings

Bradley, S. (1993) *Tex Avery Cartoons. Music from the Tex Avery Original Soundtracks Composed by Scott Bradley*. Milan [Sound recording: CD].

Cage, J. (2000) *Williams Mix* from *OHM: The Early Gurus of Electronic Music 1948–1980*. Ellipsis Arts [Sound recording: CD].

Cage, J. and Patchen, K. (2000) *The City Wears a Slouch Hat*. Organ of Corti [Audio recording: CD].

Negativland (1991) *U2: Special Edit Radio Mix and A Capella Mix*. Negativland [Sound recording: MP3 file]. Available from: <www.negativland.com> [Accessed 19 November 2005].

Pauline, M. and Jupitter-Larsen, G. (n.d.) *Survival Research Laboratories*. SubRosa [Audio recording: CD].

Rockmore, C. (1987) *The Art of the Theremin*. Delos [Sound recording: CD].

Schaeffer, P. (1990) *Etude aux chemins de fer* (1948) from *Pierre Schaeffer: l'oeuvre musicale Vols 1–4*. INA-GRM [Audio recording: CD].

Scott, R. (1992) *The Music of Raymond Scott. Reckless Nights and Turkish Twilights*. Columbia [Sound recording: CD].

Semper, J. (n.d.) *Kenotaphion*. Charrm [Sound recording: CD].

Stalling, C. (1990) *The Carl Stalling Project: Music from Warner Bros. Cartoons 1936–1958*. Warner Bros. [Sound recording: CD].

Stalling, C. (1995) *The Carl Stalling Project Volume 2*. Warner Bros. [Sound recording: CD].

Stravinsky, I. (1958) *Ebony Concerto*, The London Symphony Orchestra. Everest [Audio recording: vinyl].

Varèse, E. (2004) *Déserts* (1954) and *Poème électronique* (1958) from *Varèse: the Complete Works*. Royal Concertgebouw Orchestra, ASKO Ensemble, Ricardo Chailly. Decca [Audio recording: CD].

Selected film and video distribution sources

Anthea Kennedy
57 Ravensworth Road
London NW10 5NP
UK
Email: Anthea.Kennedy@btopenworld.com

British Film Institute
21 Stephen Street
London W1T 1LN
UK
Tel.: 020 7957 8935
Fax: 020 7580 5830
Email: bookings.films@bfi.org.uk
Web: www.bfi.org.uk

Electronic Arts Intermix
535 West 22nd Street, 5th Floor
New York, NY 10011–1119
USA
Tel.: +1 212 337 0694
Fax: +1 212 337 0679
Email: info@eai.org
Web: www.eai.org/eai/

Lux
18 Shacklewell Lane,
London E8 2EZ,
UK
Tel.: +44 (0)20 7503 3980
Email: mike.sperlinger@lux.org.uk
Web: www.lux.org.uk

Scott Rankin
Illinois State University
College of Fine Arts
Campus Box 5600
Normal, IL 61790–5600
USA
Tel.: +1 309 438 8090
Email: sdranki@ilstu.edu
Web: www.cfa.ilstu.edu/sdranki/

Video Data Bank
112 S. Michigan Avenue
Chicago, IL 60603
USA
Tel.: +1 312 345 3550
Fax: +1 312 541 8073
Email: info@vdb.org
Web: www.vdb.org

Index